Mastering Corporations and
Other Business Entities

Carolina Academic Press Mastering Series
Russell L. Weaver, Series Editor

Mastering Bankruptcy
George W. Kuney

Mastering Civil Procedure
David Charles Hricik

Mastering Corporations and Other Business Entities
Lee Harris

Mastering Criminal Law
Ellen S. Podgor, Peter J. Henning, Neil P. Cohen

Mastering Evidence
Ronald W. Eades

Mastering Intellectual Property
George W. Kuney, Donna C. Looper

Mastering Legal Analysis and Communication
David T. Ritchie

Mastering Negotiable Instruments (UCC Articles 3 and 4) and Other Payment Systems
Michael D. Floyd

Mastering Products Liability
Ronald W. Eades

Mastering Professional Responsibility
Grace M. Giesel

Mastering Secured Transactions
Richard H. Nowka

Mastering Statutory Interpretation
Linda D. Jellum

Mastering Tort Law
Russell L. Weaver, John H. Bauman, Ronald W. Eades,
Andrew R. Klein, Edward C. Martin, Paul J. Zwier II

Mastering Corporations and Other Business Entities

Lee Harris
UNIVERSITY OF MEMPHIS
CECIL C. HUMPHREYS SCHOOL OF LAW

CAROLINA ACADEMIC PRESS
Durham, North Carolina

Library of Congress Cataloging in Publication Data

Harris, Lee, 1978-
   Mastering corporations and other business entities / Lee Harris.
      p. cm.
   Includes index.
   ISBN 978-1-59460-444-7 (alk. paper)
   1. Business enterprises--Law and legislation--United States. I. Title. II.
Title: Mastering corporations and other business entities.

   KF1355.H37 2008
   346.73'066--dc22

                                           2008041490

Carolina Academic Press
700 Kent Street
Durham, NC 27701
Telephone (919) 489-7486
Fax (919) 493-5668
www.cap-press.com

Printed in the United States of America

Contents

Table of Cases

Series Editor's Foreword

The Carolina Academic Press Mastering Series is designed to provide you with a tool that will enable you to easily and efficiently "master" the substance and content of law school courses. Throughout the series, the focus is on quality writing that makes legal concepts understandable. As a result, the series is designed to be easy to read and is not unduly cluttered with footnotes or cites to secondary sources.

In order to facilitate student mastery of topics, the Mastering Series includes a number of pedagogical features designed to improve learning and retention. At the beginning of each chapter, you will find a "Roadmap" that tells you about the chapter and provides you with a sense of the material that you will cover. A "Checkpoint" at the end of each chapter encourages you to stop and review the key concepts, reiterating what you have learned. Throughout the book, key terms are explained and emphasized. Finally, a "Master Checklist" at the end of each book reinforces what you have learned and helps you identify any areas that need review or further study.

We hope that you will enjoy studying with, and learning from, the Mastering Series.

Russell L. Weaver
Professor of Law & Distinguished University Scholar
University of Louisville, Louis D. Brandeis School of Law

Preface

The title of the basic business law course — Corporations, Business Associations, Business Organizations, or Business Entities — varies from law school to law school and from year to year. However, in these courses, the core coverage is essentially the same — agency principles, partnership law, fiduciary duties, securities fraud, and changes in corporate control. This relatively concise book is intended to reach students in the basic corporate law course, regardless of course title. This book attempts to make the usual coverage as easy and straightforward as possible. Although the vast majority of law students take a business law course, there are surprisingly few attempts to systematically organize the most important doctrine and theories covered. Of the few books that track the basic business law course, even fewer still are of recent vintage. This book attempts to fill those lacunae.

The book intends to aid students, of course, in the basic Corporations or Business Organizations courses. Additionally, though, I should like to think this book would be a useful resource to students in other closely-related courses in law school, like Agency & Partnership, Closely-Held Firms, Mergers & Acquisitions, and Securities Regulation, to name just a few. Outside of law schools, I am also writing with an eye toward the graduate student in business administration who are frequently enrolled in a basic business law course and the newly-minted corporate attorney who wants a refresher text. In addition to a review of the doctrine, I also want to give the reader a sense of the theory and history behind the more complicated concepts. With any luck, the book's contribution to the theory and history of corporate law is as pervasive as the concentration on doctrine.

Acknowledgments

I must acknowledge the University of Memphis, my permanent academic home, and George Washington University, where, as a visiting professor, I was in residence while writing much of this book. Both institutions are full of creative thinkers, top-flight support staff and, of course, challenging students. I thank the intrepid deans of those institutions, former dean Jim Smoot at the U of M and Dean Fred Lawrence at GW, for their generosity in providing me with a wonderful place to complete this work. Additionally, I should like to thank those who have been particularly helpful along the way, including Alena Allen, Regina Burch, Lawrence Cunningham, Janet Richards, Kevin Smith, Steve Schooner, and Russ Weaver. Lastly, I have had a handful of research assistants over the course of my writing this book, all of whom have been particularly adept at turning inchoate assignments into gold. My research assistants have included Jon Barnes, Michael Gore, Jason Koch, and Deric Ortiz at GW; and Lea Mullins, Jennifer Longo, and Bruce Shanks at the U of M.

LAH

Mastering Corporations and Other Business Entities

Chapter 1

Agency Law

Roadmap

- Agency Formation
- Liability in Tort
- Liability in Contract
- Agent-Principal Duties
- Disclosed, Partially Disclosed, and Undisclosed Principals
- Co-Agents and Sub-Agents
- Agency Termination

A. Introduction to Agency Law

Business leaders, entrepreneurs, and even active parents have only so much time. They routinely rely on managers, employees, day care providers, and other "agents" to take care of tasks that they cannot. An agent operates on behalf of another individual or entity. In technical legal jargon, the person or entity that "hires" the agent is the agent's principal. An individual or firm may hire an agent to perform tasks that she does not have the time to perform, the expertise to execute properly, or the ability. For instance, public corporations are legally recognized entities, but can do very little without the help of agents. Public corporations have hundreds, sometimes thousands, of employees or agents. They rely on these agents for countless tasks from negotiating contracts on the firm's behalf to hiring more agents.

1. Legal Consequences of Agency Relationship

When tasks or duties are delegated to another party, an agency relationship, with special legal consequences, may be formed. A typical agency relationship is commercial, such as the relationship between an employer and her employee.

For instance, someone shopping for a home in a new city may retain the services of a real estate agent to cull listings, scout properties, make an offer, and negotiate terms. However, an agency relationship does not depend on whether the parties are in an employment relationship or, for that matter, whether the relationship is commercial at all. Thus, a teacher who loans her car to a school football coach on his way to transport players to an away game may create an agency relationship. *See, e.g., Gorton v. Doty*, 69 P.2d 136 (Idaho 1937). In addition, although there is substantial similarity between agency and contract, an agency relationship can be created more easily than a contractual relationship. Unlike with a contract, consideration — that is, a return promise made in exchange as in a bargain — is not a requirement for creating an agency relationship. Also, unless state law is to the contrary, an agency need not be formalized or reduced to writing. Broadly put, this Chapter explores how an agency relationship is formed, the legal consequences that arise from such a relationship, and how an agency relationship is terminated.

2. Economic Consequences of Agency Relationship

When a principal hires an agent to work on her behalf, she not only creates legal consequences, but also economic consequences. Agents have divergent interests and better information regarding the agency. These disadvantages are frequently referred to as agency costs. To start with, the most important of these disadvantages is that the agent may have interests different from the interests of her principal. As a result, the agent may pursue choices that differ from the choices her principal would have made. Many of these choices are opportunistic, because the agent realizes that the choice, while permitted, would create benefits to him. However, not all agents are opportunistic. Some of the agent's choices can be described as benign attempts to maximize private benefit to the agent. This is because it is probably impossible for the agent to always recognize her own self interests, much less always use her discretion to maximize value to her principal while separating out other motivating factors. The agent, acting within the confines of the relationship, may unintentionally champion a cause that is not the best course for her principal.

Another related problem of the agency relationship that may result in losses for the principal is the problem of information asymmetry. That is, the agent is tasked to do something very specific and, as a result, may develop specific access to information in that area. For instance, the firm may hire a chief financial officer to manage the books of the firm. The CFO may always have more information regarding the financial reporting of the company than others at the firm. The agent may be able to use the information advantage to redirect firm resources or the agent might use the information to cover up her misconduct, like, say, abuse of the company credit card or company car.

The tendency of an agent to pursue her own interests at the expense of the principal can be resolved by effective contract design. Notably, to align the principal and agent's difference, some firms have tried to tie the agent's compensation to the principal's objective. A public corporation may compensate high-level executives with stock options, for instance, in order to create such an incentive. A second way a principal may reduce the problems of agency costs is by monitoring and screening of agents. Direct monitoring takes place when the principal checks up on the agent with an eye toward curbing abuse. The principal could also indirectly monitor her agent's potential for mischief by setting up effective governance parameters. For instance, principals might spend a substantial amount of time to screen agents to ensure that only the most trustworthy, diligent individuals are hired in the first place.

B. Formation of Agency Relationship

The Restatement (Third) of Agency is an attempt by law professors, judges, lawyers and others to compile court precedent and common law rules on the law of agency. Although courts are not bound by the Restatement, the drafters intended for it to be a solid reflection of the current state of the law of agency. Thus, most judges can be expected to follow Restatement provisions. Under the Restatement, an agency relationship is formed when two parties agree that one party (the agent) will act, subject to control, on behalf of the other party (the principal). RESTATEMENT (THIRD) OF AGENCY § 1.01. Thus, for an agency relationship to be formed, the principal must agree or consent that the agent shall act on the principal's behalf; the agent must agree to act on the principal's behalf; and control must be vested with the principal. Additionally, under the Restatement, a party may agree to have an agent act on her behalf by words or conduct. The test is an objective one; that is, what objective evidence of assent is there. RESTATEMENT (THIRD) OF AGENCY § 1.03.

1. Consent to Act

First, agency relationships cannot be formed without the consent of the parties. The principal consents to the agent acting on her behalf, while the agent agrees to do as directed. In order to create an agency relationship, the parties must show through their conduct, words, or the circumstances that they intend to be in an agency relationship. Circumstances that have been used to show consent to form an agency relationship have been wide-ranging and do not depend on the parties subjective intention. Instead, as mentioned, courts look to objective evidence to determine whether the parties intended to form an agency relationship.

For instance, in *Green v. H & R Block* the court held that there could be consent based on the parties' conduct, even though at least one of the parties, H & R Block, may not have intended to consent to an agency relationship. 735 A.2d 1039 (Md. 1999). Specifically, *Green* is a relatively recent class action in which several H & R Block customers filed suit when they learned that the company was receiving a commission from their "Rapid Refund" program. Under the terms of the tax refund program put on by H & R Block, customers who wanted to use the cash from their tax refund immediately could receive it in the form of a loan from a third-party bank, Beneficial National. However, customers did not know that H & R Block would receive a share of Beneficial National's finance charges from those loans. Importantly, in that case the court had to determine whether an agency relationship existed between H & R Block and its customers. If there was an agency relationship, H & R Block would owe certain fiduciary duties to its customers, including an obligation to disclose the company's relationship with the bank.

Although the court's decision is not without some contrary authority, the court in *Green* decided that an agency relationship could be created between the tax preparation agency and the public it served. The court's theory suggested that H & R Block, in many ways, resembled an agent and the customer a principal. Further, the court found that the parties' conduct suggested that they consented to an agency relationship. According to the court, H & R Block's national media campaign created a reasonable impression that the company wanted to serve as the taxpayer's agent. The court noted that H & R Block, in its ad campaign, exhorted customers to trust the company and, as a consequence, the company could not now disclaim consent when customers took them up on their offer:

> Through its national and local efforts advertising its tax preparation and refund services, H & R Block strives to convince potential customers that it can be "trusted" to obtain both the highest and fastest possible refunds for its customers. Its advertisements call on consumers to "Do what millions of Americans do. Trust H & R Block." H & R Block declares that it "watch[es] over" its customers and that "you can trust H & R Block." H & R Block promotes itself as having the expertise to achieve the maximum allowable tax return, with the customer secure in the knowledge that, if necessary, an experienced tax

preparer "will appear with you at [an] audit and explain how your refund was prepared...." Finally, H & R Block's advertisements promoting its ability to secure a "Rapid Refund" constitute an integral part of its promotional efforts. Customers who enter the doors of the local H & R Block office therefore may reasonably believe that H & R Block is acting on their behalf—to obtain the highest and fastest return possible—in the preparation and filing of the tax returns with the IRS and, in the case of the RAL [rapid refund], in acting as the intermediary to the transactions with the lending bank.

735 A.2d at 1053. Thus, the consent element of an agency relationship only refers to consent to form an agency, not necessarily consent to the legal consequences that follow. That is, H & R Block consented to act on behalf of its customers and the customers, in turn, consented to H & R Block serving as their agent. Once such consent has been manifested, legal consequences follow, like the fiduciary duty to disclose, discussed here briefly by the court. Additionally, another important takeaway on consent is that the parties' conduct is the measuring stick. Written evidence of consent is not necessarily required. If the parties' conduct is sufficient to infer their consent, an agency relationship with concomitant legal consequences may be formed, regardless of the parties' subjective beliefs or whether there is a writing.

2. Control Is Vested with the Principal

Second, in order to form an agency relationship, the principal should have "control" over her agents. Courts have interpreted the requirement of control in an agency relationship broadly. The vast majority of courts agree that a principal need not micromanage the tasks of the agent in order to create control. This is logical because if the principal had to manage each of the tasks of the agency, the relationship would be of little benefit to the principal. Further, it is impossible for a principal to ever have total control of an agent, because the agent will have her own mind, interests, and style of accomplishing tasks.

Rather, court opinions suggest that the principal need only be in control in a much broader sense. Control sufficient to establish an agency relationship is based on a range of conduct, from the principal's ability to oversee the day-to-day tasks of an agent to, more broadly, the principal's ability to set the agenda or set objectives for an agent to accomplish. In all these cases, however, a principal gives directives and an agent, with varying levels of oversight, attempts to implement them. Frequently, the issue of control comes up in lender cases. The issue in these cases is whether the lender's advice, counsel, and directives to a borrower are within the usual scope of the lender-borrower relationship or whether the lender's conduct is evidence that the lender was in control of the borrower's conduct, such that an agency relationship may have been created.

For instance, in *Gay Jenson Farms v. Cargill*, a perennial darling of business law professors, dozens of farmers contracted with a local grain elevator operator, Warren Grain & Seed Co., for the sale of their grain. 309 N.W.2d 285 (Minn. 1981). Warren would re-sell the farmer's grain to other companies or trade the grain on the Minneapolis Grain Exchange. When Warren could not make good on its debts to the farmers and the company collapsed, the farmers sued Warren's financier, Cargill. Their theory was that Warren was actually Cargill's agent.

At the time of the case, Cargill ran (and continues to run today) a lending and financial services arm, alongside an even larger grain processing operation. Cargill frequently called Warren to make recommendations regarding the operation of the business. Cargill audited Warren's books. Cargill got a right of first refusal for Warren's supply of grain. Warren agreed not to enter into any mortgages, purchase stocks, or pay dividends without Cargill's approval. Cargill could enter the premises to conduct periodic audits. Cargill criticized the salary structure, inventory levels, and Warren's financial arrangements. Although many of the features of "control" — review of the financial statements, for instance — look like a lender exercising a traditional monitoring function, the court held that these factors should not be "considered in isolation." Considered together, the *Cargill* court held that this was more than a typical lender-borrower relationship:

> We deal here with a business enterprise markedly different from an ordinary bank financing, since Cargill was an active participant in Warren's operations rather than simply a financier. Cargill's course of dealing with Warren was, by its own admission, a paternalistic relationship in which Cargill made the key economic decisions and kept Warren in existence.

309 N.W.2d at 292–93. Thus, the court interpreted Cargill's acts as that of a manager or principal directing the operations of an employee or agent. The issue of lender versus principal routinely creates instances of close calls. However, it is worthwhile to highlight one of the more important indicators of whether a lender may be liable for exercising too much control — the right to veto ordinary decisions. That is, often such cases may turn on whether the lender has veto rights over normal operational decisions of the borrower. For instance, here the lender had veto rights on some decisions that could be described as being taken in the ordinary operations of the business, like the decision to issue div-

idends. Further, because Warren was in the business of selling grain, Cargill's right of refusal with respect to Warren's grain could also be analogized to a strong veto right. That is, under the terms of the agreement, Cargill could, in effect, deny Warren the right to enter into ordinary sales contracts with others. In the end, lenders that have broad veto rights are probably more like principals than traditional lenders, because the borrower-firm cannot operate without first getting the lender's approval.

C. Imputed Knowledge

If the elements of consent and control are present and an agency relationship is formed, the agent becomes an extension of the principal. The agent's acts are the principal's and the agent's knowledge is imputed to the principal. RESTATEMENT (THIRD) OF AGENCY § 5.03. Specifically, if the agent acquires information that is significant and relevant to the nature of the relationship, the common law rule is that the principal is presumed to also have such knowledge. For instance, it is assumed under this rule that in a large corporation, with many agents assigned to different tasks, a principal has knowledge commensurate to each and every agent, regardless of whether that is actually the case. *See* RESTATEMENT (THIRD) OF AGENCY § 5.03 cmt. b, illus.5. Thus, a principal, regardless of whether she has actual notice, can be held liable for knowledge known by her agent.

Such a presumption makes sense for two reasons. First, the rule of imputed knowledge matches up with the duty of an agent to disclose all relevant information to her principal. Second, the rule seems to have a strong economic justification as well. That is, without a presumption of imputed knowledge, third parties who deal with agents could not merely convey information to agents. Third parties would have to speak directly with principals to deliver relevant information, a costly proposition.

The general rule that an agent's knowledge is imputed to her principal has two exceptions. First, the principal will not be assumed to have knowledge similar to her agent if the agent acts adversely to the principal's interest. RESTATEMENT (THIRD) OF AGENCY § 5.04. That is, if the agent uses the knowledge to compete with her principal or frustrate her principal's interest, then the rule of imputation does not apply. Still, even this exception is very narrow and the imputation rule may still be relevant. For instance, in cases in which the principal learns of the agent's disloyalty and retains the agent despite it, the principal can be said to have ratified the agent's tactics. As such, the principal would not be able to avoid the rule of imputation. Further, if another party dealing with the agent has no reason to suspect that the agent is acting adversely to the principal and deals with the agent in good faith, most courts will not rely on this exception to the detriment of the third party.

Second, a principal avoids imputed knowledge if the agent has a prior agreement or duty not to make relevant disclosures. In these cases, if an agent has agreed with another person (or is duty-bound) to not make a disclosure to her principal, it will not be assumed that the principal has also acquired that knowledge. For instance, an agent serving multiple principals may have agreed to keep the confidences of one of the principals. In this case, because the agent has a duty of obedience to her principals, there is no assumption that the other principals have the agent's knowledge.

D. Contract Liability

One of the important legal consequences of forming an agency relationship is that the principal will be bound to the contracts formed by the agent on the principal's behalf. In these cases, the party who the agent contracted with may sue to enforce the contract against the principal. There are several ways an agent can have authority to bind a principal to a contract.

1. Express Actual Authority

Actual authority or true authority for an agent to bind the principal to contracts can be created expressly. That is, the most straightforward and simple way for a principal to give an agent authority to act on her behalf is by stating it frankly and directly. According to the comments to the Restatement, express actual authority is created when the principal has stated her wishes "in very specific of detailed language." RESTATEMENT (THIRD) OF AGENCY § 2.01 cmt. b. In these cases, the agent is said to have express actual authority to act on behalf of the principal.

2. Implied Actual Authority

The Restatement provides that an agent has implied actual authority or, simply, implied authority to take on such tasks that are necessary to accomplish the principal's express instructions. RESTATEMENT (THIRD) OF AGENCY § 2.01, cmt. b. The rationale is that the agent should not have to waste time asking for minute instructions. To require such would be inefficient, a waste of time and money. Implied actual authority can also be created in instances in which the agent has a good faith belief or reasonable belief as to what the principal's wishes are, based on the principal's conduct, the principal's goals, and other relevant facts.

One problem of whether an agent has implied actual authority to enter into contracts on behalf of the principal usually arises in cases in which an agent is given broad express authority, but few step-by-step instructions. Exactly this circumstance occurred in *Mill Street Church of Christ v. Hogan*, a dispute that developed after a church hired a handyman, Bill Hogan, to paint the church building. 785 S.W.2d 263 (Ky. Ct. App. 1990). To complete the painting job, Hogan hired a helper, his brother Sam. In his first half-hour of work, Sam climbed a ladder to reach a ceiling corner, when he fell and broke an arm. The issue was whether Bill's hire was authorized by the church such that the hire could look to the church for recovery and worker's compensation. According to this court (and others), implied actual authority is based on whether the agent reasonably believes, based on conduct and the circumstances, that the principal desired a certain task be done or that the agent had proper authority. Since the church had permitted Bill to hire helpers in the past to complete church work and Bill could not realistically finish the job by himself, the court found that there was implied actual authority for Bill to make the hire:

> First, in the past the church had allowed Bill Hogan to hire his brother or other persons whenever he needed assistance on a project.... Further, Bill Hogan needed to hire an assistant to complete the job for which he had been hired. The interior of the church simply could not be painted by one person. Maintaining a safe and attractive place of worship clearly is part of the church's function, and one for which it would designate an agent to ensure that the building is properly painted and maintained.

785 S.W.2d at 268. The opinion in *Mill Street Church* is a good illustration of implied actual authority. As the court says, the handyman in the case, Bill, had implied actual authority to hire a helper because (among other reasons) painting the building was not a one-man job. In order to complete the task, he necessarily had to get some help. In the same way, for instance, regardless of whether it was expressly discussed with church leaders or not, Bill likely had implied actual authority to buy the supplies necessary to get the job done, like paint, brushes, and perhaps a tall ladder. Also, the case provides a sufficient backstory for illustrating express actual authority. That is, the handyman in the case, Bill, had express actual authority to paint the church interior, because the leaders of the church had so instructed. Whether an agent's actual authority is created by way of express instructions or implied by the principal's man-

date, conduct, or other circumstances, the agent may legally bind her principal to contract.

3. Apparent Authority

In addition to actual authority, an agent may have authority to act on behalf of the principal, based on conduct or "holding out" by the principal suggesting that the agent has the authority to act on her behalf and the third party's reasonable belief that the agent has the power to act on the principal's behalf. Specifically, according to the Restatement, apparent authority might create legal consequences when a "third party reasonably believes that the actor has authority to act on behalf of the principal" and when "that belief is traceable to the principal's manifestations." RESTATEMENT (THIRD) OF AGENCY § 2.03. In such cases, the agent is said to have apparent authority and the principal is bound. Thus, the third party must have a reasonable belief that the agent is vested with authority. The reasoning here is that it would be unusually costly for a third party to make an inquiry regarding whether there is actual authority. The third party should be able to reasonably trust a principal's conduct. Additionally, this rule creates an incentive for the principal to speak up to disclaim authority if she has a suspicion that her conduct could be misunderstood.

The federal appeals court of the Fifth Circuit, in *Three-Seventy Leasing Corporation v. Ampex*, notes such authority is created whenever "the principal acts in such a manner as would lead a reasonably prudent person to suppose that the agent had the authority he purports to exercise." 528 F. 2d 993, 996 (5th Cir. 1976). In that case, Kays, a salesman for Ampex, a computer maker, negotiated with Joyce, a representative of Three-Seventy Leasing, for the purchase of six supercomputers. At the direction of his boss at Ampex, Kays submitted a written document to Joyce memorializing the parties' understanding, but with the signature block for an Ampex representative left blank. Later, Kays sent a subsequent letter to confirm deliver of the six computers. Kays did not have actual authority to bind the company, since company internal policy required approval for contracts from a supervisor or comparable executive.

Still, according to the court, Ampex could be held to the sales contract because there was a holding out and it was reasonable to believe that Kays represented the company. Kays' boss asked Kays to send the initial letter laying out the terms of the deal. Evidence showed, furthermore, that Kays' boss agreed with Joyce that Kays would be the point-man on this deal and all company communications would come from Kays. For instance, during the negotiations Kays' boss sent an intra-office memorandum that said as much. Also, it was reasonable for Joyce to believe that Kays, a salesman, had the power to bind the company to sales contracts.

Therefore, even if the agent does not have actual authority, a principal can be held liable for the contracts entered into by her agent under the doctrine of apparent authority. In these cases, the principal's liability would turn on whether the principal has held the agent out as having actual authority. Also, apparent authority turns on whether it was reasonable to believe the agent was so authorized. Like in *Three-Seventy Leasing*, a holding out that creates a reasonable assumption could be based on a variety of manifestations by the principal, including company memoranda. At the same time, however, much smaller manifestations may create apparent authority. For instance, giving an employee a public title may suggest to outsiders (ignorant of company internal policy) that the employee has authorization to pursue tasks associated with the title. As in *Three-Seventy Leasing*, thus, a "salesman" might be reasonably perceived as having the power to enter sales contracts.

4. Inherent Authority

Although the latest Restatement of Agency does not specifically include agency derived from inherent authority, many courts continue (and will likely continue) to rely on this doctrine. Under the doctrine of inherent authority, an agent has the authority to do such as things as would normally or customarily flow from the agent's position. *See generally* RESTATEMENT (SECOND) OF AGENCY § 8A. The doctrine, thereby, protects third parties who may enter into contracts with an agent because they reasonably believe the agent to have the normal range of powers. Straight inherent authority cases are rare because in the vast majority of cases, the third parties' reasonable belief can be linked to the principal's conduct. In these cases, an argument could be made for apparent authority. Thus, in cases where inherent agency comes up, it's likely to be in combination with other theories of authority, particular apparent agency. Yet, some cases, like the next one, are tough to make based on a holding out, the touchstone of apparent authority.

Watteau v. Fenwick best elucidates the common law rule of inherent authority. 1 QB 346 (1892). The defendants in this case purchased a microbrewery called the Victoria Hotel from Humble. Presumably, as they were interested in keeping the customer base intact, they kept Humble on as the bar's manager. They even left Humble's name on the door. Humble was directed by the new owners to buy almost all of the bar's supplies from them. However, Humble violated this directive and ordered cigars and a non-alcoholic drink from an unauthorized vendor. When the vendor who had supplied the orders over the years learned that Humble had no right to enter into these contracts, since he was no longer the owner, the vender sued the defendants. Humble could not have had actual authority to enter into these contracts because the defendants told him that supplies should not be ordered from outside venders. Further, the plaintiffs would have a tough time showing apparent authority because the defendants had not actively held out Humble as its agents. The plaintiff, Fenwick, never even knew that Watteau existed. Thus, one of the plaintiff's only ways to make out an agency relationship such that the pub's owners would be answerable for Humble's debts was inherent authority. The court found that a principal is "liable for all the acts of the agent which are within the authority usually confided to an agent of that character."

To be frank, the rationales for keeping inherent authority are fading, though not completely vanquished. As mentioned, inherent agency has been left out of the latest Restatement. Instead, the latest Restatement relies on a more specific and narrower statement of a rule that purports to create liability only in the case of an undisclosed principal. *See* RESTATEMENT (THIRD) OF AGENCY § 2.06. Additionally, the cases relying exclusively on the doctrine are few and far between, as apparent authority seems to cover the vast majority of the cases. For instance, even in *Watteau*, the vendor may have been able to recover on apparent agency grounds, because there was arguably at least some "holding out" on the part of the principal in letting the manager keep up, say, a sign. Thus, even in cases where it appears to be a poor fit, apparent agency can still be stretched to cover the conduct in question. Finally, it seems a bit harsh to impose liability when there has been no act on the part of the principal and the principal has given express instructions to the agent to the contrary, like in *Watteau*.

5. Agency by Estoppel

An agency relationship can also be created based on estoppel principles. RESTATEMENT (THIRD) OF AGENCY § 2.05. These cases are even a broader interpretation of agency liability, since there may not be an actual agency relationship at all. Yet, third parties can still recover against a principal on the basis of agency principles. The theory here is that based on some act (or failure) of the principal the principal should be estopped from disclaiming an agency. In these cases, a party who mistakenly believes that they are dealing with an agent may be able to recover against the principal, if she has good reason to believe that the imposter is an agent; the principal creates the impression that an actor is its agent (*e.g.*, the principal is unreasonably lax in ridding imposters); and the mistaken party suffers some losses as a result. Agency by estoppel is similar, although not identical, to an agency created by apparent authority. In both cases, legal consequences follow a manifestation or other conduct on the part of the principal. However, in agency by estoppel the principal's conduct leads to an ascertainable loss on the part of another party. This requirement of ascertainable loss or detrimental reliance is not a necessary prerequisite in apparent authority cases. For instance, consider *Hoddeson v. Koos Bros.*

In a satirically written opinion, the court held a furniture store bound to sales entered into by an imposter salesman. 135 A.2d 702 (N.J. Super. Ct. App. Div. 1957). In that case, the plaintiff, Joan Hoddeson, visited a local Koos Brothers furniture store to shop for bedroom furniture. She claimed she was shown around the store by man wearing a gray business suit. The man, according to the plaintiff, appeared to work at the store and over the next half hour, she said, he took her order for several items. All told, he "sold" her $168.50 in items, took her payment, and promised her that the items would be delivered to her in a short time. When Hoddeson never got the furniture, she realized that the "tall man with dark hair frosted at the temples" was a phony and brought this lawsuit. In that case, the court agreed that Ms. Hoddeson could recover against the furniture company just as if she had dealt with an actual agent of the company who had absconded with her money.

According to the court, an agency relationship was created by estoppel because Ms. Hoddeson had reason to believe that the man in the suit operating in the furniture store was actually employed by the store, the store had (indirectly) held the man out as an employee of the store, and Ms. Hoddeson had detrimentally relied:

> That which we have in mind are the unique occurrences where solely through the lack of the proprietor's reasonable surveillance and supervision an impostor falsely impersonates in the place of business an agent or servant of his. Certainly the proprietor's duty of care and precaution of the safety and security of the customer encompasses more than the diligent observance and removal of banana peels from the aisles. Broadly stated, the duty of the proprietor also encircles the exercise of reasonable care and vigilance to protect the customer from loss occasioned by the deceptions of an apparent salesman.

135 A.2d at 706–07. As the court mentions, one of the goals of the rule of agency by estoppel is to induce principals to police their place of business — the rule creates an important incentive for the owner of the shop to watch who is on their floor making sales. In the end, as found in *Hoddeson*, agency by estoppel turns on a holding out and a change of position. However, as to the first principle, holding out does not necessarily depend on an affirmative act

on the part of the principal. It could also be a failure to take reasonable pre-cautions to prevent a reasonable person from believing there has been a hold-ing out. In addition, the theory requires a "change in position." An important consequence of this requirement is that only the principal would be estopped from disclaiming an agency relationship. In other words, the third party can bring a claim against the principal, but the principal cannot bring claim against the third party.

Recall from the *Hoddeson* case, the store owner was not paid; the imposter escapes with the shopper's money. Yet, the store is still liable to the shopper for her loss. The store must either return the money (though it never received it) or deliver the furniture (though the imposter has run off with the money). Thus, though the store was never paid, the store cannot use the theory of agency by estoppel to bring a claim against the shopper, Ms. Hoddeson, for fail-ure to pay. The notion that agency by estoppel is really a one-way street makes sense. Otherwise the policing incentive would be undermined. That is, why would a shop owner police his business if the courts would compensate him in the end regardless?

6. Agency by Ratification

As previously mentioned, an agency relationship created by actual author-ity depends on the principal's *prior* consent that the agent should act on her be-half. However, in some cases, a principal's conduct *after* the agent acts can be used to create legal consequences. RESTATEMENT (THIRD) OF AGENCY § 4.01 That is, a party can also be bound to the contracts of her agent (as if her agent has actual authority) if her subsequent conduct, either expressly or implicitly, can be interpreted as a ratification or approval of the agent's actions. Ratifica-tion is effective regardless of whether there is a claim for apparent authority or whether the third party had reason to know that the agent had no actual authority.

In some cases, a third party attempts to avoid the contract on the ground that the principal has not made an effective ratification. To this point, a prin-cipal does not have an unfettered right to ratify, without any costs. For in-stance, a party does not have unlimited time to ratify an agent's otherwise unauthorized acts. RESTATEMENT (THIRD) OF AGENCY § 4.05. A third party may withdraw from a transaction it believed to be with an agent's principal if the agent really had no authority to make the transaction. Thus, a principal must manifest her intent to ratify the contract before the third party withdraws. Ad-ditionally, a principal cannot ratify the most beneficial part of the transaction; she must ratify the whole or nothing. RESTATEMENT (THIRD) OF AGENCY § 4.07. Finally, if there has been ratification, the principal can no longer sue an agent for acting without her authority. RESTATEMENT (THIRD) OF AGENCY § 4.08. In probably more cases though, a third party tries to enforce the contract against the principal by showing evidence of ratification. In order to show ratification by a principal, as the court in *Botticello v. Stefanovicz* notes below, the principal must demonstrate intent to ratify and must have knowledge of the material circumstances of the transaction.

In *Botticello*, a husband and wife, Walter and Mary Stefanovicz, owned a farm together. Walter, the husband, sold Botticello an option to purchase the farm. 411 A.2d 16 (Conn. 1979). However, Walter never told Mary or received her authorization for the transaction. When Botticello wanted to enforce the option and purchase the farm, the court confronted the issue of ratification, whether Mary had implicitly (or expressly) consented to Walter's acts. The court held that there was little convincing evidence that Mary's subsequent conduct amounted to ratification. Mary knew very little about the terms of the contract. Further, her actions did not suggest that she intended to ratify the lease agreement, though Mary did receive the benefit of rental payments. According to the court, the fact that Mary did not object to the payments received from the tenant did not show ratification, because she could have reasonably interpreted the payments otherwise—for example, perhaps the payments reflected an agreement between Walter and Botticello under a traditional lease agreement. Thus, although whether the party has received a benefit from the transaction supposedly ratified is a factor, it is not dispositive. More important, the party must also have intent to ratify the contract and must have known the important terms of the contract. This rule mirrors the requirement of intent in contracts and the economic justification in both cases is the same. That is, it is important for courts to have some sense that the agreement was in the best interest of the parties and the 'intent requirement' serves that function. When there is intent, courts can be sure that the party wants it; when intent is lacking or questionable (*e.g.*, no knowledge of the terms), courts have no good reason to suspect the agreement is a beneficial agreement. Additionally, the 'intent requirement' is also rooted in philosophical and moral justifications. That is, it protects individual autonomy and freedom to contract.

E. Tort Liability

Of course, a principal, like any person, may have direct tort liability if the principal's conduct in some way caused injury to another. In addition to direct liability, a principal may be vicariously liable for the torts committed by her agent while performing tasks on behalf of the principal. Under the Restatement, a principal is vicariously liable when an employee commits a tort while "acting in the scope of their employment." Restatement (Third) of Agency § 2.04

1. Scope of Agent's Authority

For an injured party to recovery against a principal for acts of an agent, the agent must have been acting on behalf of the principal at the time of the conduct that caused the injury. Restatement (Third) of Agency § 7.03. In many cases, this is a critical but not easily-decided issue, because a person who is an agent that commits an act may be an agent, but may appear to be acting outside of the scope of their duties or authorization.

For instance, in *Ira Bushey & Sons v. United States*, a federal appeals court gives a broad interpretation to acts occurring within the scope of an agent's authority. In *Bushey & Son's*, a seaman returning from shore-leave to his docked vessel caused significant property damage after a night of drinking. 398 F.2d 167 (2d Cir. 1968). In his drunken state, the seaman, Lane, opened a set of valves that controlled the dock, causing his Coast Guard ship to topple and causing significant damage to the dock. The Coast Guard did not dispute that Seaman Lane was its agent. However, the Coast Guard argued that they should not be liable, because Seaman Lane was not operating within the scope of his duties. In one of the broadest findings of scope of employment, the court in *Bushey & Sons* said the Coast Guard could be held accountable, because Lane's conduct was "characteristic" of the seaman activities and, therefore, could have been foreseen by the Coast Guard and prevented:

> Here it was foreseeable that crew members crossing the drydock might do damage, negligently or even intentionally, such as pushing a Bushey employee or kicking property into the water. Moreover, the proclivity of seamen to find solace for solitude by copious resort to the bottle while ashore has been noted in opinions too numerous to warrant citation.

398 F.2d at 172. Thus, in an opinion famous for its language, facts, and written by the erudite appeals Judge Friendly, the court holds that a principal can be held liable for some acts, which are not obviously within the scope of their employment. In addition to looking at whether the conduct was characteristic or foreseeable as the type of activity that the agent might pursue, courts have applied at least three other tests to discern whether an act of an agent was within the scope of the agents duties such that it would create vicarious liability for the principal. First, the most straightforward test of whether the employee's tortious conduct was within the scope of her employment is when she

acts as instructed or under the direction of her employer. In the case of Seaman Lane, the act was unquestionably outside the course of his official duties, as instructed.

Second, courts evaluating whether an agent has acted within the scope of her duties have looked to the motive of the actor, the so-called "motive test." In these cases, courts are concerned with whether the agent took on the act in service of the principal or the principal's interests. In *Ira S. Bushey & Sons*, the court could not find that Seaman Lane, in his barely ambulatory condition, thought he was acting for the benefit of the Coast Guard. However, the court held that the motive of serving his principal was not the only method of determining whether he acted within the scope of his employment.

Third, courts have looked to whether the conduct was intentional or criminal. If the agent commits an intentional tort or flagrantly breaks the law, courts are less likely to find that the employee acted within the scope of her employment. Still, in some cases of even intentional torts or law-breaking, courts have found that the act occurred within the scope of the agency relationship. For instance, a bouncer may commit an intentional tort after she is instructed by her employer to eject someone from a discotheque; a pizza delivery driver may violate the speeding law because she believes his employer's emphasis on "on-time" deliver requires it; or a saleswoman may make intentional misrepresentations to customers because she believes it is related to her sales performance. Nevertheless, this factor tends to undercut vicarious liability, because the agent would, in most cases, be motivated by her own ends when intentionally law-breaking.

2. Independent Contractor Exception

A principal is not liable for the acts of her purported agent unless there is control and assent to control. In some cases though, as previously noted, although a party may have hired someone to do a specific task, they may not exercise sufficient control to create an agency relationship. In these cases, the agent cannot bind the principal to contract. Additionally, in these cases, the principal is not vicariously liable for the hire's misconduct. Put differently, the hire is said to be an independent contractor and liability does not flow back to the principal. Whether a party is an agent or independent contractor frequently comes up in franchisor-franchisee relationships, wherein one side argues that the franchisee/owner managed the day-to-day operations of the store, while the other side argues that there was control from the franchisor creating liability.

Take *Hoover v. Sun Oil*, a case where the court found that there could be no liability for the corporate conglomerate, Sun Oil, after an accident at one of their franchised stores. 212 A.2d 214 (Del. 1965). The facts in that case are simple, but explanatory. The plaintiffs brought suit after they suffered injuries when a fire started as they received a fill up at a full-service Sun Oil station. The court rejected plaintiff's argument, finding that Barone, the store's operator, was an independent contractor, not under the control of Sun Oil corporation. According to the court, Sun Oil could not be liable, since it had no control the day-to-day operations of the store.

On the other hand, a company that exercises too much control over its franchises can be held liable for the operator's negligence. In *Humble Oil & Refining Co. v. Martin*, a court held that the gas company could be liable for the negligence of an attendant at one of its franchises. 222 S.W.2d 995 (Tex. 1949) In that case, the gas station attendant failed to set a parking break for one of the cars waiting for repairs. As a result, the car rolled out of the station and into Martin, a passer-by, and his children. The court held that Humble was liable for the acts of its operator and his employees, since Humble controlled the operation of the store.

Importantly, courts evaluate whether there is control based on an objective review of available evidence, with no single piece of evidence being conclusive. For instance, in *Humble Oil*, the evidence showed that the parties themselves did not think of Humble Oil Company as in control, and they even signed a franchise agreement that reflected that understanding. However, other evidence did suggest control. Humble set the store hours, paid some of the stores' operating costs, and held legal title to the goods that were sold in the store. In the end, these cases turn on things, among others, like whether the franchisee/operator could hire and fire employees at her discretion, was forced to carry only one kind of merchandise, could set her own prices, or whether the franchisee/operator could set store hours.

3. Limits of Independent Contractor Exception

Even though principals are not normally liable for the mistakes of their independent contractors, courts have hammered out several notable exceptions to this rule. To begin with, a principal cannot outsource all duties to independent contracts and expect protection from liability. Some duties cannot be delegated without frustrating important public policy concerns or law. For instance, courts have held that a principal cannot seek protection from liability if she hires an independent contractor to engage in hazardous activities. Thus, a large oil and gas company will not able to insulate itself from liability for a massive oil spill by claiming that its tanker operator was an independent contractor.

Majestic Realty Associates v. Toti Contracting makes this point plain. 153 A.2d 321 (N.J. 1959). In that case, Toti Contracting was retained to demolish a building in New Jersey. While operating the wrecking ball, a Toti employee negligently caused significant damage to the roof of the wrong building, which was owned by Majestic. In fact, according to the published opinion, when asked for an explanation by one of the building's employees at the scene, the contractor responded, "I goofed." Majestic wanted to reach beyond Toti Contracting and sue the city agency that hired the crew for the job. Although Toti would normally be an independent contractor, the court held that the city agency could be held liable, because Toti Contracting was engaged in a dangerous activity. According to the court, the city could not be immune from suit on the theory that Toti was an independent contractor over which the city had no control. To summarize, because some duties are non-delegable, a principal is not always able to escape liability by hiring an independent contractor.

In addition, a principal can not rely on a protection based on control in cases in which the principal hires a contractor ill-equipped to the task. *See* Restatement (Second) of Torts §411. Thus, a principal cannot hire an independent contractor that is completely incompetent or without the financial ability to insure against reasonable mistakes. This creates incentives for the principal to screen and monitor her hires. To take an example, consider *Page v. Sloan*, a case in which the owners of a motel hired a plumber instead of an electrician to repair the electrical element of the motel's water heater. 190 S.E.2d 189 (N.C. 1972). When the water heater exploded, resulting in the death of a motel guest, the court held that the jury was entitled to decide whether the motel owners were liable, with the dispositive factor being whether the owners knew or should have known that the plumber was unqualified to make the electrical repair.

F. Agent Duties

1. Agent Duty of Loyalty

According to the Restatement, agents have a duty to be loyal to their principals in "all matters connected with the agency relationship." Restatement (Third) of Agency § 8.01. Thus, while acting in the agency relationship, the agent should act in the interests of the principal or for the principal's benefit. This duty of loyalty continues even in cases in which the employee or agent may contemplate leaving the principal. Those employees still owe their employers loyalty until the relationship formally terminates. Therefore, the agent should not agree to receive any outside compensation or "secret profits," without the consent of the principal. When an agent breaches the duty of loyalty and receives secret profits, the principal may (in addition to normal damages caused by the breach) be able to recover in a suit against the agent the amount of the agent's profits or other benefits from the disloyal acts. This principle of disgorgement attempts to remove the incentive the agent has from taking impermissible outside compensation in the first place. Thus, the right to an agent's improper profits arises even where the principal is not directly hurt by the agent's acts, as in the next case.

For instance, consider *Reading v. Regem*, an early common law case. 2 KB 268 (1948). In *Reading*, a British soldier stationed in Egypt, a British colony at the time, was able to use his station to help a group of smugglers pass through checkpoints unmolested and transport their wares through Cairo. The soldier was paid 20,000 pounds for his services. The soldier did not abandon his post. Nor was the smuggling transaction something England would have entered into. Still, the court held that England had a right to keep the money and denied the soldier's plea for recovery.

The *Reading* case stands for the rule that an agent must be loyal in all aspects connected with the agency. If she is not, the principal may bring suit to recover any profits the agent derived from the disloyal acts. At the same time, the rule of loyalty to your principal is not without limits, including cases where the acts are not connected to the agency and acts where the agent obtains her principal's consent. In some instances, thus, even an agent may moonlight or hold down a second job without fear that she will be hauled into court and accused of disloyalty.

To ascertain whether the agent is moonlighting or impermissibly collecting secret profits, courts look to two issues. First, courts look to whether the agent was acting in her official capacity or a capacity connected with the agency. Thus, a soldier in uniform cannot use her position or official influence to collect outside compensation during the agency relationship. Second, courts look to whether the agent disclosed the relationship with a third party to the principal. That is, if the agent discloses the outside contract and obtains consent, either implicitly or expressly, there is no violation of the agent's duty of loyalty.

2. Other Agent Duties

In addition to a duty of loyalty, an agent owes her principal much more, including candor, diligence, and obedience. First, the agent, regardless of whether she has an interest, owes a general duty of candor to the principal. In these cases, an agent has a duty to inform her principal of any fact that may be relevant to the principal's decision-making. *See, e.g.*, RESTATEMENT (THIRD) OF AGENCY § 8.11. (For a discussion of the obligation of candor, *see Community Counseling Service, Inc. v. Reilly*, 317 F.2d 239 (4th Cir. 1963); *Hamburger v. Hamburger*, 1995 WL 579679 (Mass. 1995).)

Second, an agent has a duty to her principal to act with due care and diligence in executing tasks. RESTATEMENT (THIRD) OF AGENCY § 8.08. The agent's duties of care are usually enforceable under contract or tort principles. On the one hand, an agent has a duty of care that is synonymous with any contractual arrangement that the parties have. For instance, an agent and principal may agree to certain performance standards, which could create a cause of action for breach of contract if the agent is unable to meet the standards. Like with all contracts, the level of performance agreed to can be memorialized in writing or implied based on the circumstances or the parties' conduct. On the other hand, regardless of any formal contractual arrangement, because an agent has a duty, an injury caused by the breach of that duty may also create a potential action that sounds in tort. Third, an agent has a duty to follow the instructions of her principal. RESTATEMENT (THIRD) OF AGENCY § 8.09. Thus, an agent would likely violate her duty on this front, if she acted outside of the scope of the authority granted by her principal. At the same time, however, an agent has no duty to follow instructions that would require the agent to break the law or cause injury or violate standards of professional conduct.

G. Principal's Duties to Agent

Principals also have duties to their agents, including a duty to observe any contractual terms of the parties' agency agreement, to compensate their agents, to indemnify their agents for any losses suffered in connection with the agency, and to act in good faith. RESTATEMENT (THIRD) OF AGENCY §§ 8.13–8.15. Most of the principal's duties are uncontroversial. For instance, though there are gratuitous agencies in which there is no compensation to agents, many agents expect compensation for the services they render the principal. The requirement that a principal pay the agreed compensation is unremarkable. However, it is worth noting that the Restatement suggests that the principal's duty of good faith encompasses a duty to be relatively candid with her agents. As such, a principal should stay reasonably aware of dangers or risks connected with the agent's tasks, and warn their agents about such risks or dangers.

H. Disclosed and Undisclosed Principals

In many cases, an agent freely discloses that she is operating on behalf of someone else and, usually, has little hesitation in disclosing who that someone is.

In the most obvious scenario, a third party who transacts business with an agent knows that the agent only speaks for another, her principal. If the third party knows who the principal is, the principal is said to be disclosed. RE-STATEMENT (THIRD) OF AGENCY § 6.01. When an agent contracts on behalf of a known or disclosed principal, the agent is not a party to the contract and faces no direct liability. RESTATEMENT (THIRD) OF AGENCY § 6.01.

However, some principals are careful about whom they share their identity with and expect their agent to stay mum. In some cases, a third party may know that the agent speaks for another, but have no concrete idea who the principal is. In such cases, the principal is unidentified or only partially disclosed. RESTATEMENT (THIRD) OF AGENCY § 6.02. In other cases still, a principal may want to keep the third party completely in the dark regarding their existence. The third party has no reason to know that it is dealing with an agent of some-one else at all. In these cases, the principal is said to be undisclosed. RE-STATEMENT (THIRD) OF AGENCY § 6.03. For instance, to avoid a bidding war, a well-heeled and well-known real estate investor may want to keep it a secret that she is buying up property along the shore. This way, the famous buyer can prevent potential sellers from holding out for a higher price. Others may want to maintain customer relations and goodwill that are attached with third parties' continued belief that they are dealing with a certain agent. It may be a good idea to leave the mom-and-pop look to a business in order to maintain the store's customer base. Recall, for instance, the facts of the *Wattean* case.

1. Undisclosed Principals

A principal need not disclose herself. In fact, the failure of a principal to disclose does not create a fraud or a reason for avoiding enforcement, as *Hirsch v. Silberstein* should illustrate shortly. Still, a third party may have grounds to avoid a contract if the agent knew (or had reason to know) that the third party would not have wanted to do business with the principal. RESTATEMENT (THIRD) OF AGENCY § 6.11(4).

Hirsch is a fascinating (but also depressing) nugget of agency law from the segregated residential days of the 1960s. 227 A.2d 638 (Pa. 1967). A white agent purchased a piece of property on behalf of an African-American couple. The seller sought to cancel the purchase contract on the grounds that they had no idea that the real purchasers were the Crosses, the African-American couple. However, the court rejected their argument, holding that Mr. Silberstein had no reason to believe that the Hirsches would object to having the Crosses as their neigh-bors. Keep in mind, the contract to sale had a limitation on the right to assign-ment, which provided that there could be no transfer without the seller's consent.

The court held that there had been no assignment *per se* by Silberstein to the Crosses, since Silberstein had at all times been operating on behalf of the Crosses. Further, the court in the case goes so far as to suggest that even though the defendant misrepresented his intention (*e.g.*, he never had any intention to occupy the property himself), misrepresentation was immaterial and created no damage to the plaintiffs. Thus, in that case, the court resolved firmly that there was no blanket duty on the part of the principal to disclose her identity. The only exception to the court's strong holding in *Hirsch* is if the undisclosed principal (or her agent) has good reason to believe that the other party would not enter the contract if the principal's true identify were revealed. Perhaps overly optimistic given the time period, the court in *Hirsch* suggests that there was no such reason to suspect the Hirsch's might be prejudiced against the Crosses.

In summary, regardless of whether the principal is disclosed or not, she becomes a direct party to contracts entered into by her agent on her behalf. If the third party wants to limit their assent to only the agent, as in *Hirsch*, an anti-assignment clause is not enough. They must go further by, for instance, limiting their assent and specifically excluding assent to contract with other parties. Also, an agent of an undisclosed (or unidentified) principal can have direct liability for a breach of contract or non-performance. In both cases, both the agent and the principal can enforce the contract against the third party.

2. Disclosed Principals

An agent who makes a contract on behalf of a disclosed principal will not be the party to the contract. In these cases, only the principal is liable in contract. However, even in these cases, the agent and the third party may make a special agreement such that the agent and the principal are jointly liable for the terms of the agreement. RESTATEMENT (THIRD) OF AGENCY § 6.09. For instance, the third party may be leery of the principal's finances or otherwise wary that the performance will be completed in time. The third party may want the agent to guarantee performance in her individual capacity, in which case both the agent and the principal are liable for a breach. Further, an agent will still be liable in tort, even where the principal is disclosed and acts with authority.

I. Co-Agents and Sub-Agents

Not all agents are created equally. Some agents have a direct reporting line to the principal. There can be several such agents. As long as each acts directly on behalf of the principal and under the direct control of the principal, these individuals are most likely "co-agents." RESTATEMENT (THIRD) OF AGENCY §§ 1.04(1), 3.15 cmt. b. Other agents are appointed, not by a principal, but by yet another agent. These so-called "sub-agents" usually report to their appointing agent who, in turn, reports to the principal. Thus, a sub-agent is any person or entity appointed by the original agent to act on the agent's behalf and under the control of both the original principal and the appointing agent. RESTATEMENT (THIRD) OF AGENCY § 3.15. For example, consider a principal that agrees that a corporation or other legal entity can operate on the principal's behalf and under the principal's control. The principal has an agency relationship with the corporation as its agent. Since the corporation cannot act without hiring directors, officers, and other employees, the corporation has to hire others to execute tasks. These other individuals are sub-agents.

Interestingly, a sub-agent acts on behalf of the principal, but is answerable to both the principal and the appointing agent. The sub-agent's appointment of an agent creates a new agency relationship, wherein the original agent functions like a new principal and the sub-agent the new agent. In fact, in a sub-agency, the appointing agent bears primary responsible for monitoring and controlling the sub-agent. Nevertheless, although most directions in a sub-agency come from the appointing agent, the sub-agent, like the appointing agent, must at all times be answerable to the principal. In the end though, principals can be liable for the acts of a sub-agent or a co-agent. Thus, the legal consequences for the principal for the acts of a sub-agent are the same as they for an appointing agent or co-agent.

J. Termination of Agency Relationship

An agency relationship can be terminated at the election of either party, principal or her agent. The Restatement provides several ways an agency relationship may be terminated, including termination by death of either the principal or agent, by the loss of capacity of the principal, by the term of agency ending, by renunciation by the agent, or by revocation by the principal. RESTATEMENT (THIRD) OF AGENCY § 3.06. If the agency terminates, the agent can no longer bind the principal. Once the agency is terminated (but not before), the agent may compete with her former principal and the principal with the agent. However, the parties' duties related to the agency largely continue. For instance, a departing agent may not disclose confidential or proprietary information learned during the agency. RESTATEMENT (THIRD) OF AGENCY § 8.05 cmt. c. Further, a former principal has a duty to continue to indemnify the departing agent for conduct occurring during the agency.

In several cases, the process of determining whether an agency has ended is straightforward. If the agent or principal dies or is judged to be without capacity, the agency relationship ends, so long as the agent (or third parties) receive notice of the death or loss of capacity. This makes sense, because the principal, in the case of death or incapacity, cannot control the agent or desire for the agent to continue to operate on her behalf. Or if the parties have agreed explicitly to a time period for the agency and that time has run, the agency ends.

In other cases, determining whether an agency is at end requires a reasonable, objective appraisal of the parties' conduct. First, in cases in which the parties have set no particular time period for an agency to end, the agency continues until a reasonable time period has elapsed. Second, it is reasonable to presume (absent conduct to the contrary) that an agency ends when the agent has accomplished the goals set out by her principal. For instance, a homeowner may hire an agent to make particular home improvements, like re-pave the driveway, changing the locks, or re-painting a bedroom. Absent a manifestation by the principal to the contrary, the agency would end, when the particular home improvement is completed. Second, an agency is at an end if the agent can no longer reasonably expect to accomplish the principal's goals because of supervening frustration. As above, a homeowner may hire an agent to make improvements. However, the agency is likely at an end if the home is destroyed by fire.

As stated, generally an agency relationship can be terminated at the election of either party. However, the one exception, discussed by the United States Supreme Court in *Hunt v. Rousmanier's Administrators*, is in cases where the relationship creates a security interest. In *Hunt*, the U.S. Supreme Court opined about whether the parties to an agency have an absolute right to terminate an agency relationship at any time. 21 U.S. 174 (1823). According to the high court, the general rule is that a principal may terminate an agency relationship at any time. But, the court noted that an agency relationship is irrevocable if the agency relationship was created as a security interest:

> The act of the substitute, therefore, which in such a case is the act of
> the principal, to be legally effectual, must be in his name, must be such
> an act as the principal himself would be valid if performed by him.
> Such a power necessarily ceases with the life of the person making it.
> But if the interest, or estate, passes with the power, and vests in the
> person by whom the power is to be exercised, such person acts in his
> own name. The estate, being in him, passes from him by a conveyance
> in his own name. He is no longer a substitute, acting in the place and

name of another, but is principal acting in his own name, in pursuance of powers which limit his estate. The legal reason which limits a power to the life of the person giving it, exists no longer, and the rule ceases with the reason on which it is founded. The intention of the instrument may be affected without violating any legal principle.

21 U.S. at 204–05. To be sure, some terminations of an agency are wrongful and can create a breach of contract. Still, the rule that an agency can be terminated is broad and permissive. Under the law of agency, the parties to the agency can still terminate the relationship, even though the termination may create a breach. A principal has virtually unfettered authority to determine who speaks on her behalf. Equally, an agent may abandon an agency at any point. The only slim exception is for agencies created as security interests as noted in *Hunt*. In these cases, which are more about securitizing transactions than agency principals, the security interest predominates and the agency relationship may be irrevocable, until the interest is satisfied. Thus, besides the scenario described in *Hunt*, a principal (or agent) can terminate an agency relationship at any time for any reason.

Checkpoints

- An agency relationship is formed when two parties agree that one party (the agent) will act on the other party's (the principal) behalf, and the principal provides general control over the agent's actions.

- An agent's authority to bind the principal in contract may be created by an express statement of the principal (express authority), the circumstances or the principal's conduct (implied authority), a "holding out" by the principal that suggests authority (apparent authority), or from the customary powers of an agent's position (inherent authority).

- A principal may face vicarious liability when her agents act within the scope of their employment. Acts outside the scope of an agent's authority are not normally attributable to the principal.

- A principal is generally not liable for the acts of an independent contractor, unless the contractor's activities are non-delegable or the principal is negligent in hiring the contractor.

- Principals may be disclosed, partially disclosed, or undisclosed. Regardless, the principal is a direct party to the agreement. An agent of a disclosed principal is not a party to an agreement, but may be bound if the principal is undisclosed or only partially disclosed.

- In almost all cases, the parties to an agency can terminate the agency at any time, for any reason.

Chapter 2

General Partnerships

Roadmap

- Formation of a General Partnership
- Rights of Partners to Manage
- Rights of Partners to Share in Profits (or Losses)
- Partnership Liability
- Partnership Duties: Loyalty, Care, Good Faith and Fair Dealing
- Partnership Changes in Control

A. Introduction

The general partnership is still an attractive business vehicle. For one thing, a general partnership is the easiest type of business organization to form. It does not take any paperwork, filing, or advice from a lawyer, accountant or other professional. In fact, forming a partnership does not require any real knowledge of partnership law. Furthermore, in a general partnership, investors ordinarily have a formal role in the management of the business. The default rules make the partners at once investors and mangers, each with an important say-so in how the entity is run. Lastly, many individuals elect partnership as their organizational form, because the partnership offers the benefit of pass-through taxation. The profits or losses of a partner, in other words, are passed from the entity or partnership to the partners without any taxation on the entity level. However, the main disadvantage of a general partnership is that the partners are all individually and jointly liable for partnership contracts and torts. A partner's personal assets can be at stake. Despite this shortcoming in terms of liability, the partnership, with the rather casual formation requirements, is probably the most widely used organizational vehicle.

B. Sources of General Partnership Law

Partners face several legal consequences when they co-join forces and create, even by accident, a partnership. To begin with, the legal consequences of the acts of the partners are frequently resolved by state law. One of the most important sources of state partnership law is the Uniform Partnership Act (UPA), which has been adopted in its most recent version by thirty five states (at the time of this writing).

List of States Adopting Various Versions of Uniform Partnership Act			
State Adoptions of UPA (1992) (1996)	Connecticut West Virginia Wyoming		
State Adoptions of UPA with 1997 Amendments *Substantially Similar*	Alabama Alaska Arizona Arkansas California Colorado Delaware District of Columbia Florida Hawaii Idaho Illinois	Iowa Kansas Kentucky Maine Maryland Minnesota Mississippi Montana Nebraska Nevada New Jersey New Mexico	North Dakota Oklahoma Oregon Puerto Rico South Dakota* Tennessee Texas* U.S. Virgin Islands Vermont Virginia Washington

Nevertheless, despite the coverage of the Uniform Partnership Act, probably the most important arbiter of partnership disputes comes from the parties themselves, rather than from any state law. The parties may privately contract around the vast majority of legal obligations created by courts or state legislatures. In most cases, the UPA only represents a set of default rules. For instance, one of the early provisions of the Revised Uniform Partnership Act (RUPA), provided that "relations among the partners and between the partners and the partnership are governed by the partnership agreement. To the extent the partnership agreement does not otherwise provide, this [Act] governs relations among the partners and between the partners and the partnership." REVISED UNIF. P'SHIP ACT § 103(b) (1997). The only significant limitations on private parties' ability to define privately the scope of their joint venture are when the partnership unreasonably over-reaches. A partnership agreement, for instance, may not unreasonably eviscerate the duty of loyalty, duty of care, or obligation of good faith and fair dealing, all of which are discussed in detail below. Besides these duties (and a handful of other non-waiveable obligations), partners may privately contract around state law or the common law regarding their partnership relationship.

Finally, common law or case precedent is also an important source of partnership law. As will be seen throughout this Chapter, courts are frequently called on to make decisions on how state partnership law is to be interpreted or the scope of the parties' private agreement. For example, the UPA provides that courts may, as always, look to principles of law and equity, unless the UPA otherwise displaces those principles. Revised Unif. P'ship Act § 106(a) (1997).

C. Definition of Partnership

Two or more persons will have formed a partnership, with accompanying legal obligations, whenever they come together to create a business for profit. Thus, parties who collaborate on a non-profit venture are not considered partners. Based on objective evidence, the parties need only manifest intent to carry on a for-profit business together for a general partnership to be created. For instance, did the partners memorialize their understanding by entering into a partnership agreement? Even less formally, a partnership may be created if the parties have allocated responsibilities for the business enterprise. Accordingly, forming a general partnership is a snap. In fact, formation of a partnership is the default organizational form. Though co-profiteers have the option to organize their collective effort in another statutory form, if the parties say nothing, they will have formed a general partnership.

D. Evidence of Formation

According to the RUPA, which has been adopted by a majority of states, evidence of formation of a partnership is based on an objective review of the parties' conduct, regardless of "whether or not the persons intended to form partnership." Revised Unif. P'ship Act § 202(a) (1997). Thus, though the distinction is subtle, it is consequential: What is important to determining whether the parties have formed a partnership is whether they have an intent to operate a business together, not a question of whether they have an intent to be in a partnership (with the corresponding legal obligations and duties that come with it).

Because courts rely on objective evidence to determine whether a partnership was formed, it is conceivable that the legal characterization of the relationship might not match even what the parties intended. In other words, the legal characterization of the parties' acts may be inconsistent with their subjective or internal intention vis-à-vis their co-partner. Since whether a partnership is formed depends on objective evidence, courts have found a partnership in cases in which the parties did not intend one and have refused to find a partnership existed, even when the partners wanted to create one. In the next case, in particular, the court finds that the parties had not created a partnership, even though they intended to create one and even though they were sharing profits of the enterprise.

In *Fenwick v. Unemployment Compensation Commission*, the owner of a beauty shop, Fenwick, attempted to form a partnership with his receptionist, which would have meant that he could avoid certain employment taxes. 44 A.2d 172 (N.J. 1945). The court held that Fenwick and his receptionist had not formed a partnership. The court found that, though the so-called partnership agreement provided that the receptionist would be entitled to a small share of the profits, she was not exposed to the possibility of any losses. Further, the court noted that the receptionist had no real interest in partnership property. If there were dissolution of the partnership, in other words, all unencumbered partnership assets would flow to Fenwick. Finally, and perhaps more important, the court noted that the receptionist had no management control over the operations of the company.

Thus, in order to determine whether the parties have formed a partnership, the parties' stated intention is but one piece of evidence. Also, courts, as in *Fenwick*, look to see whether the purported partner has the typical indicia of a partner, like control, a claim on business property, or shares in profits and losses of the partnership. As to the first point, control, courts look to determine whether the purported partner has a right to participate in partnership decision-making. Second, courts may attempt to ascertain whether the parties have a claim on partnership property upon dissolution, as you would expect if it were a real partnership. For instance, in *Fenwick*, the receptionist, Mrs. Cheshire, upon a winding up of the partnership would be treated no differently from an employee who was dismissed: her wages would stop and she would not receive a share of partnership property. However, control and ownership do not always overlap. Mere co-ownership of the same property does not necessarily create control, since some co-owners will exercise no oversight over their property. Third, courts evaluate whether the partnership shares in profits. On this point, merely sharing in profits, as in *Fenwick*, is not enough to signal that the parties have created a general partnership. For instance, it is not uncommon for a landlord to receive rents as a proportion of the profits that the tenant is able to generate from use of the property. Such an arrangement does not necessarily suggest a general partnership. Other important factors for determining whether the parties have successfully formed a partnership include the language that the parties used to characterize their agreement and the parties conduct of holding themselves out as partners to third parties.

E. Right to Control and Share in Profits

Once a partnership is formed, partners (by default) have two important rights: the right to control or manage the operations of the partnership and the right to an equal share in the profits that the partnership generates.

1. Right to Control

First, the right to control partnership operations makes a partnership unique from other types of business organizations, such as the corporation. In the corporate context, as discussed later, investors have no clear line of management authority over the corporate enterprise. Instead, shareholders have to rely on executives, officers, directors, and other agents to manage the daily affairs of the business entity. By contrast, in a partnership, unless the parties agree otherwise, all partners have an equal right to participate in management of the partnership business. This right to control means that each partner has both a right to be informed of the operation of the partnership and a right to participate in decision-making.

At this point, it is worth mentioning that partnership decision-making can be grouped under two types, broadly speaking. On the one hand, some decisions by the partnership are extraordinary and represent significant changes (*e.g.*, the admission of new partners) to the business entity. Such extraordinary decisions are only adopted by the partnership through unanimity. Unless the partners agree otherwise, the default rule is that if just one of the partners disagrees, the extraordinary change will be halted. On the other hand, other proposals to change the partnership arrangement are not extraordinary at all. They are proposals to change something in the ordinary course. A partner may propose a change in how customers are greeted in a retail partnership (*e.g.*, a change from "Welcome" to "Howdy") or change the uniforms of employees or any number of other changes that arise in the ordinary course of business operations. In these cases, a simple majority of the partners may stop a change in the management of the partnership proposed by one of the parties.

2. Right to Share Profits (or Losses)

Second, partners have a right to an equal share of the profits from the partnership. The natural corollary to that rule is that by default partners are equally liable for partnership losses. At the same time, however, if the partners agree to an alternative arrangement for the sharing of profits, but say nothing about how losses are to be shared, losses would be allocated in the same way as profits were split. An illustration is in order. Consider a three member partnership, with no agreement with regard to how profits or losses are to be split. The default rule is that one-third of both profits and losses would be allocated to each of the partners. However, imagine if the three member partnership fails to agree on losses, but agrees that Partner A should get half of the profits, while the other two members, Partner B and Partner C, are to split the other half of the profits. In that case, Partner A would, by default, be liable for one half of the partnership losses, while Partner B and Partner C would each be liable for twenty-five percent of losses. Of course, the partners could always contract around the default rules and come up with any number of their own private arrangements.

Allocation of LOSSES in Hypothetical Three-Person Partnership			
	No Agreement on Losses	Agreement on Profits (*i.e.*, 50% of Profits to Partner A)	Complete Agreement on Profits and Losses (*i.e.*, 50% of Profits to Partner A and equal split of Losses)
Partner A	One-third	One-half	One-third
Partner B	One-third	One-fourth	One-third
Partner C	One-third	One-fourth	One-third

However, the rule of equal sharing of partnership profits and losses does lend itself to at least one interesting exception. That is, in cases in which one partner contributes only labor and another contributes only capital, the labor partner might not be liable for losses. For example, consider the next case, *Kovacik v. Reed*. 315 P.2d 314 (Cal. 1957). In this pearl of partnership law, one partner, Kovacik, was the "deep-pocket" and funded Reed's talent for remodeling kitchens. Kovacik would find the customers and keep the books. Reed would do the work. Thus, the parties agreed that Kovacik would contribute the capital to the business and Reed would contribute the know-how. Importantly, Reed would take no salary for his labor. The parties agreed to share profits equally, but made no agreement regarding losses. When the partnership was dissolved with some debt, the court had to grapple with whether Reed should be liable for partnership losses under the traditional default rule that partners share in profits *and losses* equally. However, in this case, the court acknowledged an exception to the default rule in cases in which the parties have a true services-only partnership. In these cases, the services-only partner is not liable for losses, because he was never compensated for his labor. According to the court, all such losses are to be borne by the capital-contributing partner.

The court's logic in *Kovacik* makes sense. If the labor-only partner was also forced to contribute one-half of losses, he would be a double-loser. That is, if the business declines, the labor-only partner would lose not only his labor contribution to the partnership (which, recall, was not compensated), but would also have to contribute to make-up half of the partnership's losses. This result is probably not the result that most services-only partners would have anticipated. Surely, if Reed were forced to take up one-half of the losses, he would have asked to be compensated by the partnership for that increased risk, perhaps by taking a fixed salary for his labor.

This exception for services-only partners, however, is on the wane, if not moribund. That is, although some courts may continue to view *Kovacik* as good precedent, the vast majority of courts today would not make a services-only exception in light of the recent changes to the Uniform Partnership Act, which specifically disclaims *Kovacik*. In those states, which have adopted the revised UPA, the following comment to the equal sharing rule, is the most telling:

> If partners agree to share profits other than equally, losses will be shared similarly to profits, absent agreement to do otherwise. That rule, carried over from the UPA, is predicated on the assumption that partners would likely agree to share losses on the same basis as profits, but fail to say so.... The default rules apply ... where one or more of the partners contribute no capital, although there is case law to the contrary.

REVISED UNIF. P'SHIP ACT § 401 cmt. 3 (1997) (citing *Kovacik v. Reed, inter alia*). According to other comments, the drafters acknowledged that eliminating the exception for the services-only partner might not be what unsuspecting partners desire. However, the drafters believed that the uniform rule of equal sharing by default would act as a penalty default. In other words, the rule would incentivize partners who do not want the rule to contract around it: "In entering a partnership with such a capital structure, the partners should fore-see that application of the default rule may bring about unusual results and take advantage of their power to vary by agreement the allocation of capital losses." *Id.* The logic of the drafters makes sense among sophisticated parties, considering that such parties are likely to know the content of legal rules or be well-advised. However, the argument loses some cogency in the case of unso-phisticated parties, who might be subject to equal sharing of losses by default, even though they had no inkling such an outcome was possible. For instance, in *Kovacik*, the services-only partner, Reed, likely had little knowledge of part-nership law or financial accounting. The other partner, after all, agreed to keep the books, drum up business, and all Reed had to do was remodel kitchens. The issue is whether eliminating the exception for services-only partnership cre-ates a trap for many unwary individuals, like Reed.

F. Partnership Liability

1. Introduction to Partnership Liability

Each partner is at once an agent and principal of the partnership and the other partners. In a general partnership, the rules of agency normally apply. Thus, a partner is liable for the acts of her co-partners when such acts are within the ordinary course of the partnership or the partnership has authorized such acts. As mentioned, partners (by default) have the power to control the part-nership, receive a share of the profits, and are responsible for a share of losses. Because partners (by default) have the power to manage or control the affairs of the partnership, they may also enter into contracts on behalf of the partner-ship. In most of these cases, partners have apparent authority to bind each other in contract. Thus, as in other apparent authority contexts, one of the only lim-itations on their right to bind is whether their acts were (1) done on behalf of the partnership and (2) done within the ordinary course of business like that nor-mally carried on by the partners. Thus, a partner's authority under principles of apparent agency cut broadly. A partner can arguably bind the partnership to transactions that are customary or traditionally carried on by partners in sim-ilar businesses, regardless of whether the acts are in the ordinary course of the particular partnership. In cases in which a partner does not have apparent au-thority to bind the partnership to contract, she may still have actual authority, if the other partners have authorized the act. The other partners may have au-thorized the act by formalized partnership agreement or implicitly based on their conduct.

2. Limiting Partners' Authority to Bind

Partners may blanch at the thought of the acts of their co-partners. In these cases, well-advised partners may attempt to limit the ability of their partner to enter into contracts that bind the entire partnership. How the partners go about limiting the ability of a partner to enter into contracts depends on whether the partner has actual authority to enter into such contracts or merely apparent authority. For instance, one way for partners to limit the reach of the partner's authority to act under apparent authority is to notify third parties of the partner's limited authority. If the partnership so notifies third parties, third parties usually operate at their own risk, when dealing with an overly eager partner. Second, a partnership may limit the partner's actual authority to act by calling for a vote among the majority of the partners. As mentioned, if the partner's act occurs within the ordinary course of business, the partnership can likely limit a partner's actual authority by majority vote of the partners. (Keep in mind the partners can only modify the partnership agreement or make changes to partnership beyond those taken in the ordinary course only by unanimous consent.) The next two cases show that whether contracts are binding on the partnership, depends importantly on whether the partner acts with actual authority (*National Biscuit Company v. Stroud*) or apparent authority (*Summers v. Dooley*).

In *National Biscuit Company v. Stroud*, Stroud, one member of a two-man partnership informs a third party, National Biscuit or Nabisco, that the partnership would no longer be entering into contracts for bread. 106 S.E.2d 692 (N.C. 1959). However, despite the warning, Nabisco took another order from Freeman, Stroud's co-partner. When Nabisco sues the partnership for payment, the issue is whether Nabisco can recover against Stroud, even though Stroud warns Nabisco. The court holds for Nabisco on the ground that Freeman had actual authority to bind the partnership.

In *Nabisco*, the court's opinion helps unscramble at least two important concepts dealing with actual authority in partnership law. First, absent agreement to the contrary, partners have actual authority (as opposed to apparent authority) to enter into contracts in the ordinary course of business on behalf of the partnership. Accordingly, since Freeman, the overly-eager partner, had not been formally limited, he had actual authority to enter into contracts with Nabisco, since these contracts fall within the ordinary range of conduct for a partner in a grocery partnership. Of course, the partners could enter a partnership agreement that contracts around this default rule. However, without an agreement, if a partnership wants to circumscribe the ordinary authority of one of the other partners, such a limitation must be decided by a majority of the partners.

Perhaps a second point of *Nabisco*, therefore, is that in a two-member partnership, a majority vote to limit your co-partner's actual authority is technically impossible. At least one of the partners is certain to vote against it! Put another way, in the case of two-member partners, like in *Nabisco*, a deadlock is reached when the partners cannot agree on the reach of actual authority to conduct ordinary partnership business. In cases of deadlock, the change-agent partner (*i.e.*, the partner proposing the limit on conduct in question) loses.

Nabisco is also a useful backdrop to take up the issue of apparent authority. As mentioned, in addition to actual authority, a partner has apparent authority to carry out such tasks as would normally fall within the normal range of a partner's responsibilities. Thus, in the last case, Freeman might also have apparent authority to make contracts with Nabisco. However, as mentioned, a third party, like Nabisco, can only rely on apparent authority unless they are warned that no such authority exists. For instance, imagine that the facts of *Nabisco* were slightly different and Freeman had no actual authority to order goods from Nabisco. For the sake of argument, imagine the parties had a secret, undisclosed partnership agreement that provided that Freeman may *not* do business with any local bread vendors. Nabisco may still attempt to seek recovery from the other partner on the grounds that there was apparent authority to enter the contracts. However, a big problem for Nabisco's argument is that the company was notified that Freeman should not be making bread contracts. In theory, therefore, Nabisco could not justify its claim that it relied on a notion of apparent authority, after they had received notification.

The next case explores a situation where the partner does not have actual authority. In these cases, a partner cannot make a unilateral decision to bind his co-partners unless they approve. As mentioned, ordinary decisions can be approved by a simple majority. This default rule effectively gives each partner veto rights over decisions in a two-member partnership.

Specifically, in *Summers v. Dooley*, where one of the partners in a two-man trash collection business hires a third individual to help out, the court held that the additional hire was improper, since it was not approved by a majority of the partners. 481 P.2d 318 (Idaho 1971). When the hiring partner, Summers, sues his co-partners for expenses related to the hire, the court held that the hiring would not be an obligation of the partnership. As the court reasons, the hiring partner had no actual authority to make a permanent hire, because the parties had an agreement that each would pull his own weight. Nevertheless, even though there was not actual authority, the decision to hire the extra man to help with the trash collection was not extraordinary by any stretch. Thus, in a case by the new hire against the partnership, both partners might have liability for, say, unpaid wages, if the new hire's claim was based on ap-

parent authority. However, in this case, is it is the partner Summers who sues
his co-partner for his expenses in hiring the third man. He could only recover
against his co-partner if there was no actual authority to make the hire. Because
the decision was taken in the ordinary course, in order for it to become a decision of the partnership, it would have needed to be approved by a majority
of the partners. In a two-man partnership, a single dissenting partner can
avoid these changes.

To summarize, in order to evaluate whether all the partners are liable for the
acts of their co-partners, two critical issues have to be resolved. First, answer
whether the partner had authority under the parties' agreement to make the
decision to bind. That is, partners generally are given authority to bind the
partnership at the time of the formation of the partnership. Their right to bind
is spelled out in their agreement. If no limits on authority are outlined by
agreement, the partners have actual authority to bind the partnership to contracts taken in the ordinary course. Second, if the decision to bind is beyond
the scope of the partner's authority under agreement, figure out whether the
partners may have subsequently approved of the decision. When a change-
agent partner who has no actual authority wants to bind the partnership to a
relatively significant business venture, no liability for the other partners will at-
tach unless the partners have unanimously approved the venture. By contrast,
when a change-agent partner who has no actual authority wants to bind the
partnership to a contract taken within the ordinary course, liability attaches if
a simple majority of the partners approve or if there are grounds for apparent
authority.

3. Other Limits on Partnership Liability

Even though a partner may face significant exposure for the debts and other
obligations that her co-partner enters on behalf of the partnership, some protections exist. For instance, in many states, a creditor must have exhausted the
assets of the partnership before pursuing a co-partner individually. Therefore,
a creditor cannot usually elect to go beyond partnership property, since such
property in many cases would be substantial and in the usual case enough to
satisfy a creditor. Additionally, co-partners are protected by time. Specifically,
under the RUPA, a partner is not personally liable for transactions or partnership conduct that predates the partner's arrival. REVISED UNIF. P'SHIP ACT
§ 306 (b) (1997). However, an incoming partner still risks any investment in
the partnership she has made, since partnership assets (regardless of origin) are
the first source to satisfy outstanding obligations. Further, a departing partner
may still be liable for obligations incurred by her former partners, if those ob-

ligations were incurred while the departing partner was still part of the partnership. To summarize, a creditor cannot come after a new partner's personal assets, if the debt obligation was created prior to the partner joining the firm; only the new partners' investment in the partnership is at risk in such a case; and after a partner leaves she only stands liable for obligations incurred by the partnership while she was part of it.

G. Partnership Fiduciary Duty

The partnership relationship is one of cooperation, trust and confidence. Partners, tied together by shared business objectives, are fiduciaries of one another. Of course, partners should not abscond with the partnership's property. But, a partnership is something more significant than a simple prohibition against theft. True partners should also disclose opportunities with their co-partners, and perhaps even share them. They should treat their co-partners with respect and avoid put-downs or slights. In the end, partners owe each other several obligations or duties, including loyalty, care, and good faith. Although these duties can be modified by contract (*i.e.*, the parties' partnership agreement), the parties cannot completely eliminate these core duties to one another. How far parties can go to privately decide the scope of their fiduciary duties is a question to be decided by courts.

1. Duty of Loyalty

To begin with, under both common law and state partnership acts, partners owe one another a duty of loyalty. For instance, the RUPA provides that the duty of loyalty is duty to refrain from misappropriating partnership property, avoid conflicts of interest, and refrain from competition with the partnership. REVISED UNIF. P'SHIP ACT § 404(b)(1)-(3) (1997).

As mentioned, the partners may enter into a partnership agreement that outlines the outer parameters of the fiduciary duty of loyalty they owe to one another. Specifically, partners can enter a partnership agreement that provides that certain categories of activities or certain specific acts do not violate the duty of loyalty. It is not unusual, for example, for partners to agree that certain transactions that produce a conflict of interest will not be a breach of the fiduciary duty. Yet, partners may not enter into a contract that unreasonably circumscribes or completely eliminates the duty of loyalty. REVISED UNIF. P'SHIP ACT § 103(b) (3) (1997). Whether a particular agreement does so is a judgment for courts. For some courts, the duty of loyalty that partners owe one another has relatively far-reaching implications. Unarguably, all courts would agree that a partner would violate her duty of loyalty to other partners if she were to lie or equivocate on matters related to the partnership.

One important implication of the duty of loyalty is that a partner is required to hold partnership property (*e.g.*, real property, profit, or partnership opportunities) for the benefit of the partnership. One relevant preliminary issue courts must confront in these cases is what is "partnership property"? For instance, in many cases it is unclear whether some property or benefit belongs to the partnership as an entity or to one of the individual partners. The RUPA provides several nuggets for determining what "partnership property" means. Begin with the simple case: Partnership property is resolved in favor of the partnership if title to the property references the partnership. Thus, partnership property would include any property that is acquired in the name of the partnership or in the name of one of the partners in their capacity as a partner. REVISED UNIF. P'SHIP ACT § 204(a)(1)(2) (1997). Additionally, property is presumed to belong to the partnership if the property is paid for with partnership funds, regardless of what the title of the property says. REVISED UNIF. P'SHIP ACT § 204(c) (1997). What is clear though is that a partner who misappropriates a benefit that arises out of the partnership business (as *Meinhard v. Salmon* shows) violates the duty of loyalty. When partnership property is misappropriated by one of the partners, the partnership property should be disgorged and shared among the partners.

One of the most famous partnership cases is *Meinhard v. Salmon*. 164 N.E. 545 (N.Y. 1928). In this case, Meinhard and Salmon go into the inn-keeping business together. Early in the twentieth century, they entered a long-term lease for a plum piece of property in Manhattan, between Grand Central Station and the New York Public Library. Meinhard, a wool merchant, would be the main investor in the project and Salmon, a real estate entrepreneur, would manage the day-to-day operations. They agreed that the profits of the venture would eventually be split right down the middle, fifty-fifty. With the lease about to end in the next few months, their landlord approached Salmon about a big construction project for the site and Salmon was ready to run with it. In an opinion by Cardozo, the court held that Salmon's actions were a breach of his fiduciary duty to Salmon:

> Joint adventurers, like copartners, owe to one another, while the enterprise continues, the duty of the finest loyalty. Many forms of conduct permissible in a workaday world for those acting at arm's length, are forbidden to those bound by fiduciary ties. A trustee is held to something stricter than the morals of the market place. Not honesty

alone, but the punctilio of an honor the most sensitive, is then the standard of behavior. As this there has developed a tradition that is unbending and inveterate.

Meinhard v. Salmon, 164 N.E. 545, 546 (N.Y. 1928). According to Cardozo, the duty of loyalty requires a partner to disclose to his other partner opportunities arising out the partnership. In his next move, Cardozo describes a partnership opportunity as something related to the "subject-matter" of the original endeavor, inn keeping. Cardozo reasoned that the developer approached Salmon, because he managed the day-to-day operations and wrongly assumed he was a sole operator.

Therefore, partnership property, including opportunities that arise out of the partnership, should be used for the benefit of the partnership. However, there are exceptions; not all opportunities need be shared. For starters, some opportunities, as the court notes, are not of the same subject-matter as the original partnership. Thus, if the developer in *Meinhard* had offered Salmon a lease for property in, say, New Jersey one might argue that this is not a partnership opportunity, because it is not closely related to the partnership for the management of a hotel in Manhattan.

Additionally, a partner may be able to keep an opportunity for herself if she discloses the opportunity to his co-partners and all have an opportunity to compete on equal footing. For instance, if Salmon had disclosed the existence of the opportunity, Cardozo reasons, Meinhard would have had an opportunity to bid on the opportunity. In this way, the disclosing partner has shown no disloyalty to the partnership, since there is no real additional requirement that a partner be prepared to share all with her co-partners *ad infinitum*. A partner is not penalized for having self-interest. She is penalized only when her tactics ensure that partnership benefits flow to her alone. Thus, partners have a duty of loyalty to one another, which requires disclosure to one other regarding partnership opportunities. When a partner does not disclose partnership opportunity, the duty of loyalty may command that such opportunities (once they are found out) are shared.

A second legal consequence of the duty of loyalty is that a partner has a duty not to compete with his co-partners during the partnership. A partner may still view the partnership as a vehicle to further the partner's own personal interest. For instance, a partner does not violate her duty of loyalty if she loans money to the partnership and expects a fair rate of return. However, as the next case shows, a partner, even a departing one, may not further her own personal interest at the expense of his co-partners or at least without giving her co-partners an opportunity to compete as well.

The reaches of the duty of loyalty were again explored in *Meehan v. Shaughnessy*. 535 N.E.2d 1255 (Mass. 1989). In that case, two partners at a large law firm plotted to leave the firm and go it on their own, but without disclosing their plans to their other law partners. In fact, while still employed and without informing their partners, they made preparations for their new shop, which they anticipated would compete with their firm for clients and business. They approached several lawyers about leaving with them, created lists of potential clients they might poach, and executed a lease agreement for office space, among other things. Additionally, when rumors start to swirl and they were asked by other parties whether they intended to leave the firm, they extemporized or lied.

The firm and the departing partners ended up in court with the issue whether their actions of building a competing business even before departing their former firm violated the fiduciary duty of loyalty. The court held that some of their conduct did not violate their duties to their co-partners. The court advised that the logistical arrangements — finding office space for their new firm, obtaining financing for the new firm, and making a list of prospective clients, for example — that the departing made were not improper. According to the court, the attorneys had a duty to be prepared to serve their clients and this ground-laying was merely prudent preparation. However, the departing attorneys, the court found, did make some improper preparations to solicit clients and lied to their partners about their intentions. By not disclosing their intentions to the firm fully and completely, their co-partners were on unequal footing and, possibly, unable to compete to keep many of the clients that ultimately left the old firm. Even on this score though, the court held that a technical breach of fiduciary duty alone is not enough to require the departing attorneys to pay damages. The court found that, in addition to breach, the breaching parties may be able to avoid damages if they can show that the clients would have left anyway.

Thus, a departing partner may have a duty to inform his co-partners about his plans by, first, giving reasonable notice of their departure and, second, giving their co-partners a reasonable opportunity to compete. First, in these cases, a departing partner should give reasonable notice to her co-partners of their departure. What is reasonable notice is essentially a determination that must be made by courts. Still, factors courts will consider to ascertain what is reasonable notice include the partners' past practices at the firm, any agreement between the parties regarding notice, and any losses that the departing attorney may suffer by a pre-mature disclosure. Second, as discussed above, a departing partner has a duty to avoid competition with their firm, as long as they remain a member of the partnership. If the departing partner cannot avoid some incidents of competition, she must permit her co-partners to compete for opportunities arising out of the partnership on equal footing. Thus, in *Meehan*, the departing attorneys breached their duty when they failed to give their co-partners a real shot at competing for several clients.

However, it is noteworthy that even misconduct or a breach of a partner's fiduciary duty does not necessarily create a reason to grant recovery, since it may not create or "cause" a loss to the other partners. In the case of the law firm just discussed, some clients would leave, regardless of the tactics used, which means that the breach of fiduciary may be a technical violation with no corresponding damages created. Whether or not the breach of the duty not to compete creates a real loss for the partnership depends on several factors, according to courts, including the level of sophistication of the parties, how the client came to the firm, and the departing attorney's skill set.

First, to determine whether a breach of the duty not to compete creates any damages, courts consider the client's level of sophistication. For instance, if the client is a highly sophisticated corporation, it is unlikely, most courts would reason, that the improper solicitation of a departing attorney caused the client to leave. Sophisticated clients are rarely gulled by silver-tongued attorneys. They are aware of the full range of representation options and likely to only consider what is in their best interest. In these cases, courts reason that the sophisticated client would have left the firm anyway, regardless of whether the departing attorney waited until before she departed to make her pitch.

Second, in considering whether the solicitation has caused any damage courts look to how the client relationship was established and maintained. If the departing lawyer was the main contact person for the client or brought the client to the firm in the first place, it is less likely the firm can suggest that improper solicitation caused it to lose the client. The theory here is that the client had no relationship with the other members of the firm and, thus, was likely to leave with the departing attorney, regardless of the improper solicitation. Third, courts look to the departing attorney's skill level. If the departing attorney had particular and unique set of skills, it is unlikely the improper solicitation caused any damage. For instance, if the departing attorney was an international tax specialist and no other members of the former firm had similar skills, it's likely that a client who relied on this talent was not unduly swayed by the pre-departure entreaties.

2. Duty of Care

Also under the common law and state partnership acts, partners have a duty of care to one another. To be frank though, the partners' duty of care to their co-partners is a relatively low standard. Many courts have suggested that a partner cannot be liable for negligent acts. Instead, a partner violates the duty of care if she intentionally or recklessly engages in misconduct that is a violation of the law. Moreover, although the duty of care in partnership law is mostly a creation of the common law, the most recent version of UPA now also mentions that a partner has a duty to refrain from gross negligence, reckless conduct, or violations of the law. Revised Unif. P'ship Act § 404(c) (1997). Thus, absent an agreement to the contrary, a partner cannot be held liable by her co-partners for simple mistakes. Notably, this protection from liability in cases of simple negligence tracks the business judgment rule protection afforded directors in the case of corporate organization, which is discussed in several subsequent chapters. It appears that the partners cannot contract to lower this duty of care to their co-partners. Revised Unif. P'ship Act § 103(b) (4) (1997). However, the partners may agree that the standard of care should be higher. For instance, partners may agree that a partner violates his duty of care for ordinary negligence.

In *Bane v. Ferguson*, one of a law firm's former partners sues the old firm for negligence after the firm dissolved. 890 F.2d 11 (7th Cir. 1989). In particular, Bane, the plaintiff, was promised a pension from his former firm, which would continue until the partnership was dissolved. When the firm dissolved and the pension that the retired plaintiff depended on stopped, he sued his former firm on the theory that their negligent conduct caused the firm's demise and the end of his much-needed pension. The court, in an opinion by the venerable Judge Richard Posner, did not disagree that the partner's negligence may have precipitated the end of the firm. However, Posner rejected the notion that negligence of a co-partner is an actionable offense. First, in Posner's view, Bane was owed no fiduciary duty of care at all by these former partners, because fiduciary duties end with the partnership. Second, Posner contends that managers of business could not be liable for good faith decisions, even if the decision was careless.

Thus, *Bane's* most important point for these purposes is that the duty of care does not provide a cause of action for the negligent conduct of co-partners. Perhaps the logic behind this protection is to encourage decision-making and avoid stalling. Without the protection, in other words, partners would be leery to take many decisions for fear that they may be liable for them.

3. Obligation of Good Faith and Fair Dealing

Under the common law, in every contract, there is an implied obligation of good faith and fair dealing. Whether implied or formalized, agreements to form a partnership are no different. Under the RUPA, partners owe to one another an obligation of good faith and fair dealing in all respects for the term of the partnership. REVISED UNIF. P'SHIP ACT § 404(d) (1997). However, because "good faith" and "fair dealing" are not specifically defined, the scope of these obligations is inevitably determined by case law. In such cases, courts have been loathed to define good faith *per se* and have been more apt to suggest what type of conduct is not in good faith. For instance, a party may violate the obligation of good faith if she fails to make full disclosure, even though no such disclosure may be required under the duty of loyalty (standing alone). Further, the obligation of good faith is at least a duty not to lie or misrepresent the truth to a counterpart. Similar to other duties, the partners may by private agreement limit the scope of the obligation of good faith and fair dealing, so long as they do not unreasonably limit the obligation.

H. Partnership Change in Control

Fundamental changes in a partnership can occur in several ways. New partners may be added, partners may be expelled, or the partnership may be dissolved or terminated. At the same time, partners die or retire or transfer their stake in the partnership to their heirs. All of these decisions could affect the partnership's ability to manage the business and many of these decisions are major ones requiring unanimous consent. It is commonly said, for example, that the admission of a new partner or the departing of a single partner effectively dissolves the old partnership and creates a new partnership. Thus, in virtually every case of a new partner or the expulsion of an old one, the default rules is that there has to be unanimous consent of the partners. Other changes in partnership dynamics might not require such a dramatic step.

1. Transfer of Partnership Interest

To begin with, an important, but not earth-shattering, change in the partnership occurs when the financial rights of one of the partners is transferred to another person. A partner's interest in the partnership comprises of many rights, including, most significantly, the right to participate in partnership decision-making and share in partnership profits (or losses). However, rights related to control are inalienable and cannot be transferred, at least not without the consent of all the other partners. The rule makes sense, since otherwise a partner might have to share the reins of control with a stranger or, worse still, a foe. Thus, this rule ensures that partners are able to have a voice in the selection of their co-partners. Similarly, a partner may not transfer partnership property to a third party without her co-partners agreeing to the transfer. This rule protects partnership property from claims by creditors. That is, a partner cannot shift partnership assets to her creditors. Thus, a creditor cannot pursue partnership property to satisfy a debt obligation that an individual partner has incurred, one which has nothing to do with the partnership.

However, a partner's financial interest in the partnership can be transferred or assigned. That is, a partner may transfer their right to profits or losses. A partner may, for instance, assign his rights to receive profits in the partnership to his children or grandchildren. The rights could also be used by an individual partner to satisfy a personal credit obligation, like an obligation to a former spouse. In fact, a creditor may pursue legal action (*i.e.*, referred to as a "charging order") to get the benefit of an individual partner's share of profits in order to satisfy a debt obligation. In either event, the party receiving the benefit of the transfer does not have a right to make decisions. Those rights are still lodged with the transferor or original partner. Generally, the assignment of a financial interest by one of the partners is not a fundamental change that requires consent of the other partners or that would effectively dissolve the partnership. (I say "generally" here to take account of those exceptional cases where a transfer of a partnership interest may create reason to dissociate or "fire" a partner. See below discussion of Expulsion of Partner.) Thus, the transfer of the financial interest in a partnership does not effect a change in the how the partnership is operated; the partnership continues with its same structure.

2. Admission of New Partners

Successful partnerships, like other business entities, grow and expand. One way to grow a general partnership is to admit new members. Under the same principles, new partners are personally liable for the acts of their co-partners, for any acts occurring after the new admit joins the partnership. The new admit's capital contribution to the partnership is also at risk for any acts occurring, regardless of when they occurred. However, in return the new partners get all the benefits of the partnership previously discussed, including a right to portion of partnership property (net of liabilities), profits, and right to participate in decision-making. The admission of new partners is considered a major decision of the partnership. It would undermine the freedom of association to permit a small number of partners or even a majority of the partners to force a dissenting partner to work with a new admit. Thus, as a general rule the admission of new partners can only occur with the assent of all the partners. As with most rules in partnership law, the partners can contract around this default by memorializing an alternative understanding in their partnership agreement.

3. Dissolution

Dissolution is the beginning of the end of the partnership. That is, when a partner calls for the dissolution of the partnership, the partnership is not immediately terminated. Instead, the partnership is said to wind up. Debts are settled, outstanding receivables collected, and partnership property sold. Absent agreement to the contrary, partnership assets are liquidated with the partners sharing in any surplus after the sale of partnership property or partnership revenue. Technically, the partnership continues as long as the partnership is being wound up and partnership assets are being liquidated. Of course, many partnership dissolutions are governed by the partnership agreement, which will likely provide explicit procedures for both windup and dissolution. In these cases, the partners may prefer not to actually liquidate the assets of the firm, but instead to continue the partnership and simply pay the departing partner her share of partnership income and capital contribution.

A partnership is ended or dissolved by any one of three possible ways: (1) one of the partners declares the partnership dissolved; (2) the partnership is dissolved pursuant to the partnership agreement; or (3) the partnerships becomes impractical based on court order, legislation or other supervening cause. First, unless there is an express or implied agreement to the contrary, partnerships are at-will agreements. This means that any of the partners can call for dissolution at anytime for any reason.

Second, a term partnership, or partnership with a specific objective at its core, is considered to be dissolved once the term has run or the objective reached. When the parties have expressly agreed as to the term of the partnership (*e.g.*, one-, two-, or five-years) or a specific objective (*e.g.*, partnership until a certain level of profit is made or a partnership until debt obligations are paid off), it's straightforward to tell when the partnership can be dissolved. However, in many cases, courts hold that a partnership should continue to run until a specific objective is met even though there may be no express or formal agreement between the parties. In these cases, courts have suggested that parties have by their conduct implicitly agreed to enter into partnership until the objective is met. Additionally, a term partnership is dissolved if all the partners agree that the business should end. REVISED UNIF. P'SHIP ACT § 801(2)(ii) (1997). The evidence in these cases needs to be strong, as the next case shows.

That is, in order to find a partnership for a particular term or undertaking by implication, the evidence has to be relatively robust. In *Page v. Page*, for instance, two brothers associated to create a linen supply business. 359 P. 2d 41 (Cal. 1961). Although the business initially suffered significant losses, it would ultimately rebound and begin to show a profit. But, by this time, one of the brothers, H.B., had resolved to dissolve the joint endeavor. The co-partner argued that the call for dissolution would be wrongful, since the parties had implicitly agreed that the partnership would continue until the two had were able to pay off partnership debts. Because the business, which was starting to turn a profit, still had significant debts, the co-partner suggested that the partnership could not be properly dissolved. The court, in this case, held that no evidence suggested an implicit agreement to form a partnership for a particular undertaking. In the court's view, any understanding that the business would one day be able to satisfy its obligations was aspirational, not contractual. Absent clearer evidence to the contrary, according to the court, the default rule would apply: The parties simply entered a partnership at will, terminable at the election of either part at any time. Thus, although courts have suggested that parties have by their conduct entered partnerships for a specific term or to accomplish a specific objective, such evidence needs to be clear and specific.

In cases whether the parties have either implicitly or expressly agreed that the partnership shall be for a specific term or until a specific objective is met, a party cannot usually terminate the partnership early without liability for damages to their co-partners. To be sure, nothing can stop a partner for calling for dissolution of the partnership, even if their call for dissolution contradicts the parties' agreement. Yet, the general rule is that if the parties terminate a partnership and such termination is in violation of the partnership agreement, then the wrongful termination may create a cause of action for damages.

Third, as under general contract principles, a partnership agreement also becomes unenforceable if operation of the partnership enterprise becomes unlawful because of supervening legislation or the purpose of the partnership is substantially frustrated, or it becomes impracticable to carry on the partnership. For instance, a partner, despite an agreement, may still request an order from a court to dissolve the partnership, if a continuation of the partnership is not practicable. In these cases, a partner will not be liable for an early dissolution, if such dissolution is pursuant to a court order. In these cases, courts may find, as in the next case, the partners have very little trust or confidence in their other partners and cannot manage the business enterprise together.

In *Owen v. Cohen*, two individuals partnered to open a bowling alley. 119 P.2d 713 (Cal. 1941). Although the parties did not a have a writing memorializing how long the partnership was to continue, it appears, based on their conduct, they assumed the partnership would continue until the business could afford to pay off its start-up debts. However, the two partners did not get along, to put it charitably. For instance, Cohen told his co-partner and target of abuse, Owen, that he should do the manual work, while Cohen would "wear the dignity." After enduring Cohen's criticisms for three months, Owen moved to have the partnership dissolved immediately. The court held that dissolution was appropriate, regardless of their understanding that the partnership should continue. Thus, a partner, regardless of agreement to the contrary, can bring a suit for dissolution in case of extreme misconduct by his counterpart. In fact, according to RUPA, the right of a partner to bring an action to dissociate is immutable or, in other words, cannot be contracted away. REVISED UNIF. P'SHIP ACT § 103(b)(6) (1997.) This permanent right to dissociate makes some sense, as it it is unlikely truly incongruous personalities will be able to successfully run a business.

4. Dissociation

Dissociation occurs when a partner is no longer to be associated with the partnership, though the partnership may continue without that partner. Dissociation can be either voluntary of involuntary (*i.e*, an expulsion). A partner may choose to dissociate from the partnership for a number of reasons and that partner's decision would effectively terminate the departing partner's fiduciary obligations to the partnership. Further, the departing party is no longer liable for the acts of his former partners after notice of the dissociation has been received. The right of a partner to dissociate at any time is a non-waiveable right, though (as with an early dissolution) may give rise to damages if the dissociation contravenes the partnership agreement. A departing partner may choose to dissociate by giving a notice of withdrawal to other partners. Further, a partner may be dissociated when a certain triggering event occurs. Like in other contracts, the parties to a partnership agreement may agree to a condition subsequent, the occurrence of which may trigger dissociation.

If the partnership continues after dissociation, which is likely, the partnership must buy out the partnership interest of the dissociated partner. As a general matter, the partnership must make the buy out soon after receiving the demand from the dissociated partner. For instance, the RUPA provides explicitly that the buy out should be made within 4 months after the demand for payment. REVISED UNIF. P'SHIP ACT § 701(e) (1997). The price that is to be paid to the dissociated partner is supposed to equal the partner's *pro rata* share of the partnership as if it were sold as of the date of the dissociation. At the same time, however, a wrongful dissociation can create liability for the dissociating partner. For instance, a partner may dissociate before the term of the partnership agreement has run. In these cases, the RUPA provides if the partnership is for a specific term or for a particular undertaking and the dissociation is wrongful, the partnership can defer making a buyout payment "until the expiration of the term or completion of the undertaking." REVISED UNIF. P'SHIP ACT § 701(h) (1997). Even in this case though, the dissociating partner is still entitled to a fair buyout and is entitled to interest on the deferment. If a wrongful dissociation, the remaining partners may charge any losses created in the wrongful departure against the buyout amount owed to the departing partner.

Importantly, also, the partnership will likely want to notify third parties of the dissociation to avoid continuing liability. (The partnership may also accomplish this by filling a statement of dissociation, which creates constructive notice to third parties.) That is, under the Uniform Partnership Act, the partnership is still liable for the acts of the departing attorney for two years after the dissociation. REVISED UNIF. P'SHIP ACT §703(b) (1997). Interestingly, the departing partner may also be liable for the same two-year period for contracts the partnership enters. However, in either case, liability is limited to parties who had reason to believe the departing partner was a part of the firm.

5. Expulsion of Partner

Finally, a partner may be dissociated or expelled from the partnership by force. Like the power to discharge an at-will employee, the power to expel a partner is relatively broad. For instance, a partnership may expel a partner with or without cause, if the partnership agreement permits it. Alternatively, in some special cases, a partner can be expelled even without a provision providing for expulsion in a partnership agreement, if there is unanimous consent among the partners. Here, the most noteworthy case where a unanimous vote would work is after a partner has transferred substantially all of her financial interest in a partnership to another firm.

Even when expulsion is permitted under a partnership agreement, the power to expel a partner is not completely without checks, however. When expelling one member of a partnership, the partnership is still bound by the partnership agreement and the obligation of good faith and fair dealing. This limitation on the power to expel though is not particularly far reaching and usually only means that a partner cannot be expelled so that the other parties can reap a clear financial reward.

In *Bohatch v. Butler*, for instance, a partner was expelled after she suspected (and accused) one of her co-partners of over-billing. 977 S.W.2d 543 (Tex. 1998). Among other causes of action, Bohatch sued under the theory that her expulsion violated the common law fiduciary duty that partners owe to one another. Her theory was that the partners could not expel her for attempting to stop unethical billing practices. The majority opinion held that no fiduciary duty was violated by the firing, because the partners had a legitimate reason for the termination: trust and personal confidence were shattered between the partners as a result of the accusation. Thus, partners have no obligation to continue to associate with someone against their will and have significant latitude to terminate a relationship, particularly pursuant to the partnership agreement. Still, a partnership may not exercise discretion under a partnership in bad faith. For instance, in *Bohatch*, it would likely certainly be a breach of good faith for her partners to have fired for petty financial gain.

Additionally, as discussed in *Owen* above, a partner can be dissociated by force or expelled from a partnership by court order based on extreme misconduct. A partner may also be expelled if she files bankruptcy or conclusively demonstrates financial irresponsibility. As in contracts, a partner can also be discharged from the partnership if the partner is no longer capable of taking on partnership responsibilities, because of supervening illegality, mental incapacity or death (in the case of an individual partner) or filing of a certificate of dissolution (in the case of a corporate partner), for instance. As above though, a partner expelled from the partnership is entitled to a buyout of her partnership stake.

Checkpoints

- The general partnership is the default organizational form. Thus, the parties need not make a formal filing to form a general partnership.

- The majority of rules in general partnership law are default rules, which the parties may contract around in the partnership agreement.

- Partners in a general partnership have an equal right to ordinary operational management of the partnership. Similarly, partners in a general partnership have an equal right to share in profits (or losses) of the partnership.

- Partners have a duty of loyalty to one another to hold partnership property (including partnership opportunities) for the partnership's use, avoid conflicts of interest, and make reasonable disclosures to their partners.

- A partner's duty of care is a relatively low standard and a breach is only created when a partner acts intentionally, recklessly, illegally, or is grossly negligent.

- A partner may leave or dissociate from the partnership at any time, although if the partner's departure is a breach of the partnership agreement, she may liable for damages.

Chapter 3

Introduction to Limited Liability Entities

Roadmap

- Introduction to Limited Liability for Investors
- Advantages of Rule of Limited Liability
- Disadvantages of Rule of Limited Liability

The remainder of the book discusses business organizations that share one common and important characteristic: limited liability. Limited liability is not usually used in reference to whether the entity itself can escape debts and obligations. Instead, notions of limited liability usually describe the protection afforded investors in these entities.

In all these entities — the limited partnership, limited liability company or LLC, and the corporation — investors generally do not bear the risk of inappropriate conduct by company managers. Investor protection from suit is a profound phenomenon for the modern business, but this has not always been the case. Historically, investors in business organizations, even corporations, were treated like partners in a general partnership and held liable for entity misdeeds. Today, however, in the event of suit for recovery that is unsatisfied by the entity, most investors lose only their investment or capital contribution. Their losses are, in effect, capped at the level of their investment. Also, limited liability can also be used to describe the protection afforded managers, like the officers and directors of a corporate entity, for their actions on behalf of the firm. Although a party always remains liable for her own misconduct, if the employees or other persons were merely acting on behalf of the firm they are insulated from liability for any errors or mistaken judgment.

The protection from liability that is afforded to investors in the entities discussed in this next group of chapters is pronounced and unique. For instance, imagine an investor of enormous wealth who takes a chance and invests $1,000 in a fledgling Internet limited liability company. The start-up expands fast by borrowing money to buy a large office building and hiring legions of employees to work in it. If the start-up fails just as fast, the creditors (*i.e.*, the lender and the employees) can only go after the assets of the company for payment. If those assets are insufficient to pay the mortgage on the building or employees who might be owed back wages, these creditors cannot recover against the investor's personal assets. In a world of limited liability, the investor will only be in jeopardy of losing the $1,000 invested. In a world of unlimited liability, such an investor could file for bankruptcy protection, but probably would not, at least not if she truly is very wealthy. Only if the losses represented a significant share of the investor's personal wealth would it be worth it to her to try to avoid these debts through bankruptcy protection.

These losses do not, of course, disappear. If the losses are greater than the assets of the limited liability entity, the creditors are forced to take on those losses. As one source puts it, "[l]oss is swallowed rather than shifted." Frank Easterbrook & Daniel Fischel, *Limited Liability and the Corporation*, 52 Chi. L. Rev. 89, 98 (1985). Thus, a consumer who is injured by a tort of the corporation can only seek recovery from corporate assets. When those assets fail to make the injured victim whole, the consumers cannot pursue the investors and may end up being forced to manage their own losses if the corporation becomes insolvent. The same is true for employees who have unpaid wages from a bankrupt limited liability company. And the same is true for the lender who contracts to loan money to an entity that has squandered its assets and can no longer make payments on the loan.

A. Advantages of Limited Liability

Thus, before proceeding to discuss these organizations in greater detail, it is prudent to analyze some of the economic rationales for protecting investors. Some of the theoretical benefits of limited liability are plain, while others are not as obvious. In fact, the virtues of limited liability have been widely debated amongst the most prominent academics in corporate law. Importantly, Federal Appeals Judge Frank Easterbrook and University of Chicago Professor Dan Fischel in a classic corporate law article give arguably the most thoughtful and comprehensive analysis of the benefits of limited liability. Easterbrook & Fischel, *supra*.

1. Investment

One economic rationale for the rule of limited liability, which protects investors from suit, is that the rule likely encourages investments in business.

The logic is straightforward: If investors do not bear company losses (beyond their own investment), they will be more likely to invest than if those same investors had to bear the costs of company misconduct. This is because investors with vast resources will be leery to invest in companies that might put their personal assets in jeopardy. If, say, an unsatisfied tort claim came along, which the company could not satisfy, such investors might be wiped out. Thus, rather than face the prospect of personal liability, it reasons that investors, particularly those with vast wealth, may be wary of making investments in the first place, unless there is liability protection.

Furthermore, unlimited liability might change or distort investors' decision about which companies to invest in. For instance, investors will likely be disinclined to invest in larger companies. That is, one might expect that investors will prefer smaller companies to larger companies (all else being equal) since smaller companies have fewer opportunities to make risky decisions. By contrast, the view may be that larger companies have unlimited opportunity to make a mistake that could put the investors' asset in jeopardy. With limited liability, however, both the wealthy and not-so-wealthy will be more likely to make investments, regardless of firm size, since their personal assets are not at risk.

Related to this last point, limited liability may also encourage diversification of portfolios. In a world of unlimited investor liability, investors bent on investing in companies would likely invest in just one company or one particular industry. For instance, they would invest in the company with the management they trust most or the management they could easily monitor. Investing in too many companies would surely spread their monitoring ability too thin. However, in a world of no liability for shareholders, investors have no good reason to concentrate their investment in a single company. Thus, limited liability encourages investment and diversification.

2. Monitoring

Without the shield of limited liability, many investors will have to spend a significant amount of time monitoring managers, since their managers' misconduct puts their own personal assets in jeopardy. This monitoring, one would expect, will be directly correlated with the wealth of the individual: the wealthier the individual means that more personal assets are at stake if there is firm misconduct and, therefore, the more monitoring such individual will be apt to undertake. Furthermore, in addition to monitoring the conduct of managers, shareholders would have an incentive to monitor the composition of ownership. In a world of unlimited liability, shareholders will take notice, for instance, if a shareholder with significant wealth sells her shares, since those personal assets can no longer be used to satisfy an adverse judgment against the corporation. *See* Easterbrook & Fischel, *supra* at 95.

This monitoring is potentially excessive since the social gains from monitoring are likely outstripped by the costs. For instance, since it might be tough for all shareholders to effectively band together in order to monitor management, it is likely that there will be overlapping and duplicative monitoring activities by shareholders. In a world of limited liability, by contrast, the need for monitoring the conduct of management is reduced (although not completely eliminated). Since investors do not have more exposure than their original contribution to capital, they have less need to police the activities of managers of the company. To be sure, even in a world of limited liability, investors will still monitor management to some extent. However, in world of limited liability, the monitoring activities of investors are re-directed toward watching for a different type of conduct. Instead of keeping an eye on management to be able to anticipate and head-off outsized losses, investors in a limited liability company assess management for their ability to produce gains. Thus, rather than value managers who are careful and unlikely to produce significant losses, investors have more reason to value managers that take chances in an effort to increase share price, earnings, and dividends to investors.

3. Fairness

Another reason for the rule of limited liability arises out of notions of fairness. Specifically, the idea that people should be responsible for their own conduct or those things in their control and should have to pay for their misdeeds, but not for things outside of their control. The ability of most shareholders, as will be shortly discussed, to affect the decisions of management are limited. Briefly, they can vote to elect directors of the corporation and veto change-in-control transactions, among other limited powers. Thus, though shareholders may be able to monitor and protect themselves from company misconduct by selling their shares, they cannot easily stop manager wrongdoing. As such, it would be a little unfair to impose liability that could wipe out investors, when investors have only limited authority to affect firm managers.

4. Valuation

Further, limited liability helps investors assess the value of ownership of the company. That is, without limited liability the value of ownership would be directly related to the level of wealth of the individuals. All things being equal, individuals with vast wealth might exact a sizeable discount for investments in Company A, since their investment will also mean that their personal assets are in jeopardy should Company A have any unsatisfied tort or contract claims. Compare that with how an individual with virtually no wealth will value an investment in Company A. Since this individual has no wealth to speak of, he or she will value investments in Company A based on the present expected value of income flows from the company. To come up with a target price for a share, he may, for instance, pore over Company A's annual report, cash flow, balance sheet, and other financial statements. Thus, limited liability puts the two investors on an even playing field and they need not make individualized assessments of value. Others have even argued that the ability to come up with objective valuations of company shares makes it possible to have a public exchange. *See, e.g.*, P. Halpern *et al.*, *An Economic Analysis of Limited Liability in Corporation Law*, 30. U. TORONTO L.J. 117 (1980).

At the same time, differential valuations might also distort allocations of capital. That is, individuals with substantial personal assets might be more inclined to invest in companies that already have other wealthy investors. This would reduce the chances that one wealthy investor might have to satisfy claims that exceed corporate assets. Investment dollars will not necessarily chase the best investments. Put differently, in a world of unlimited liability, investors choose companies to invest in, not with an eye toward which companies they expect to do well. Instead, they seek out companies with wealthy investors. In this way, the differential valuations contribute to a socially counterproductive investment strategy.

B. Disadvantages to Limited Liability

At the same time, for all the benefits created by a liability shield, limited liability does create some unique challenges as well.

1. Monitoring

In a way, one of the unique advantages of unlimited liability is it gives investors a reason to be wary. In other words, investors who face full liability will be cautious about where they invest their capital and will monitor underlings for misconduct. This notion of caution and monitoring may enhance some types of businesses. For instance, consider a law firm in which each of the partners faces unlimited liability for the acts of her law partner. When each of the partners has liability, they probably do a better job monitoring their colleagues' performance. This may reduce the incidence of mistakes and increase business to the firm, particularly in the business like, law where mistakes are costly. With limited liability between and among partners, there would be less incentive to monitor the conduct of law partners.

2. Moral Hazard

Since investors are insulated from liability, the notion of limited liability may also create some incentive for wrongdoing. That is, to the extent the players do not realize the actual expected value of the losses caused by their actions, they may not take due precautions. In this case, the firm might take risks that exceed the expected benefit from those risks. Perhaps the best example of this is in the parent-subsidiary context. That is, a parent corporation might create a wholly-owned subsidiary to take advantage of some business opportunity, but also to insulate the parent corporation from the risk of liability from the activity. Thus, an oil company may form a subsidiary to do excavation, another to do the transportation, another to do the refinery work. With each separate subsidiary, the parent corporation may transfer just enough funds for operations to be completed, in order to avoid a large payout in the event of a suit. Because they realize that their losses from the subsidiary's operations will be modest, they may take excessive risks. They may, for instance, use short cuts when excavating a worksite or be careless with their labor bill.

Checkpoints

- In all these entities — the limited partnership, limited liability company (or LLC), and the corporation — investors generally do not bear the risk of inappropriate conduct by company managers.

- The rule of limited liability creates several advantages. The rule encourages investment, reduces the need for monitoring, matches up well with notions of fairness, and creates the opportunity for uniform valuation.

- At the same time, there are at least two disadvantages of limited liability for investors. The rule might create a pretext for some investors to forgo monitoring manager behavior and may cause managers to take unnecessary risks.

Chapter 4

Limited Partnerships

Roadmap

- Formation of a Limited Partnership
- Fiduciary Duties of Partners
- Management Control in Limited Partnerships
- Liability of Limited Partners versus Liability of General Partners
- Change in Control of Limited Partnerships
- Dissolution of a Limited Partnership

A. Introduction

According to some commentators, the limited partnership as a form of business organization is moribund, slowly being replaced by an alphabet soup of other limited liability entities, like the LLC, LLP or LLLP. This narrative, however, misses the reasons for the likely continued allure of the limited partnership. To start, the limited partnership seems to fit a unique niche not always met by other organizational forms. The limited partnership provides for centralized management, like a corporation. But, unlike a corporation, the limited partnership is run by owners of the entity, the general partner. Also, unlike a corporation, the limited partnership still retains the benefits of pass-through taxation of a general partnership—*i.e.,* profits and losses of the partnership are passed through to the partners as ordinary income. Unlike a general partnership, a limited partnership is not easily dissolved. In many states, a limited partnership continues indefinitely (unless otherwise agreed). When a limited partner leaves a limited partnership, there is no automatic call for dissolution.

Further, the limited partnership will likely continue to be a useful business form because it has developed an intrepid following among the relevant interest groups—lawyers, judges and savvy business persons. Many members of these groups appreciate the limited partnership because a significant amount

59

of case law has developed around the limited partnership, which tends to make limited partnership law clearer. All the states have a set of limited partnership statutes, with the first statute adopted in New York almost two hundred years ago. By comparison, the number of significant cases discussing the issues in the context of other limited liability entities, like LLCs, is smaller and less widely-known.

Accordingly, business activity is still organized in this form. In fact, many high-profile private investment activities continue to be organized as limited partnerships. Venture capitalists and other private equity funds, for instance, frequently organize their activities into limited partnerships. In these enterprises, pension funds and other large institutional investors invest in the fund as limited partners. The investors or deep-pockets have no operational say-so in how the money is invested. They are so-called passive investors. The general partner, usually a cadre of investment bankers and other financial professionals, puts some of their own money in the fund. But, more important, the general partner allocates the fund's money to different ventures and receives hefty profits for their successes. The general partner realizes returns based on management fees (usually 2%) of the fund, but also profits generated (usually 20%) if the ventures rise in value.

Typical Venture Capital Organizational Structure

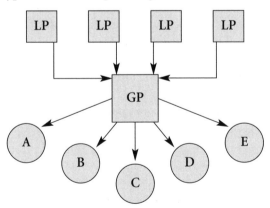

Portfolio Companies A–E

B. Sources of Limited Partnership Law

In some ways, the law of limited partnership law is complicated. At this writing, in the majority of states the law of limited partnership is governed by the Revised Uniform Limited Partnership Act of 1985 (RULPA). The RULPA has always relied on the general partnership law to resolve some disputes. In fact, the RULPA specifically "links" or cross-references the Uniform Partnership Act; and vice versa, the Uniform Partnership refers expressly to the RULPA. To be more specific, the RULPA provides that "in any cases not provided for ... the provisions of the Uniform Partnership Act govern." REVISED UNIF. LTD. P'SHIP. ACT § 1105 (1985). Similarly, the Uniform Partnership Act (UPA) provides that it covers cases of limited partnership law. In relevant part, the Uniform Partnership Act states that the Act "shall apply to limited partnerships except in so far as the statutes relating to such partnerships are inconsistent herewith." REVISED UNIF. P'SHIP. ACT § 6(2) (1997). Thus, in a majority of states, the Uniform Partnership Act governs in any cases not covered by the RULPA. In a majority of states, the law of limited partnership is a mash-up, which mixes principles of general partnership (previously discussed) and the relevant uniform body of limited partnership law.

However, in a minority of states the law of limited partnerships is governed by the most recent uniform act—the Uniform Limited Partnership Act of 2001 (ULPA). The ULPA is a free-standing uniform act, without cross-reference to another uniform body of law. According to the notes introducing the ULPA, the drafting committee expressed two reasons for their decision to de-link limited partnership law from general partnership law. UNIF. LTD. P'SHIP. ACT prefatory note (2001). First, the committee calculated that the historical link between the two bodies of law would produce ambiguity over the legal standard that governed the parties to a limited partnership. Courts would come to varying opinions as a result of the ambiguity. Second and related, the complexity of interpreting a party's obligation because of the cross-reference to general partnership law would produce bad case law. If the two bodies of law remained linked, some courts would, no doubt, utilize principles of general partnership law inappropriately, without fully considering the distinctions of a limited partnership. Over time, it is likely that the majority of states will adopt this free-standing body of law to govern limited partnerships. For now, though, at least three bodies of law govern the legal relations of parties in a limited partnership—the RULPA, the UPA, and the ULPA.

Finally, as in the case of general partnership law, the law of limited partnership is informed and developed a great deal by court opinions. In particular, courts have opined on the meaning and scope of limited partners' partnership agreements, as will be shown throughout this Chapter. In the end, this Chapter will often refer to the 2001 uniform act, even though the act has been adopted by a minority of states at this writing, because it is particularly important to note the significant revisions to the law of limited partnership under the free-standing act. Still, unless otherwise noted, this Chapter's principle concern is with limited partnership law under the RULPA, since most states have adopted it. In any event, as could be expected, the law of limited partnership builds on and expands the law of general partnership.

C. Formation

A limited partnership consists of at least one general partner and one or more limited partners. The general partner controls the operation of the business and is personally liable for partnership debts. Thus, the general partner's liability is normally the same as the liability of a partner for partnership debts in a general partnership. However, in a limited partnership, limited partners are not ordinarily liable for partnership debts beyond their contribution to the partnership. Of course, there are exceptions, which will be discussed shortly. For now, a limited partner who is a passive investor and who does not exercise any operational control over the enterprise is also free from liability outside of her investment.

1. Certificate of Limited Partnership

A limited partnership is formed upon the filing of a certificate of limited partnership with the appropriate state secretary and payment of a nominal filing fee. All told, the process of creating a limited partnership is a relatively simple one, and the information that the partners need to disclose in the certificate of limited partnership is relatively modest.

For instance, unlike prior law, the parties no longer need to disclose the name of limited partners and their respective contributions. Instead, under the RULPA, the certificate of limited partnership should include information about the name and address of general partners; the duration of the partnership; the name of the limited partnership; and contact information for service of process. REVISED UNIF. LTD. P'SHIP. ACT § 201(a)(1)-(4) (1985). The notion of a duration term means that the parties have to specify a date-certain when the limited partnership will be dissolved. For instance, private equity funds frequently agree that a limited partnership should last for only 10 years. However, under the ULPA, a limited partnership is considered to be perpetual, like a corporation. Unless the parties agree to a date for dissolution, under the ULPA, the limited partnership does not dissolve upon a date-certain and continues in perpetuity. UNIF. LTD. P'SHIP. ACT § 801(1)(2)(3)

(2001). Arguably, the filing of the certificate gives all interested parties (constructive) notice that what they are dealing with is a limited partnership. The certificate of limited partnership gives interested partners express notice of the names of the general partners and, thus, their general liability. At the same time, the filing implicitly provides that all other partners (not therein named) are limited partners with limited liability.

Although the parties' obligations to disclose in a certificate of limited partnership are limited, the parties' obligations are on-going. Thus, a limited partnership must amend its certificate if the ranks of its general partnership changes—*i.e.,* the limited partnership adds a general partner or a general partner withdraws from the limited partnership. Other records, including the in-house list of general and limited partners, must also be kept current. For instance, under the ULPA, the limited partnership must annually file a report with the state that gives current contact information for the enterprise. UNIF. LTD. P'SHIP. ACT § 210(a)(1)-(4) (2001). In all events, a failure to keep the records current could lead to liability. That is to say, if the limited partnership has a certificate that contains false or non-current information that is relied on by another, the limited partnership and its partners could be liable for losses. For instance, a general partner might have liability, if such general partner had a reasonable opportunity to correct the erroneous filing. Also, any partner, general or limited, might be liable if that partner was responsible for submitting the information she knew to be false. Finally, a party who fails to file a certificate of limited partnership or fails to substantially comply in filing a certificate with the respective state office will be deemed to be liable under principles of general partnership law. In the following case, the court finds that the defects in the filing of a certificate were too severe and, thus, were not in "substantial compliance."

In *Direct Mail Specialist, Inc. v. Brown,* for example, all the partners to a limited partnership were sued to recover for an outstanding balance with one of the limited partnership's vendors. 673 F.Supp. 1540 (D. Mont. 1987). The court held that the limited partners would not be protected from suit, because their certificate of limited partnership failed to comply with state law in a number of respects. Among the defects with the filing, the court noted that the filing was not even made with the Secretary of State's office. The court reasoned that the defects were too severe to put even a diligent vendor, such as the out-of-state corporate plaintiff, on notice of the limited partnership's legal status. Thus, as in *Direct Mail,* the parties must file a certificate of limited partnership with the appropriate Secretary of State and show substantial compliance in order to form a limited partnership with concomitant liability protections.

2. Partnership Agreement

As mentioned, in the case of a limited partnership, the partners must file a certificate of formation with the state. By comparison in the case of general partnership law, the parties may form a general partnership without any filing whatsoever. In fact, parties may have formed a general partnership without extended deliberation or even by accident. Because in a limited partnership the partners have to make an official filing with the state, partners to a limited partner are also more likely to also come to terms on a formal partnership agreement. Also, unlike a general partnership, a limited partnership is required to keep more detailed, in-house records regarding the organization of the limited partnership. Most importantly, these records must include the names and designation (*i.e.*, limited or general) of each of the partners and information regarding the amount of capital contributed to the partnership by each of the partners. Although such records need not be publicly disclosed, they should be available should any partner, litigant, or court need to review them.

Typically, therefore, the parties to a limited partnership enter into a partnership agreement that outlines the respective rights and obligations as participants in the partnership. Thus, creditors interested in specific information regarding a limited partnership are likely to find it, first, in the partnership agreement. Perhaps for this reason, in the certificate of filing, the parties need not include much information to make a proper filing of a certificate of information, since the partnership agreement will contain most of the pertinent information that interested parties will need. Shortly, although there is no specific requirement that the parties have a partnership agreements, the vast majority of partners in limited partnerships probably have such an agreement, in contrast to the context of a general partnership.

3. Incongruent Writings

Sometimes the parties' partnership agreement and the information in public filings may not match. For instance, the partnership agreement may list several new general partners who are not mentioned in the publicly-filed certificate of limited partnership. Or, conversely, the certificate of limited partnership may list several new partners as general partners, when in fact they have recently withdrawn from the partnership. In circumstances of disagreement between the two documents, the partnership agreement trumps the public filing with respect to partner obligations *vis-à-vis* other partners. Thus, in a dispute between partners, the partnership agreement governs. However, in cases of third parties, the partnership agreement is not necessarily known. The public filing would likely trump the partnership agreement, if the third party reasonably relied on it to her detriment.

D. Introduction to Fiduciary Duty

Partners in a limited partnership owe one another a fiduciary duty, like the duty of loyalty, duty of care, or obligation of a good faith and fair dealing, previously mentioned in Chapter 2. In a few limited ways, these duties effectively mirror the duties covered in the general partnership context. For instance, all partners, both limited and general ones, in a limited partnership must discharge their obligations in good faith. Further, even though the general partner may have control under the partnership agreement, the general partner cannot use her power in order to effect a self-deal without disclosure. Finally, like in the case of a general partnership, members of a limited partnership cannot completely eliminate by contract the traditional fiduciary default rules.

1. Duty of Care and Loyalty

Recall that limited partners are typically passive investors, not day-to-day managers. In contrast to general partnership law, therefore, a limited partner has no duty of care and loyalty by default. A general partner in a limited partnership has duties of care and loyalty patterned after the same duties under general partnership law. Thus, a general partner in a limited partnership will only breach the duty of care if her misconduct is grossly negligent, reckless, or intentional. Similarly, a general partner in a limited partnership has a duty of loyalty that matches the duty of any partner in a general partnership. Namely, the general partner has a duty to hold and use partnership property (including partnership opportunities) for the benefit of the limited partnership and to avoid conflicts of interests. The extent to which a general partner can, by contract, restrict these fiduciary duties is explored in the next case.

Gotham Partners, L.P. v. Hallwood represents a relatively complicated, but still typical, limited partnership arrangement. 817 A.2d 160 (Del. Supr. 2002). In that case, Hallwood Realty Partners, L.P., a limited partnership with investments in commercial properties, had several investors whose interests were allocated on the basis of partnership units. The units were traded on the American Stock Exchange. The general partner was a corporate entity, Hallwood Realty

Corporation, which was wholly-owned by another corporate entity, HGI. The controlling directors and officers of Hallwood Realty Corporation were the same as the people in charge of HGI. The general partner, Hallwood Realty Corporation, initially had only a small stake, 5.1%, in the partnership. The most important limited partner in the case was another limited partnership, Gotham Partners, which initially owned 14.8 % of the partnership.

With partnership units trading at a low price, several directors promoted a scheme to shore up the trading price of the units, which would require a deep-pocketed backer. The directors were serving simultaneously in controlling positions at both HGI and its subsidiary, Hallwood Realty Corporation. As a result of several of these transactions, Hallwood Realty Corporation's stake in the limited partnership rose from 5.1% to 29.7%. Among other things, Gotham alleged that Hallwood Realty Corp. orchestrated self-deals whereby Hallwood Realty Corp. could increase its stake in the limited partnership at fire sale prices. As such, Hallwood Realty Corp., according to Gotham, had violated its fiduciary duty.

At least two important issues discussed in this case are relevant. First, the court noted that the parties could privately contract around any default fiduciary obligations, as they had. For example, parties may privately agree to limit the extent of their fiduciary duties to one another, change the standard of actionable conduct, or list the types of actions that might violate fiduciary duty. The court noted that the parties had agreed in their partnership agreement that self-deals were not a violation of fiduciary duties if the transaction met the standard for entire fairness — the insider should pay a fair price and deal fairly, for example. Although the court endorses the view that the parties may contract around to limit the reach of many fiduciary obligations, the court goes out of its way to note that parties cannot privately contract to completely eliminate fiduciary duties in a limited partnership. Thus, the parties may not by contract agree that there should be no fiduciary duties whatsoever, but they can privately agree to parameters.

Second, the court noted that the directors and officers of the general corporation could be held liable personally for aiding the breach of fiduciary duty. The important point here is not that the court suggested that these officers and directors could be held liable, although it is a remarkable conclusion. The important point here is to note the fact the some of the limited partners had dual capacities as limited partners and directors/officers of the general partner corporate entity. Thus, as in *Gotham Partners,* the limited partners cannot usually be held liable for breach of the fiduciary duties of loyalty or care in *that* capacity, but may be found liable for breach of those duties in their capacity serving as a general partner.

2. Obligation of Good Faith and Fair Dealing

Both general and limited parties owe each other an obligation to act in good faith and deal fairly. Importantly, the obligation is not a fiduciary duty. Instead, the obligation to discharge a duty in good faith arises under normal contract principles, which provide that in every contract there is a duty of good faith. For instance, consider the scope of a general partner's responsibility to make a full and complete disclosure before undertaking a self-deal. Specifically, in *Jerman v. O'Leary*, the general partners, the O'Learys, wanted to purchase several acres of unimproved land from the partnership. 701 P.2d 1205 (Ariz. Ct. App. 1985). The land was currently zoned for a suburban ranch, but the O'Learys had been pushing to have the land re-zoned as "TH", travel trailer park. The change in designation would have likely pushed up the value of the land and the O'Learys had managed to win a provisional change in the land's designation. However, the O'Learys did not inform the appraiser. A handful of the limited investors complained that the O'Learys had violated their fiduciary duty by failing to give the appraiser full information, which conceivably could mean an under-appraisal and an under-bid for the land. Importantly, the partnership agreement vested the general partner with the sole power to dispose of partnership property. Nevertheless, the court held that the defendant's conduct could potentially be a breach of duty. Accordingly, a general partner in a self-deal may have a strong duty to disclose all facts to its limited partners and can probably not restrict this right by contract.

E. Right to Control

Power in a limited partnership, like in a corporation, is highly centralized. The general partner normally makes all operational decisions for the partnership, while the limited partners are merely passive investors. The right to control that flows to the general partner in a limited partnership mirrors the power of any partner in a general partnership. For instance, the general partner can enter into contracts on behalf of the general partnership, just as any partner would be able to in a general partnership. If a limited partnership has more than one general partner, then decision-making is by a majority vote of those serving as general partner. Decisions outside the ordinary scope of company obligations require the consent of all the partners, including the limited partners. For instance, the consent of both limited and general partners is necessary to amend the partnership agreement or dispose of substantially all of the partnerships assets.

F. Right to Share in Profits and Losses

As stated, the limited partnership is required to maintain records reflecting each partner's capital contribution. By default, partners in a limited partnership share in profits and losses according to their capital contribution to the partnership. REVISED UNIF. LTD. P'SHIP. ACT §§ 503–504 (1985). This contrasts with how profits and losses are allocated, absent agreement to the contrary, in a general partnership. Recall that under default principles in a general partnership profits and losses are normally shared equally without regard to a partner's capital contribution. For instance, a partner in a 10 member limited partnership that makes a 50% of the capital contributed to the partnership is, by default, entitled to half of the partnership profits. Of course in a general partnership, such a partner would only be entitled to one-tenth of the profits generated from the enterprise.

G. Right to Sue

Normally, like other operational decisions, a general partner makes decisions on whether to sue on behalf of the limited partnership. However, another partner can bring a legal action in the name of the limited partnership, if the general partner has decided not to pursue the action. As in derivative actions in corporate law, the net proceeds of the lawsuit will flow to the limited partnership. Additionally, a partner can pursue a direct action against one or more of the other partners or the limited partnership for wrongful conduct. In these cases, the suing partner would have to show (or allege) that the wrongful conduct created special harm independent from any harm that may be felt by the general partnership.

H. Limited Partner Liability

Limited partners are protected from liability in a limited partnership. Thus, limited partners are generally treated like shareholders in a corporation or members in a limited liability company. However, the extent of their protection varies. For instance, a limited partner is always liable for her own wrongful conduct that may cause damages. Thus, if a limited partner wrongfully absconds with partnership property, there is no liability shield. For that matter, a creditor holding a debt against an individual partner can seek a court order levying that partner's financial interest in the limited partnership. Moreover, a limited partner can be liable to the limited partnership or other partners if the limited partner breaches the partnership agreement or the limited partner's duty to deal in good faith (previously discussed). Lastly, and perhaps most importantly, limited partners who participate in management decisions or control the partnership are behaving like a general partner. As a result of exercising management control, such limited partners may lose their liability protection, although these instances have become fewer and fewer.

1. The Control Rule

With only a few exceptions, the limited partners have no inherent power to enter into contracts or act as an agent in the ordinary course on behalf of the partnership. To be frank though, even these cases are flexible. To take an example, a limited partner may act in a controlling role if the limited partner is also a general partner. In these cases, the notion is that the limited partner is only acting in a controlling role in her capacity as a general partner. Further, a limited partner may end up with some control-type functions based on the agreement. However, again, in many of these cases there is no inconsistency with the limited responsibility of a limited partner. For instance, a limited partner may be designated an agent of the limited partnership for certain purposes by a general partner. Because a general partner has the power to delegate responsibility, no real exception to the notion of control would exist in this case either.

Absent those exceptions, under the partnership agreement, when a limited partner does exert control, the limited partner (as discussed below in detail) may be liable as if she were a general partner. Specifically, courts have held that a limited partner be individually liable as a general partner, in cases in which the limited partner controls the business enterprise. This is variously referred to as the "control rule." In some ways, notions of control in limited partnership law can be analogized to control under agency principles. A true principal has veto power over the decisions of an agent within the scope of any agency. In the same way, a partner that bears final responsibility for entity decisions can be said to be effectively in control.

Before describing the control rule, it is important to note that the rule has waned over time. Most importantly, under the latest version of the RULPA, which has been adopted by most states, there are several exempted activities. For instance, limited partners can vote on major decisions of the partnership, like the admission of new partners or exclusion of current partners, amendments to the partnership agreement, sale of the partnership assets, or dissolution, without implicating any control rule. REVISED UNIF. LTD. P'SHIP. ACT § 301 (1985). Further, the RULPA declares that certain activities can be undertaken by limited partners without creating liability. For instance, a limited partner may give advice or consult with the general partner about company operations or may file a direct or derivative action, without entering the ambit of control. REVISED UNIF. LTD. P'SHIP. ACT § 303(b)(2)(4) (1985).

In the latest uniform act, furthermore, liability flowing from the operation of the control rule has been completely eliminated. Thus, under the ULPA a party's liability is based on her status or designation. Partners designated as limited partners are not liable, regardless of their conduct, even conduct that arguably represents control-type actions. UNIF. LTD. P'SHIP. ACT § 303 (2001). As more states adopt the ULPA, the control rule (and the cases decided there under) will have less and less relevance, because a limited party will have no liability, even in cases where there is control. Despite the increasingly limited number of circumstances where control can create liability, courts and litigants continue to weigh what type of conduct might constitute control sufficient to warrant imposing liability on a limited partner. In many of these cases, the third party may have a reasonable belief based on another party's contact with the limited partner.

Holzman v. De Escamilla is a brief case about a short-lived limited partnership between De Escamilla (the general partner), Russell and Andrews (both limited partners). 195 P.2d 833 (Cal. Ct. App. 1948). Only a few months after the partnership was formed, the partnership went into bankruptcy, where the trustee appointed to manage partnership assets argued that the two limited partners, Russell and Andrews, should be individually liable for partnership debts. In the trustee's view, Russell and Andrews had final authority over the operation of the enterprise, a farming venture. Russell and Andrews, it was shown, had authority to withdraw partnership funds, to sign checks, and made decisions about what crops would be planted. Further, the two could require the general manger to resign. The court agreed with the trustee that Russell and Andrews were in control and, therefore, liable as a general partner would be liable. Thus, in some cases, a limited partner might be liable if the court finds that the limited partner exercised control over the limited partnership.

All things considered, *Holzman* is an easy case. In such cases, a third party creditor will allege control based on the limited partner's conduct. Less easy, however, are cases, like the next one, when it does not appear the limited partner has made any representations of control, by conduct or otherwise. More to the point of the problem, the RULPA provides that liability under the control rule will only occur if the third party had a reasonable belief that the limited partner was in fact a general partner exerting control. REVISED UNIF. LTD. P'SHIP. ACT § 303(a) (1985). Under this statement of the control rule, the reasonable belief must be based on the limited partner's conduct. However, it is not completely clear from the cases whether a third party must have *direct* knowledge of the limited party's conduct. As discussed below, therefore, it is conceivable that a limited partner may have liability under the control rule, even though the limited partner may have not had any direct contact with such third party.

To the point, in *Gateway Potato Sales v. G.B. Investment Company,* the plaintiff, Gateway sued to recover for unpaid expenses incurred by the limited partnership. 822 P.2d 490 (Ariz. Ct. App. 1991). The plaintiff argued that it should recover not only against the general partner, but also against the limited partner, G.B. Investment. Although the plaintiff had had no contact with G.B. Investment, the limited partner, the plaintiff claimed it relied on representations made by the general partner who had expressed that real control rested with G.B. Investment. The court noted that G.B. Investment could still be liable, even though it made no direct representation to Gateway. According to the court, the issue is whether the limited partner effectively has at least as much (or more) control over the limited partnership as a general partner. For instance, if G.B. Investment had at least much control over Sunworth, the limited partnership, then liability could be created. In cases like that, Gateway could reasonably rely solely on a representation from the general partner. Thus, a creditor need not have contact with the limited partner in all cases to have a good faith belief that the limited partner is in control.

2. Other Issues in Limited Partner Liability

Besides the control rule, a limited partner can also be held liable in many other circumstances that might create good reason for a third party to believe that the partner is actually a general partner. As mentioned, for instance, a partner may also be liable for damages caused by a third party's reliance on an erroneous public filing (*e.g.,* certificate of limited partnership), if the partner knew of the error or, upon learning of the error, failed to correct the error after a reasonable period of time. Also, it is worth noting a limited partner might face exposure if the limited partner permits her name to be used in the name of the business entity. The limited party, however, must knowingly agree for her name to be lent to that of the partnership for liability to be created.

I. General Partner Liability

A creditor in a limited partnership can only get at the assets of the partnership and, if those assets are insufficient, the assets of the general partners. Yet, the general partner can be insulated from liability in several ways. For one thing, the general partner can operate as a corporation that has limited liability. For instance, in *Gotham Partners,* a case discussed previously in the Chapter, recall that the general partner was a corporate entity, which means investors are normally protected from liability. An interesting case is when a limited partner may direct or control the activities of the corporate general partner. For instance, the limited partner may be the president of the general corporate entity or chairman of the entity's board of directors. Even in these cases though, the corporate protection would protect the limited partner from direct liability. Additionally, in the minority of states that have adopted the ULPA, a limited partnership may simply elect to form a *limited* liability partnership by stating in the certificate of limited partnership that the entity is to have limited liability. Unif. Ltd. P'ship. Act § 201(a)(4) (2001). A limited liability partnership would protect even the general partners from liability.

J. Change in Control

Many of the change in control issues in a limited partnership mirror the issues in a general partnership. For instance, as in a general partnership context, the default rule is that financial interest in a limited partnership is transferable, while the management interest is not (without the consent of all the other partners). Still, other issues are unique to the limited partnership context. For instance, unlike in some general partnerships, a limited partnership is not necessarily dissolved because a single partner decides to withdraw.

1. Dissociation and Admission

By default both limited and general partners to a limited partnership may withdraw at anytime. A general partner may withdraw upon giving notice to the other partners. Arguably a general partner's power to withdraw from the limited partnership agreement is stronger, particularly under the ULPA. Under the ULPA, a general partner's power to dissociate cannot be varied or eliminated by the partnership agreement. Unif. Ltd. P'ship. Act § 110(b)(8) (2001). If the partnership does not provide a procedure for withdrawal, a limited partner may withdraw after giving 6 months written notice to the other members of the limited partnership. Similarly, the default rule is that new partners can only be admitted by written consent of all the other partners. This is consistent with notions of freedom of association, which would suggest that a party cannot be compelled to continue to associate with others.

However, none of this means that a partner has an unfettered ability to withdraw from a limited partnership. First, in the vast majority of cases, the right to withdraw by a limited partner is likely governed by a partnership agreement, which probably eliminates the right to completely discretionary withdrawal. Although a partner could still withdraw from the partnership, to do so in defiance of a partnership agreement would expose the limited partner to damages for wrongful withdrawal and breach. Second, a general partner's withdrawal might also violate a term in the partnership agreement creating liability for wrongful dissociation. Once a general partner makes a decision to dissociate, she also has an obligation to see the limited partnership through termination of the entity (if applicable). If the general partner does not, the dissociation might also be wrongful and create liability. Thus, a partnership agreement can effect or restrict the right of a partner to dissociate from a limited partnership.

Additionally, a general partner can be removed *per* the terms of the partnership agreement. Interestingly, any partner's assignment of their financial interest in the partnership is tantamount to a withdrawal. As always, a partner in a limited partnership has a right to assign her financial interest—the right to receive distributions or share of profits and losses—to another. However, in contrast to the law of general partnership, in a limited partnership a partner that makes such an assignment is no longer a partner. An assignment is act of withdrawal for both limited and general partners in a limited partnership. Other acts that would normally cause a general partner to cease being a partner include financial insolvency, incapacity, or death.

2. Transfer of Corporate Partner Stock

As mentioned, the general partner in many limited partnerships is actually a corporate entity. This creates many interesting scenarios. For instance, the owners of the corporate entity may create what amounts to a change in control any time they elect to transfer ownership in the corporate entity. Since the corporate entity still has a legal status, it is not clear in all cases whether the transfer of corporate stock actually effects a change in control. Further, when the general partner is a corporate entity, a change in control could be said to have taken place when there has been significant management changes in the corporate entity—e.g., a slate of new directors, or the company hires a new CEO or President. Even tougher cases still, like the next one, are when the parties to the partnership have agreed to an anti-transfer provision. Courts have to determine whether these anti-takeover provisions cover transfers of stock in the corporate entity and changes in management.

In Re Asian Yard Partners involves whether the underlying stock in a corporate general partner could be sold without violating the parties' anti-transfer provision. 1995 WL 1781675 (Bankr. D. Del. 1995). In that case, the general partner in question was a corporate entity wholly-owned and controlled by Asian Yard Partners. Asian Yard Partners proposed selling its stock in the general partner to another party, while the other partners suggested that the partnership agreement prohibited such a transfer without consent of the partners. The court held that the transfer could not go forward based on the expansive anti-transfer provision, which restricted both "direct" and "indirect" transfers.

The point here is that when the partnership agreement includes an anti-takeover provision, courts may still be called on to determine the scope of the agreement. In the vast majority of cases, where the parties have a simple anti-transfer clause, courts have held that the clause does not bar transfers of the corporate stock of the general partner. The reasoning here is that the legal personality of the general partner remains the same — i.e., the corporate entity (albeit with different shareholders) is still in charge. However, in perhaps a minority of cases, the parties have crafted very detailed anti-transfer clause. On the basis of these detailed clauses, courts have suggested that even a transfer of corporate stock would be a breach of the partnership agreement.

K. Dissolution of a Limited Partnership

A partnership can be dissolved in a number of ways. The limited partnership can be dissolved, of course, by the procedure described in the partnership agreement.

1. Dissolution by Consent

Interestingly also, a partnership can be dissolved by a super-majority of the partners consenting to the dissolution. That is, under the ULPA the limited partnership is dissolved if all the general partners and a majority of the limited partners (based on financial stake) consent to dissolution. UNIF. LTD. P'-SHIP. ACT §801(2) (2001). The RULPA's default procedure for dissolution mirrors general partnership law — i.e., all the partners must consent to the dissolution. REVISED UNIF. LTD. P'SHIP. ACT §801(3) (1985).

2. Constructive Dissolution

Further, in some instances, a limited partnership can be dissolved by the withdrawal or removal of a general partner. Specifically, a limited partnership must have one of the partners designated as the general partner. Thus, if members of the limited partnership remove the current general partner (or the current general partner withdraws) the members must designate a replacement general partner. When a limited partnership terminates a relationship of a general partner and fails to designate a replacement, the limited partnership is considered dissolved. By contrast, if a limited partner dissociates, that does not by itself bring the end of the partnership. This makes for a good contrast with the law of general partnership, which suggests dissolution may occur in an at-will general partnership. UPA § 801(1) (1997).

In *Obert v. Environmental R & D*, the court held exactly that—to wit, a limited partnership must always have a general partner. 752 P.2d 924 (Wash. Ct. App. 1988). In this case, the vast majority of the limited partners desired to oust their general partner, ERADCO. Although these partners voted in favor of ouster, ERADCO countered that the limited partners had acted in bad faith and in breach of their fiduciary duty since they did not provide proper notice of the vote to all partners. The court rejected this view, since the partnership agreement did not require any notice. However, the court held that the ouster would result in dissolution of the partnership, because the partnership agreement did not speak clearly to the procedure for electing a successor general partner. According to the court, under applicable default principles, it would take unanimous (not merely majority) consent to elect a successor general partner. Thus, a limited partnership must always have at least one general partner and one limited partner in order to operate. If there is a defection of a general partner, the default rule is that the limited partners may continue to operate if the limited partners agree to elect a new general partner. The limited partners must do so soon (*i.e.*, within 90 days) after or else the limited partnership is considered dissolved. By partnership agreement, the parties may agree for a less daunting standard for the election of a new general partner. They may, for instance, agree in the partnership agreement that another general partner should manage company operations. But, at all pertinent times, the limited partnership must have both types of partners.

3. Certificate of Dissolution

A limited partnership can notify the public of dissolution by filing a certificate showing dissolution with the relevant state office, which provides the effective date of the end of the limited partnership. The certificate of cancellation should be filed when the partners begin to wind up the business. Such a certificate puts non-parties on notice of the dissolution. After a reasonable time has elapsed after the public filing, such parties cannot claim lack of knowledge or reliance when dealing with the dissolved limited partnership. UPA § 103(d)(3) (2001).

Checkpoints

- The limited partnership has several benefits, including centralized management, limited liability for investors, and pass-through taxation.

- The general partner in a limited partnership controls operations of the limited partnership, while the limited partners are usually passive investors.

- If a limited partnership has more than one general partner, than decision-making is done by a majority vote of the general partners. In a limited partnership, significant decision-making requires the consent of all the partners, both limited and general.

- The general partner is liable for the unsatisfied obligations of the limited partnership. However, the limited partner is generally shielded from liability, except for the limited partner's investment in the limited partnership.

- The general partner has a duty of care and loyalty to the partnership. However, the limited partners have no significant default fiduciary duties.

- A limited partnership is not necessarily dissolved by the departure of one of the limited partners.

Chapter 5

Limited Liability Companies

Roadmap

- Historical Role of LLC
- Source of LLC law
- Forming an LLC
- Governance of an LLC
- Fiduciary Duties in an LLC
- Limited Liability
- Winding Up an LLC

A. Introduction

In many ways, the LLC is something of a chimera, composed of the best parts of the partnership (pass-through taxation and investor control) and the best of the corporation (liability shield). Thus, it is only fitting that the LLC should be discussed in between the two, after a discussion of partnership law and before discussion of corporate law.

1. The Appeal of LLCs

In recent years, the limited liability company has begun to displace the partnership and even the corporation to become one of the most appealing organizational alternatives for investors. In a recent study, for instance, one author finds that close to half (45%) of company formations were LLCs. *See* Howard Friedman, *Silent LLC Revolution*, 8 CREIGHTON L. REV. 35(2004). Although the first limited liability company was organized thirty years ago, most state limited liability acts came into fruition only in the last decade. Now, in states across the country, LLC filings are up and even moving past the number of registered filings to organize as a corporation in many states. *See* Friedman, *supra.* Three basic reasons are normally offered up as possible explanations for the LLC's surging popularity among the investor community.

First, LLCs protect investors from liability. As long as a separate business structure is maintained, the investors or "members" of an LLC are not liable for the contracts and torts of the company. As in corporate law, some exceptions exist for piercing the so-called corporate veil (or in this case, the LLC veil) and going directly after investor assets. Normally, though, investors in a limited liability company only have to fear the loss of their investment, not their personal assets, in the event of company misconduct. However, protection from liability is probably not the most appealing feature of the LLC, since several other business entities, including the corporation, offer a similar protection for their investors. Furthermore, investors who choose to conduct business in a form that has no liability shield can simply procure appropriate levels of insurance, which will effectively operate to protect assets. Additionally, the protection from liability is not a particularly alluring characteristic of LLCs and other limited-liability entities, judging by how frequently investors may opt to waive the shield. In fact, many of the investors in LLCs will have to waive their protection from liability in order to complete transactions. For instance, a bank might require investors to personally guarantee a loan to an LLC, which effectively contracts around the default rule of investor protection.

A second purported appeal of the LLC is related to taxes. That is, LLCs offer tax benefits, since company earnings are treated the same as partnership earnings. In other words, the LLC does not have to pay taxes at the entity level. Instead, like a partnership, the profits or losses of an LLC are passed straight through to investors. This avoids what is variously referred to as "double taxation"—*i.e.,* taxation of company earnings at the entity level and, later, income taxation on the individual level. While the LLC offers some unique tax advantages, these benefits should probably not be overstated. With proper planning, other entities might also produce comparable tax savings for investors. For instance, consider corporations. Only shareholders who receive an earnings distribution (*e.g.,* dividends) would be subject to double taxation. Firms that make no such distributions do not expose their shareholders to this cost. Shareholders still realize the benefit of retained earnings in the form of capital appreciation, which upon disposition is also taxed at a preferential rate.

A third, and perhaps most important characteristic of the LLC, is it provides investors maximum flexibility to organize their economic relationships as they deem fit. For instance, the founders of an LLC can play a role in managing the enterprise themselves; or hire non-investor, professional managers to do the job; or an amalgam of both. They can organize their economic interest flexibly as well. Like public corporations, the founders of an LLC can classify multiple ownership interests. Further, the organizers of a limited liability company can form the entity with broad purpose, to undertake a business purpose or any lawful purpose, including charitable activities.

The LLC, however, does have downside risk from a legal or regulatory perspective. In particular, though the limited liability company is a popular organizational vehicle, it is also one of relatively recent vintage. Because the LLC is a relatively new concept, the legal landscape is in some ways hazier than in the case of other organizational vehicles. As can be expected with a new legal entity, several questions have not been settled by courts and, thus, the body of LLC precedent is not well-developed. Courts have variously drawn on corporate law and partnership law to resolve many of the important questions, but at the same time have created a mixed bag of opinions. Perhaps even more troubling, states have yet to fully commit to a uniform body of LLC law. As it stands now, there is significant variation among the states when it comes to LLCs. One reason for the wide variation among the states is that the uniform company act was not approved until 1995. By that time, nearly all the states had already passed a limited liability act. Another reason for the wide variation in state statutes is the nature of what the LLC hopes to do: give investors the operational flexibility of a partnership and a shield from liability as in a corporation. As such, states that drafted LLC statutes have drawn on a wide variety of legal sources, like partnership law, corporate law, and tax regulations. This hodgepodge of sourcing led to many states making different decisions about what items should get emphasis.

2. Brief History of LLCs

The history of the limited liability company is significant as it helps to explain many of the statutory quirks of modern limited liability company law. Although the first state to pass an LLC statute, Wyoming, did so three decades ago, in 1977, it took several years for LLCs to catch-on. For one thing, whether the LLC would be taxed as a corporate entity or, more favorably, as a partnership was unsettled for at least the next decade. At the time the Wyoming legislature approved its LLC statutes, the IRS decided this taxation issue based on the so-called "Kitner rules." The rules provided that an entity was a corporation and should be taxed accordingly, if it possessed three or more of the following characteristics: (1) perpetual life; (2) unfettered transfer of ownership interests; (3) limited liability; and (4) centralized management. In other words, according to the IRS, if the company resembled a corporation, it would face a corporate tax; if it more resembled a partnership, it would be taxed as such.

Despite the Kitner rules, it was unclear whether an entity that shielded investors from liability, like Wyoming's so-called LLC, would be taxed like a corporation. The tax benefits of the LLCs were not settled until 1988, when the IRS, in Revenue Ruling 88-76, opined that a Wyoming LLC could be taxed like a partnership. Once the IRS issued this ruling, states around the country began devising their own LLC acts. More than thirty states passed LLC acts in five years after the ruling. Since the companies organized under the IRS ruling would have only received the pass-through taxation if they resembled a partnership, many of these early state LLC acts included statutory language that make that characterization much more likely. For instance, many of the early LLC acts provided unique exit rights for members. States (taking a cue from Wyoming) went so far as to suggest that a member's exit creates a dissolution of the LLC. The goal of states in this regard was to ensure that companies organized as an LLC would not have perpetual life or free transferability of ownership interest, corporate characteristics under the Kitner rules.

Thereafter, in 1997, the IRS implemented the so-called "check-the-box" rules. Under these regulations, business entities can simply chose whether they want to be taxed as a corporate entity or a partnership. Under internal revenue code guidelines, the only important exception was for publicly traded companies. No longer would the IRS be in the business of trying to ascertain whether closely-held firm resembled a corporation. Instead, the firm simply made the election. As a result, state legislatures had less incentive to consider whether entities possessed corporate characteristics. Many states began the process of revising their LLC acts to give entities greater organizational flexibility. Some states decided that LLC companies would exist perpetually, like a corporation, unless the founders decided otherwise. For instance, today under Delaware law, a dissociation of a member does not trigger dissolution, unless the parties have a private agreement to the contrary.

B. Source of Law

There is wide variation among the states regarding the legal organization of a limited liability company. Although every state has enacted their own LLC act, the states and the courts have variously drawn on general partnership law or corporate law or even the ABA's recommendations. Nevertheless, two sources of LLC law stand out meriting particularly close attention.

First, the Delaware LLC act is of particular importance to mastering limited liability companies. Interestingly, unlike in other countries, a limited liability company in the United States can make its filing in any of the states, regardless of whether the company is domiciled in that state. The law of the organizing state in most instances will govern most transactions. Given this flexibility, this means that as with other organizational forms, the state of Delaware receives a significant share of LLC filings. Among other reasons, many company founders flock to Delaware because the state has an experienced, business-savvy judiciary and an environment that makes out-of-state administration of an organization easy. For example, the filing costs and expense of organizing as an LLC (*e.g.*, business franchise tax) is relatively inexpensive in Delaware compared to other states. Further, when disputes arise, Delaware courts are stacked with a relatively high number of business-minded judges who have significant experience with business cases. Thus, one reason Delaware's approach to LLC law is important is because its laws govern a disproportionate number of cases. Second, the current uniform act on LLC is also worthy of note, as states consider whether to revise their LLC acts and move more toward uniformity. The National Commission on Uniform Law has tried at least twice to promulgate a uniform limited liability act. The latest revision was recently offered to states in 2006. This Chapter will also refer, from time to time, to their latest effort. Shortly, unless otherwise noted, this Chapter shall refer principally to the uniform act or to Delaware's.

C. Formation

The founders of a limited liability company must make an appropriate filing with the state in order to officially organize and continue to do business as a limited liability company. Undoubtedly, of the required filings, the most important is the certificate of formation. In addition to the certificate of formation, many states require LLCs to file other documents, like an annual report, statement of authority, denial of statements of authority, certificate of cancellation if the company is dissolved, among others. Interestingly perhaps, the most important document of all to an LLC and its members—the operating agreement—is never filed with the state.

1. Certificate of Formation

In order to form an LLC, the founders must file a certificate of formation with the relevant state office, usually the Secretary of State. The certificate of formation is the equivalent of the articles of incorporation in the corporate law context. It is a brief, publicly-available legal document that essentially names the entity and contact information for service of process. Unif. Ltd. Liab. Co. Act. §§ 202–203 (2006). An entity should have at least one member, but it need not have more than one to be eligible to organize as an LLC. As with a limited partnership, the founders of a limited liability company must demonstrate "substantial compliance" with the filing requirements in order to take advantage of the liability shield for investors. Once the certificate of formation has been filed, the limited liability company, by default, has a permanent existence, separate from its founders. Also, as an alternative, an LLC can make what is called a shelf-filing if the entity does not have a member yet, but expects to find one soon. In this circumstance, the founder would make the appropriate filing and return within a reasonable time (*e.g.*, 90 days) to name at least one member. Only when the entity has a member is it officially an LLC.

2. The Operating Agreement

The LLC apportions rights and responsibilities among participants through the operating agreement. The operating agreement is much like a partnership agreement, as both govern internal relations. Thus, the operating agreement controls relationships member *vis-à-vis* member and member *vis-à-vis* Company. The company is bound by the agreement, as are later members, as if they had assented to its terms. The importance of an operating agreement for the LLC can probably not be overstated. In fact, the operating agreement is so important that some states require one. For instance, the California Corporate Code provides as follows:

> In order to form a limited liability company, one or more persons shall execute and file articles of organization with, and on a form prescribed by, the Secretary of State and, either before or after the filing of articles or organization, the members *shall* have entered into an operating agreement.

CAL. CORP. CODE § 17050(a) (2006) (emphasis supplied). The operating agreement is a contract. But, still, an operating agreement is required even in cases of a sole-member LLC, even though there is technically no other member to assent. The thought here is that the single member may want to contractually change the scope of the default fiduciary duties. Also, like a partnership agreement, the investors or members need not disclose the operating agreement to outside third parties. Changes to an operating agreement can only occur under the terms therein or by consent of the members.

The members of an LLC are given breathtaking flexibility to determine how their business is run in the operating agreement. Nevertheless, though the parties' ability to contract around default rules in the operating agreement is expansive, there are some limitations. For instance, usually the operating agreement cannot unreasonably eliminate a member's ability to bring suit, or the duties of loyalty, duty of care, and contractual obligation of good faith. Additionally, the operating agreement may not condone intentional law-breaking or misconduct or theft of company assets. Still, in the end, the courts, as the next case shows, will almost always enforce the parties will as reflected in the operating agreement.

In *Elf Atochem v. Cyrus, et al*, the operating agreement provided that all disputes should be arbitrated. 727 A.2d 286 (Del. 1999). The agreement was only between the members of the limited liability company. The company itself, however, notably was not a signatory to the operating agreement. The plaintiff argued that his dispute, a derivative suit, should not be arbitrated because the limited liability company was not a party to the arbitration agreement. The company, therefore, still had a right to sue and was not bound by the arbitration agreement. In the plaintiff's view, he could properly prosecute the case on behalf of the company as a derivative action, an action on the company's behalf. The plaintiff also argued that the arbitration was invalid and against the Delaware liability act, which codified the right to sue derivatively.

Notwithstanding the right to sue on the company's behalf, the court upheld the arbitration clause of the operating agreement. In the court's view, the parties' freedom to contract should be respected, particularly, as in the case, when it when it comes to disputes between members:

> Notwithstanding Malek LLC's failure to sign the Agreement, Elf's claims are subject to the arbitration and forum selection clauses of the Agreement. The Act is a statute designed to permit members maximum flexibility in entering into an agreement to govern their relationship. It is the members who are the real parties in interest. The LLC is simply their joint business vehicle. This is the contemplation of the statute in prescribing the outlines of a limited liability company agreement.

727 A.2d 293 (Del. 1999). Thus, even in cases where the member claims to be acting on behalf of a third party (here, the LLC), the member will still be bound by the terms of the company arbitration agreement. *Elf Atochem* is also emblematic as it demonstrates the idea that courts are particularly inclined to enforce the operating agreement in a dispute among members. In disputes between members, courts are inclined to presume that members are privy to the terms of the operating agreement and have assented to the terms when they become members. On the other hand, a third party may have a little more wiggle room. In special cases, such parties may not always be bound by the operating agreement, since such a party would have no easy way gaining such information.

D. Governance

The internal affairs of a limited liability company can be managed in different ways to promote maximum flexibility of choice among company investors. Sometimes investors may organize their relationship in a way that more closely resembles how a partnership is managed and other times choosing to run the entity similar to a corporation. Equally, investors in an LLC can calibrate a member's voting or economic interest by private agreement.

1. Management

To begin with, the founders of an LLC can decide to be member-managed, like a partnership, where each of the investors plays a role in operations. Smaller companies without abundant resources are more likely to be managed directly by the investors or founders of the company. In fact, unless the parties privately agree otherwise, the default rule is that an LLC is member-managed. In terms of governance, member-managed companies are similar to general partnerships. The members of a member-managed entity, for instance, may act as agents of the company in the ordinary course of operations. They each have an equal right to decision-making, unless otherwise agreed. When a consensus cannot be reached among all the members, the decision is made by majority vote. However, if a decision is made outside the ordinary course of business operations, then the consent of all the members is needed.

Alternatively, managers of an LLC may opt to be manager-managed, like a corporation, in which case professional managers execute policy on behalf of the company. For instance, the company may hire outsiders to be the company CEO, CFO, or General Counsel and manage many of the day-to-day affairs. Although the managers in a manger-managed firm may be outsiders, they may also be investors wearing a dual hat. The managers, in either case, speak on behalf of the company in the vast majority of transactions. However, though the managers would run the operations of the company, the managers would still need the consent of all the members to make significant decisions. For instance, under the uniform limited liability company act, managers of a limited liability company would still need member assent to dispose of a significant share of company assets, or merge with another company or amend the operating agreement. In summary, the members' flexibility with respect to their internal affairs is extremely broad. As mentioned, the members can elect whether they want to participate in management or delegate those duties to a professional staff.

2. Owner Classes

Additionally, the states vary between the partnership model and the corporate model in assigning voting power to members of a limited liability company. Some states, following the partnership model, provide that unless the parties agree otherwise, the members of an LLC have an equal vote on operations. Other states suggest, as in corporate law, that members of an LLC have, as a default, a vote proportionate to their ownership interest in the LLC. In any event, members' ability to vote on matters of the LLC can also be expanded or restricted on the basis of the parties' private agreement. The founders of the entity, for instance, may devise several classes of members' interest.

E. Fiduciary Duty

Members of a limited liability company have several duties to one another, of which the most important three are the fiduciary duty of loyalty, fiduciary duty of care, and contractual obligation of good faith and fair dealing. Members of an LLC may alter the scope of their duties. For instance, they may agree that certain acts do not violate the duty of loyalty. They may privately agree to raise the standard of negligence required of members under the fiduciary duty of care. They may prescribe how the obligation of good faith is to be observed.

Significantly, in Delaware, the rights of members to alter their fiduciary duties are arguably the broadest. In that state, members of a limited liability company can now completely eliminate any fiduciary duty by private contract:

> To the extent that, at law or in equity, a member or manager or other person has duties (including fiduciary duties) to a limited liability company or to another member or manager or to another person that is a party to or is otherwise bound by a limited liability company agreement, the member's or manager's or other person's duties may be expanded or restricted or eliminated by provisions in the limited liability company agreement; provided, that the limited liability company agreement may not eliminate the implied contractual covenant of good faith and fair dealing.

DEL. CODE ANN. tit. 6 § 18-1101(c) (2008). Thus, though members cannot completely eliminate the obligation of good faith, in Delaware members of a company have unfettered discretion to delineate the reach of the fiduciary duties, like the duty of loyalty and care.

1. Duty of Loyalty

Members of a limited liability company have a duty of loyalty, which at its core requires a member to avoid conflicts of interest, avoid competition with the company, and disclose and share company opportunities. By private agreement, of course, members of a limited liability company can alter, and sometimes even eliminate, the core elements of the fiduciary duty of loyalty. As mentioned, Delaware permits the duty to be completely eliminated. DEL. CODE ANN. tit. 6 § 18-1101(c) (2008). Even when members cannot eliminate the fiduciary duty of loyalty, the members of an LLC have considerable latitude to outline the type of conduct that would represent a breach of loyalty. For instance, members may agree in the operating agreement that conflicts of interest, in of themselves, are not breaches of the duty of loyalty. The power to privately agree that certain acts do not violate the duty of loyalty extends to *ex post* agreements concluded as well. In other words, even if there is an act which could violate this duty, the parties could later ratify the act, if a method is provided in the operating agreement. Self-dealing could also be defended if it can be shown that the transaction was fair to the company.

For instance, consider *McConnell v. Hunt*. 725 N.E. 2d 1193 (Ohio Ct. App. 1999). In this case, a group of Ohio entrepreneurs formed a limited liability company for the express purpose of pursuing a National Hockey League franchise for the city of Columbus. When one of the local leaders of the group and main drivers of the venture demurred to the arena lease agreement, the venture appeared all but abandoned. The original group fractured. However, some of original group's remaining members elected to continue the drive for a NHL franchise and entered into an arena lease agreement. The new group was later awarded an NHL franchise. The departing members were extended no ownership interest in the franchise. When these departing members sued, they complained that the formation of the new group to pursue a NHL franchise was unfair competition and a violation of their duty of loyalty to their former members.

The court acknowledged that normally the duty of loyalty to members of a limited liability partnership, like to partners, creates a fiduciary duty not to compete with the other members. The court also noted that the new group only pursued the arena lease and the hockey franchise after their former partners found the deal to be objectionable. Even then, the new group was never secretive about their intentions to continue their drive for a NHL franchise.

Most significantly, the court held that the new group had not violated the duty of loyalty, because of the private agreement of the parties:

> The term "fiduciary relationship" has been defined as a relationship in which special confidence and trust is reposed in the integrity and fidelity of another, and there is a resulting position of superiority or influence acquired by virtue of this special trust. In the case at bar, a limited liability company is involved which, like a partnership, involves a fiduciary relationship. Normally, the presence of such a relationship would preclude direct competition between members of the company. However, here we have an operating agreement that by its very terms allows members to compete with the business of the company. Hence the question we are presented with is whether an operating agreement of a limited liability company may, in essence, limit or define the scope of the fiduciary duties imposed upon its members. We answer this question in the affirmative.

725 N.E.2d 1193, 1214 (Ohio Ct. App. 1999). In *McConnell*, the court recognizes that members have a fiduciary duty of loyalty to one another, which precludes unfair competition and secretive behavior. Members, in other words, generally have a duty to disclose company-related opportunities to one another and to avoid direct competition with the other members. Still, in the court's view, private contract is paramount in these business arrangements. The group had privately agreed to limit the reach of the duty of loyalty. Also important, the departing members had already expressed their disinterest in the opportunity.

2. Duty of Care

Similarly, by private agreement, members of a limited liability company can alter (but not usually eliminate) the fiduciary duty of care. The requirements of members or managers under the duty of care run the spectrum. Some state LLC acts suggest that a manger must exercise reasonable care—that is, care that a similarly situated individual would exercise. For instance, in New York the statute provides as follows: "A manager shall perform his or her duties as a manager, including his or her duties as a member of any class of managers, in good faith and with that degree of care that an ordinarily prudent person in a like position would use under similar circumstances." *See* N.Y. LTD. LIAB. CO. LAW §409(a) (2008). Other states suggest as a default rule that there is no breach of the duty of care, unless there is gross negligence on the part of the member. *See, e.g.,* CAL. CORP. CODE tit. 2.5 §17153 (2007); *see also* UNIF. LTD. LIAB. CO. ACT §409(c) (2006).

3. Good Faith and Fair Dealing

Finally, members have a contractual obligation of good faith and fair dealing, which is an immutable obligation. In fact, even in Delaware, a state that
adores flexibility for investors, the obligation of good faith and fair dealing
cannot be contracted away under the operating agreement. *See* DEL. CODE
ANN. tit. 6 § 18-1101(c) (2008). Good definitions of what is required under
"good faith" are few and far between. More helpful than definitions of good faith
are examples of bad faith, as the next case, a favorite, amply demonstrates.

In *VGS v. Castiel*, the minority member of a manager-managed limited liability company conspired to strip the majority-member of his power over
company assets. 2000 Del. Ch. LEXIS 122 (Del. Ch. 2000). In this case, the member with a majority interest, Castiel, controlled two seats on the company's
three-member board of managers. He named himself to one of the seats. He
also appointed the individual holding the second seat on the board. The third
seat was held by the member holding the minority interest, Sahagen. Sahagen's proposals for firm strategy and even offers to buyout Castiel were re-
peatedly rebuffed.

Amazingly though, Sahagen, the minority-member, was able to swoon the
majority-member's appointee. Sahagen convinced the appointee (and several other
employees) to defect and join him in planning a secret coup to take over the
company from its founder and current controlling member, Castiel. The operating agreement provided that the company's status could be changed by a majority of the managers. Sahagen and Castiel's appointee met secretly to take
action. They merged VGS, LLC, the limited liability company, into VGS, Inc.,
a Delaware corporation, and named themselves (without Castiel) to the new
company's board of directors. Sahagen ownership interest in the new company
grew to 62.5%, compared with his 25% minority position in the prior LLC.
Meanwhile, Castiel's interest slipped to 37.5% of the new company, from 75%.

The court noted that technically the Delaware LLC act does not require notification, when a majority of managers agree to take action by written consent.
However, the court held that members cannot avoid notification in order to effectively strip the majority interest holder of his rightful power to act:

> [I]t seems clear that the purpose of permitting action by written con-
> sent without notice is to enable LLC managers to take quick, efficient
> action in situations were a minority of managers could not block or
> adversely affect the course set by the majority even if they were noti-
> fied of the proposed action and objected to it. The General Assembly
> never intended, I am quite confident, to enable two managers to de-

prive, clandestinely and surreptitiously, a third manager representing the majority interest in the LLC of an opportunity to protect that interest by taking an action that the third manager's member would surely have opposed if he had knowledge of it.

2000 Del. Ch. LEXIS 122, 10–11 (Del. Ch. 2000). According to the court, provisions of the state LLC act only permit action by written consent (without notification) when the actors represent a "fixed" majority of LLC interests. Managers, therefore, cannot avoid notification to the real member holding a majority interest. Such action would violate rather general notions of good faith and fair dealing.

F. Introduction to Liability

The investors or members of a limited liability company are insulated from personal liability for the acts of the company. Thus, like limited partners, the members of a limited liability company are only exposed to the risk of loss of their investment, not their personal assets. Furthermore, the extension of liability protection in a limited liability company extends to *all* members. Thus, a limited liability company is unlike a limited partnership, where the general partner remains personally liable for the contracts and torts of the company. However, the members of a limited liability company do face liability in at least two important circumstances. As discussed in detail below, members face liability when it can be shown that the members and the company have disregarded company formalities and used the company for their own ends. Additionally, investors are still personally liable for their own wrongful conduct.

1. Piercing the Company Veil

First, members face liability in cases in which the entity is shown to be a mere shell or instrumentality, which is not distinct from its members. In these cases, for instance, a claimant might be able to pierce the company veil and sue the members directly by arguing that the members have co-mingled personal and company funds, pillaged company assets, or otherwise used the company as a mere extension of their own persona. The doctrine of veil-piercing in the context of limited liability companies mirrors the right in corporate law and, as a result, many courts rely on the same factors articulated in corporate law cases to weigh whether veil-piercing is appropriate. However, one such factor, a failure to maintain corporate formalities, arguably should not be over-emphasized in the case of limited liability companies. That is, some authorities, like the latest uniform company act, advise that this factor is not relevant in the case of limited liability companies, since such companies operate informally, without pomp and ceremony:

> The failure of a limited liability company to observe any particular formalities relating to the exercise of its powers or management of its activities is not ground for imposing liability on the members or managers for the debts, obligations, or other liabilities of the company.

UNIF. LTD. LIAB. CO. ACT § 304(b) (2006). Thus, in limited liability company law, it might be said that the substance of the transaction matters significantly more than procedure. In contrast to in the corporate context, members in a limited liability company are less likely to face liability for a failure to attend monthly company meetings or other procedural rituals that do not necessarily mean that the company is being used for an improper purpose. Notwithstanding more leeway to disregard some company formalities, members in a limited liability company can still face liability for transactions that demonstrate the entity is used exclusively to further personal, as opposed to company, objectives. Further, in making this determination, as the next case shows, courts rely in substantial part on the precedents established in the corporate law context. This invariably means that even supposedly non-factors, like observance of company formalities, tend to creep back into courts' analysis.

Kaycee Land v. Flahive is a Wyoming state Supreme Court case in which the members of the LLC defended against personal liability on the grounds that Wyoming statutes provided no such relief. 46 P.3d 323 (Wy. 2002). Thus, in *Kaycee Land*, the court addresses an important issue: What exactly is the source of the right to pierce the corporate veil? To this first question, the court answers that the right to pierce the corporate veil is a common law right, which is nearly the same as the right for corporations. Thus, veil-piercing is a remedy available in states, like Wyoming, even where the LLC statute is silent. Thus, the factors for determining when it is appropriate to veil-pierce are based on legal precedents and an individualized analysis by courts. One starting place for figuring out what conduct warrants veil-piercing is a review of corporate law cases. Specifically, according to the court, veil-piercing is to be treated like it is in the corporate context:

> We can discern no reason, in either law or policy, to treat LLCs differently than we treat corporations. If the members and officers of an LLC fail to treat it as separate entity as contemplated by statute, they

should not enjoy immunity from individual liability for the LLC's acts
that cause damage to third parties.

46 P.3d at 327. As in the corporate context, the Wyoming court advises that when
members of an LLC co-mingle funds or insufficiently capitalize the entity or
otherwise use it as a personal instrumentality, liability could follow. Thus, veil-
piercing mirrors the common law right to sue an investor directly in corporate
law. In both types of cases, courts will weigh the same issue to determine
whether the liability shield should be disregarded: whether the company was
treated as distinct entity. Investors still have a right to control the business, but
they cannot use the company as their personal fiefdom.

Similarly, in *New Horizon v. Haack*, the court relies on corporate law precedent to decide a veil-piercing issue. 590 N.W. 2d 282 (Wis. Ct. App. 1999).
In the case, the creditor, a fuel company, sued to recover for unpaid debts incurred by a former freight company. Interestingly, New Horizon sued one of
the company's members, Haack, in her personal capacity. The freight company had been dissolved and many of the assets of the company sold to pay
down company debts. However, several other company assets, like accounts
receivable and cash on hand, were apparently not accounted for by Haack
when she wound up the business. Further, Haack appears to have never contacted creditors, even known ones, like the plaintiff, about the dissolution of
the company. The court held that the creditor, in this circumstance, could
recover against Haack in her individual capacity. According to the court, Haack
could be personally liable for failing to observe procedural formalities that
would be necessary to warrant a shield. Many of the company assets had not
been accounted for. Additionally, the company had not filed a certificate of dissolution or systematically contacted creditors that might have a claim against
the dissolving company, as was required by statute and even though Haack
knew about New Horizon's claim.

Thus, a creditor may be able to recover against investors in a limited liability company that has failed to dissolve and distribute company assets in an equitable fashion. Perhaps, one of the most important things to come out of the
New Horizon opinion is the court's emphasis on maintaining certain formalities in order to get the benefit of the liability shield. The court lambastes Haack
for not notifying creditors and electing not to file a certificate of dissolution,
for example. This regard for formalities is another good example of the profound influence of corporate law cases, where this is one of the most important factor in corporate veil-piercing cases. The court suggests, in effect, that
the standard for piercing the company veil should mirror the standard for such
action in corporate law.

2. Individual Misconduct

Secondly, members of a limited liability company are not shielded from liability for their own misconduct. For instance, a member would not normally be shielded from liability for activities taken outside of the ordinary course of LLC operations. Nor would a member be shielded for conduct that occurred prior to the existence of the LLC, since such activities were taken in an individual, not member, capacity.

In *Pepsi-Cola Bottling Co v. Handy*, Pepsi attempted to reach individual members of an LLC after it found out the land they sold to Pepsi had severe environmental problems. 2000 Del. Ch. LEXIS 52 (Del. Ch. 2000). The case describes how several individuals, including the defendant Handy, purchased a large parcel of property to develop several homes. But, once they found that the property had an environmental problem that would make development impossible, they decided to attempt to sell the property. They transferred an option to purchase the property to Pepsi, without informing the beverage company of the environmental problem. Two weeks later, Handy and company formed an LLC. After Pepsi purchased the property and found out about the problem on their own, they sued the defendants in their individual capacities. Thus, the defendants in Pepsi were accused of clear misconduct. According to Pepsi, they lied, cheated, and formed an LLC after-the-fact in attempt to insulate themselves from their previous conduct.

The court agreed, noting that members can only be protected if they are sued because of the membership in a limited liability company. In this case, they were sued, not because of their status as members, but because of their conduct as individuals. Therefore, protection only begins after the LLC is formed; individual liability cannot be avoided by forming a limited liability company. Prior conduct can be a basis for suit, since the conduct could not have been done on behalf of a non-existent entity.

Regardless of the timing though, a member is not protected for his own misdeeds, acts not on behalf of the company. In another case, *Water, Waste & Land v. Lanham*, the two members, Lanham and Clark, of an LLC arranged for an engineering company to help it develop a restaurant. 955 P.2d 997 (Colo. 1998). They gave the engineering firm a business card, which included the initials of the company name. However, Lanham and Clark never disclosed that they were negotiating on behalf of the LLC, not in their personal capacity. The court held that the defendants could be personally liable. The court rejected the argument that the engineers should have been on notice that it was dealing with a limited liability company based on the company's public filing. The court held that constructive knowledge based on the filing is limited. For instance, in the court's view, a party can only be on notice if they have a reason to make inquiry. Thus, the business card failed to put the plaintiff on notice that it was dealing with a limited liability company, nor even the full name of the company.

Further, according to the court, the liability shield based on notice would only apply to suits against members based *solely* on their status as members. If the suit was based, as in *Water, Waste & Land*, on the members' actions, not just their status as members of a limited liability company, the suit could be maintained without doing harm to the ordinary operation of the liability shield. Lanham and Clark, in other words, could not be sued in their individual capacity if they were merely passive investors in the company.

Also important, the court reasoned that in cases where the members fail to disclose that they are acting on behalf of the limited liability company, the law of agency bespeaks the legal consequences. Under agency law, the court reminds, an agent acting on behalf an undisclosed agent faces individual liability:

> Under the common law of agency, an agent is liable on a contract entered on behalf of a principal if the principal is not fully disclosed. In other words, an agent who negotiates a contract with a third party can be sued for any breach of the contract unless the agent discloses both the fact that he or she is acting on behalf of a principal and the identity of the principal.

955 P.2d at 1001. Thus, the court reasons that a member acting as an agent must disclose that fact in order to insulate herself from liability. Importantly also, the court reasons that it is not enough for such agents to acknowledge that they are acting on behalf of another, the act must point out the identity of the company if they hope to establish that the third party "is conclusively presumed to know that the entity is a limited liability company not a partnership or some other type of business organization." *Water, Waste & Land v. Lanham*, 955 P.2d 997, 1004 (Colo. 1998).

In summary, under *Water, Waste*, a member or manager must disclose that she is acting on behalf of a company in order to be shielded from liability. If the member-manager does not, she possibly exposes herself to liability if the other party reasonably believes that she is acting in her individual capacity. This duty to disclose is consistent with statutory provisions under several LLC acts that require a limited liability company to use LLC in their names. However, the holding in *Water, Waste* regarding duty to disclose should not be pushed too far. For example, a member-manager has no duty to disclose the nature of the limited liability entity or that the members have status protection.

Notice of these matters is imputed, as long as the member-manager identifies the name of the company.

G. Dissociation

Simply put, one becomes a member of a limited liability company by consent of all the other members or per the terms of the operating agreement. However, the terms under which one may depart an LLC is far less simple. Under many early state LLC statutes, dissociation from a limited liability company caused dissolution of the firm. As mentioned, this made it more likely that the business entity would receive partnership-like taxation, since it undermines the perpetual life characteristic. Under other state statutes, dissociation from a limited liability causes a buyout of the dissociating member's interest. Today, under many state statutes, dissociation triggers neither a buyout nor dissolution. In fact, some states, like Delaware, have eliminated the unfettered default right to withdraw as member. Under Delaware law, a member can only withdraw when the company is dissolved and wound up. DEL. CODE ANN. tit. 6 § 18-603 (2008).

1. Buyouts

Initially, state LLC acts called for buyout rights for members similar to buyout rights in a partnership. Thus, these early LLC statutes provided that a departing member would be paid fair value for her interest, less any damages created by an early and wrongful departure. However, increasingly states have suggested that expansive buyout rights are inappropriate in the LLC context. For instance, consider *Five Star Concrete v. Klink*, a relatively recent case where a state court reined in extensive buyout rights. 693 N.E. 2d 583 (Ind. Ct. App. 1998). In the case, one member of a limited liability company sued to recover the value of his net income for the period he was a member of the company. The remaining members of the partnership had previously voted to distribute Klink, the withdrawing partner, the value of his partnership interest. However, the members refused to distribute to Klink the net income for the year, even though the partnership made an accounting entry that reflected income for Klink. The withdrawing partner, Klink, therefore argued that he was entitled to several thousand dollars of income that the limited liability company had allocated to him for accounting and tax purposes. The court noted that the operating agreement between the parties was silent on the point. Thus, the court held that just because the company made an allocation for tax purposes does not require the company to make a distribution. Thus, ironically enough, under *Five Star Concrete* the right to an allocation does not necessarily include the right to receive it.

2. Expulsion

It is tough to expel a member from a limited liability company. To be sure, the parties to a limited liability company may contract for the right to remove an obstreperous member. However, in cases in which the parties do not have the foresight to contract ahead of time, the right to removal tracks substantially the right to removal in partnership law. That is, under default principles, a member cannot be removed absent unanimous assent of the other members. UNIF. LTD. LIAB. CO. ACT § 601(5)(i)-(iii) (2006). Plus, the departing member is entitled to her fair share of the company. In sum, members that fail to privately agree as to the procedure for removal and buyout rights may face serious consequences, as the next case demonstrates.

In *Walker v. Resource Dev. Co.*, the complaining party, Randolph Walker, is a relative of a former United States president with an exhaustive Rolodex of contacts. 2000 Del. Ch. LEXIS 127 (2000). Because of his financial contacts, Walker was made a member of an oil and gas limited liability company. On behalf of the company, Walker made introductions to several seemingly deep-pocketed individuals with an interest in the oil and gas industry. However, Walker had little success in securing financing, but apparently was able to secure a side deal for himself. When Walker's contacts appeared to dry up, the other members of the company tried to oust him. They wrote Walker a letter of termination based on the side deal and an alleged breach of fiduciary duty. They continued to do business in the industry, ultimately having some apparent success and listing their interests in the company on a Canadian stock exchange. Walker claimed that the partnership agreement did not provide any means for removal. Thus, according to Walker, despite the purported ouster, he continued to be an 18% owner of the company.

The court held that the involuntary removal of Walker was wrongful, since the operating agreement provided members with no right of removal. The court rejected the argument that a member could be removed for breach of a fiduciary duty. Thus, according to the court, the remaining members could only remove Walker if they were willing to pay "fair value" for his economic interest in the company. At the same time though, the court recognized that Walker had failed to make sufficient capital contributions to the company on par with the other members. For Walker to recover, according to the court, he would have to make up that indebtedness to the company. Again, the court in

Walker emphasized the importance of the parties' ability to privately agree as to their rights and duties. When they do not, the default principles generally match those in partnership law.

H. Dissolution

Similar to early partnership law, early state LLC acts suggested that a departure of a member would create dissolution of the firm, unless there was unanimous consent to keep the business going. State legislatures crafted these early acts in order to avoid corporate resemblance in which a corporation has perpetual life. With the advent of check-the-box regulations, however, many state legislatures have revisited this decision to cause dissolution simply because of a member's withdrawal from the company. Now a member's departure usually has little effect, as long as there are remaining members or at least one member is admitted within a reasonable time. Delaware limited liability company law, for instance, presumes a perpetual life. DEL. CODE ANN. tit. 6 § 18-801(a)(1) (2008).

None of this means that a limited liability company can never be wound up and dissolved. An LLC can be dissolved by judicial order or under the terms of the operating agreement. Additionally, an LLC can be dissolved if a supermajority of members approve the dissolution. Under Delaware law, those voting to dissolve must represent two-thirds of those owning a right to profits in the LLC agrees to dissolution. Thus, a majority of the equity interest can vote to dissolve the company. DEL. CODE ANN. tit. 6 § 18-801(a)(3) (2008). A technical or administrative dissolution also occurs if there are not remaining members or if the company fails to pay applicable state taxes and fees when due or fails to make timely filings to state regulating authority.

Like with other entities, upon dissolution, the company should payoff creditors first, including creditors who may also be members of the entity. Any surplus assets are then distributed to capital contributing members. If there is still a remaining surplus after the capital contributions are paid in full, then the members should share in the surplus equally. Once dissolution has been approved, the company frequently files a certificate of cancellation to put interested third parties on notice. Under Delaware law, this filing is mandatory when the company is dissolved and wound up. DEL. CODE ANN. tit. 6 § 18-203 (2008). The certificate should state the date the limited liability company is to be cancelled.

In *Haley v. Talcott*, the plaintiff sought a court order dissolving a two-member LLC on the grounds that it was not reasonably practicable to continue to carry on the business. 864 A. 2d 86 (Del. Ch. 2004). In this case, the two members ran a restaurant together. The sole asset of the LLC was the land for the restaurant, of which Haley and Talcott were each 50% members and they split the rent received. Talcott owned the restaurant and employed Haley as its manager and gave Haley 50% of restaurant profits. Haley argued that because it was impracticable for the parties to continue in business, the LLC ought to be dissolved and the assets of the LLC (namely, the land) sold. However, as Talcott pointed out, the operating agreement provided that the LLC could continue even though one of the partners had wanted to dissolve the business. The operating agreement provided a detailed exit mechanism whereby the remaining member could elect to buyout the departing member's interest at market value.

Even though the parties had a detailed operating agreement, the court held that the parties still had right to judicial dissolution, which could not be easily contracted away. According to the court the exit mechanism provided in the operating agreement was inequitable, since fair value would not compensate the departing member for the considerable risk he would bear as a guarantor on assets that continued to be owned by the company. Without a hand in operations, the court reasoned, the mortgage guarantee created too much downside risk for a departing member. Thus, parties to a limited liability company cannot contract away the right to dissolution by court order. Regardless of the operating agreement, the court may order a dissolution for reasons of commercial impracticability. DEL. CODE ANN. tit. 6 § 18-802 (2008); UNIF. LTD. LIAB. CO. ACT §801(4)(i) (2006).

Checkpoints

- In order to form an LLC, the founders must file a certificate of formation with the Secretary of State and must have at least one member.

- The operating agreement governs internal relations in an LLC.

- The default rule is that an LLC is member-managed and each member has an equal right in decision-making. An LLC may also be manager-managed in which case professional managers execute policy on behalf of the LLC.

- Generally, members of an LLC are insulated from personal liability for the acts of the company.

- Members of an LLC may be held personally liable if the member and the company have used the company for their own ends. Members may also be held personally liable for their own wrongful conduct.

- An LLC may be dissolved either by judicial order; when the last remaining member dissociates; under the terms of the operating agreement; or administratively dissolved for failure to pay applicable state taxes and fees.

Chapter 6

Corporate Formation

Roadmap

- Sources of Law
- Pre-Incorporation (Promoter) Liability and Duties
- Corporate Formation
- Articles of Incorporation
- By-Laws
- Defective Formation
- Corporate Dissolution

A. Introduction to the Corporate Form

For good reason, the corporation, particularly the public corporation, commands a revered place in the public consciousness as the institution of choice for serious business. For starters, the corporate entity is the organizational form of choice for the majority of the largest businesses in the country. Publicly-traded entities are nearly always, invariably corporations. Many of these vast behemoths employ thousands of individuals and create the economic backbone for multiple communities, cities, and states. Further, the corporation is much older than other vehicles for limited liability, like the LLP or LLC, which are primarily inventions of the twentieth century. The growth of the corporate entity, since the country's founding to the present, tracks the country's story. Almost a hundred years before the first LLC statute was passed in Wyoming in 1977, for example, the United States could already boast thousands of corporations. Over that time, lawyers, accountants, judges, legal philosophers, and other stakeholders built up significant reverence for the corporate entity. Consequently, the corporation, despite the rise in popularity of the limited liability company and other entities, is among the most dominant organizational vehicles for investors, particularly investors who want limited liability.

Once formed, a corporation literally or, more precisely, legally takes on a life of its own.

1. History of the Firm

The corporate form dominated even early America, in contrast to the joint stock companies that dominated English business at the end of the eighteenth century. Shortly after the American Revolution, in fact, there were hundreds of corporations throughout the thirteen new states. *See* Phillip I. Blumberg, *Limited Liability and Corporate Groups*, 11 J. Corp. L. 573, 587 (1986). By 1830, there were almost two thousand corporations. *Id.* at 591. And the growth of the corporate form would continue largely unabated. At the turn of the nineteenth century, Supreme Court Justice Stephen Field speculated that corporate entities held at least three fourths of the nation's wealth. *See* Morton J. Horwitz, *Santa Clara Revisited: The Development of Corporate Theory*, 88 W. Va. L. Rev. 173, 180 (1985).

The growth of the popularity of the corporate form among investors, in large part, followed the health of industry in the country. Entrepreneurs needed to raise vast sums of money in order to bring product to market or kick-start operations. For instance, promoters of railways required large infusions of capital, which required tapping many actors. Further, investors in railways wanted their investments to be transferable. Thus, the expansion of rail line in the United States naturally increased the demand for corporate entities, which provide a ready vehicle for raising large sums and easy ability to transfer ownership. The same is true with the growth in manufacturing and other industries. Blumberg, *supra* at 587–88, 590.

In the early days, the state only granted corporate charters to public purpose firms, like those set up to build bridges or roads or railways. Many of these corporate entities had monopolistic power over their areas of business. In the beginning of the nineteenth century, the earliest corporations sowed some fear among Americans, who were particularly distrustful of corporations without a clear public bent. Few corporate chapters were granted in this period. States like New York required a two-thirds majority of the legislature before approving a corporate charter. Partly as a result of public distrust, corporations could only pursue the public purpose for which they were erected. In contrast to modern corporations, these early corporations had to list their purposes in their chartering documents and could not deviate from these. Under these early cases, any transaction beyond the narrow purposes would be void as *ultra vires*. Fundamental changes in corporate purpose, consolidation or any significant change would require the unanimous agreement from shareholders. Horwitz, *supra* at 182, 200. Further, in the early part of the nineteenth century, many states would not grant corporate charters without shareholder liability. Blumberg, *supra* at 591. Over time, of course, the entities began to push back and make attempts to expand the set of purposes they could legitimately pursue. Beginning with New Jersey at the end of the nineteenth century, states began to approve general incorporation laws. Horwitz, *supra* at 187. Still, American states were comparatively slow in providing limited liability for investors in these companies. Well into the 1960s, shareholders in many states could be liable for the unsatisfied wage bills of laborers. *See* Blumberg, *supra* at 601–02.

B. Source of Law

Corporations can be formed by making a public filing in the state where the entity intends to be incorporated. To be sure, the site of business operations is an important factor in determining place of incorporation. For instance, for the vast majority of closely-held firms, the state of incorporation is likely to also be the state where most of the business operations take place. Smaller firms will likely want to incorporate in states where they do business and maintain contacts. However, incorporation need not be the state where the corporation has most of its operations. Under the internal affairs doctrine, the corporation will be governed under the law of the state of incorporation. Thus, the corporation in choosing where to file is also simultaneously making a choice of law decision.

1. Delaware General Corporate Law

On this score, the Delaware General Corporate Law (DGCL) is perhaps the most significant state corporate code in the country. The DGCL's importance is the result of Delaware being the site of a significant share of out-of-state incorporation, with close to half of such incorporations. Delaware's popularity as a site of incorporation is the result of many factors.

First, Delaware appears to have amongst the most competent and business savvy attorneys within corporate law on the bench and as part of the bar. Delaware business cases are heard before the Delaware Chancery Court, which has several experienced judges. *See, e.g.,* DEL. CODE ANN. tit. 8, §111 (1999). Appeals from that court go straight to the state supreme court. At the same time, corporate lawyers over the years have built up significant expertise with Delaware corporate law. Law students learn Delaware cases in their business law classes and lawyers in Delaware (not to mention other states) look to Delaware precedent. Lastly, all things considered, Delaware corporate law is relatively stable. Under the Delaware Constitution, the state's corporate law cannot be changed, without the approval of two-thirds of the legislature. *See* DEL. CONST. art. IX, § 1. Further, Delaware Supreme Court judges frequently proffer unanimous opinions, which put the case law on firmer ground.

Second, there may be a valuable and positive signal sent by company founders by incorporating in Delaware. Other investors may be more inclined to invest in Delaware corporations, where they have already stored experience with other Delaware companies and Delaware law. This kind of signal might do a great deal in aiding the corporate entity raise money and its profile. It may send a signal to competitors, for instance, that a corporation has arrived and intends to be a major player in the industry. For all these reasons, many of the best-known corporate organizations incorporate in Delaware and the opinions by Delaware courts end up shaping corporate law.

2. Model Business Corporate Act

Outside of Delaware, each of the states (and the District of Columbia) has a corporate code. Although some state acts are probably more noteworthy than others—*e.g.*, the New York corporate code is relatively more important than Kentucky's—many of the state acts share several common strains. In fact, many of the state acts have the same progenitor, the Model Business Corporate Act (MBCA). The first model act was drafted by the American Bar Association in 1950 and the act underwent an overhaul in 1984. Additionally, the Committee on Corporate Laws of the ABA meets regularly to discuss revisions to the act. Although the DGCL is important, the significance of the MBCA should not be understated. Approximately half of the states have adopted the current MBCA with only slight variations. Of the remaining states, a number have adopted the previous versions of the MBCA and several other states have adopted the wording of the MBCA. In fact, only four jurisdictions (five, if you include Delaware)—Kansas, Oklahoma, Nevada, and Puerto Rico—have adopted the DGCL. *See, e.g.*, Michael P. Dooley, *Some Comparisons Between the Model Business Corporations Act and the Delaware General Corporations Law*, 56 BUS. LAW. 737, 738 (2001). Throughout this Chapter, the Model Business Corporate Act will be an important source of law.

C. Pre-Incorporation

The period prior to incorporation can be a demanding one for the not-yet-organized corporate entity. So-called promoters conduct business on behalf of the entity during the pre-incorporation period. Prior to incorporations, these promoters may enter into contracts on behalf of the entity, line up suppliers, rent office space, or begin to recruit and hire employees. All these activities present opportunities for the corporation, but may also create complex legal issues of liability and fiduciary duty for the yet-to-be-formed entity and for those who act on the entity's behalf prior to incorporation.

1. Promoter Liability

To begin with, consider the various contracts entered into by a promoter in the pre-incorporation period. Generally, promoters may be liable individually for such contracts, because no corporation existed at the time of contracting. For instance, the Model Business Corporation Act provides that promoters "knowing there was no incorporation ... are jointly and severally liable for all liabilities created while so acting." MODEL BUS. CORP. ACT § 2.04 (2005). At the same time, the general rule is that the corporation, formed thereafter, is not bound by such contracts, because it could not possibly have given assent if it were still not a legally recognized entity.

However, in certain instances, individuals who help create the corporate entity may be able to avoid these contracts. For instance, an individual can be protected from liability for a pre-incorporation contract if she can show that she acted merely as the company's incorporator, not a promoter. An incorporator (as opposed to a promoter) is not liable for pre-incorporation contracts, because the incorporator's relationship to the company is different and short-lived. An incorporator, usually a lawyer or other professional, merely makes the appropriate filing on the corporation's behalf. A promoter, by contrast, tries to make sure that the launch of the entity is a success. In so doing, the promoter may attempt to identify and solicit possible investors, may arrange for space for the operations of the entity, hire employees for the entity, and enter into lucrative contracts.

More importantly, in the right case, a promoter can escape liability for a pre-incorporation contract, when the corporation comes into being and adopts the contract. The question of enforceability of pre-incorporation contracts arises usually in three circumstances: (1) misconduct or misrepresentation by the promoter; (2) a failure to form the corporation; and (3) if formed, whether the corporation consented to the contract. First, the enforceability of pre-incorporation contracts might arise when the promoter has intentionally misrepresented some fact about the yet-to-be-formed corporate entity. The promoter, for instance, may puff up the corporation's finances to a potential supplier. In these cases, the promoter is liable for her own misconduct not related to the corporate entity.

Related to the last point, another issue occurs when the corporation is never formed, but the promoter has created several early contracts in the name of the entity. If the corporate entity is never formed, then the promoter is individually liable under a simple application of agency principles. The applicable rule here is that an agent who represents an undisclosed (or in this case, nonexistent) principal is liable for her own contracts and torts. There are exceptions, which will be discussed below.

A third issue is whether a promoter continues to be liable for pre-incorporation contracts after the corporation is properly formed. Under case law, the formation of the corporation is not enough, by itself, to relieve the promoter of liability for contracts that purport to have been made on the entity's behalf. Incorporation is not evidence that the entity consents to the contract. However, if the right steps are taken, a promoter may escape liability. The issue of promoter's continuing liability after the corporation is formed turns on whether the parties intended that performance should exclusively be an obligation of the corporation and if the corporation, once formed, replaces the promoter as party to the agreement based on contract principles.

Among other theories, courts have described a successful substitution of a corporation for a promoter as a novation or new contract between the corporation and the creditor or ratification of the contract by the corporate entity. Once the corporation adopts or ratifies the contract, the corporate entity can enforce the contracts' terms. However, if the corporation has not adopted or ratified the contract, then the promoter remains liable. Further, the parties must by conduct or expressly assent that the promoter is not to be continuously liable. If it cannot be shown that the parties did intend by the ratification to relieve the promoter of liability, both she and the corporation are liable, as the next case shows.

In *Moneywatch v. Wilbers*, the defendant, Wilbers, entered a lease agreement for commercial space with the plaintiff, Moneywatch. 665 N.E. 2d 689 (Ohio Ct. App. 1995). At the time of the negotiations, Wilbers indicated that he intended to form a corporation to pursue a golfing business. The space would be used for that purpose. The landlord required Wilbers to submit a business plan and personal financial statement. Wilbers signed the agreement as "Jeff Wilbers, dba Golfing Adventures". After Wilbers had formed his corporation, he asked that "J & J Adventures Inc., dba Golfing Adventures" be substituted as tenant, which the landlord agreed to do. During the period of the lease, checks were drawn on a corporate bank account. However, when the corporation defaulted on the lease agreement, the landlord attempted to recovery against Wilbers individually. Wilbers argued that he could not be personally liable for the lease, because the corporation was substituted as tenant, a substitution both parties agreed to. The court held that there was no clear evidence that the landlord intended to give up personal liability by substituting the tenants. To the contrary, the court found that the acts of the landlord — for instance, requesting a personal financial statement — suggested that he intended for Wilbers to remain personally liable on the lease.

Thus, if a corporation is formed, whether the promoter continues to be liable on pre-incorporation contracts depends on three factors: (1) the intent of the parties at the time of pre-incorporation transaction; (2) whether the corporation was ultimately formed; and (3) whether the corporation "accepted" the contract once it was formed. First, the parties must have intended that, once formed, the corporation (not the promoter), would become the obligor under the terms of the contract. For instance, this could be the case where the parties explicitly contract for corporate liability as part of the pre-incorporation contract. Alternatively, the parties' post-formation contract could have made a similar stipulation. In *Moneywatch*, there is little evidence, either pre- or post-incorporation, that the landlord intended that the promoter should be free from liability. Second, the corporation must be formed. As mentioned, the promoter is personally liable for pre-incorporation contracts when the corporation does not come into existence. Third, the corporation must adopt the contract implicitly by its conduct or expressly. For instance, the corporation may expressly assent to pre-incorporation contracts by acknowledging such contracts in its articles of incorporation. Such contracts might be implicitly adopted by the entity, if it continues to accept benefits from the pre-incorporation contracts after it knew about the contracts.

2. Promoter Duties

Additionally, prior to incorporation, there is ample opportunity for promoters to use their position to unreasonably re-direct benefits to himself or herself at the expense of other parties with an interest in the entity. Thus, under case law and statute, once there is intent to form a corporate entity, promoters of a yet-to-be formed corporate entity have some obligations to the entity, the other promoters, and investors. For instance, as the *Topanga v. Gentile* case (below) shows, promoters must deal with the entity in good faith. Most courts have suggested that the obligation of good faith requires that promoters ensure fairness in transactions with the corporation. In addition to the obligation to deal in good faith, courts have said that promoters of a soon-to-be-corporation are also required to disclose relevant information, like opportunities and conflicts to the entity, to other relevant parties.

In *Topanga Corp*, several individuals arranged for the promotion of a corporation to purchase a dump site. 58 Cal. Rptr. 713 (Cal. Ct. App. 1967). The promoter, Gentile, who was doing the negotiation for the land for the site told his other co-subscribers (*i.e.*, the individuals who had agreed to buy the first share issue in the corporation) that a plot could be purchased for $210,000. He told the other investors in the corporation that he would use a ranch in Fresno he owned to pay one-third of the price, in exchange for one-third of the corporation's shares. The other investors in the corporation could pay the balance. This was all memorialized in a pre-incorporation contract. However, Gentile had told his co-investors several lies. For one thing, it turns out that his Fresno property was only worthy $10,000, not $70,000 as originally represented. In addition, the seller's asking price for the dump site was much lower than what was originally represented. The seller was only asking $150,000 for the site. Once the corporation was formed, it brought a suit against the Gentiles for fraud. However, Gentile claimed that no action could lie, because the corporation was not formed at the time of the alleged misrepresentations. According to the court, however, promoters owe their co-investors a fiduciary duty, even while the corporation is in its basic, embryonic stages:

> Well established is the principle that promoters of a corporation formed for the express purpose of purchasing a particular piece of property occupy a fiduciary relation to their co-subscribers, requiring that they truthfully disclose to their associates any personal interest they may have in the matter of the purchase. Without such disclosure they may not legally profit at the expense of their associates; and if they were guilty of any misrepresentations of fact or suppression of truth in relation to their personal interest in the property, the corporation is entitled to set aside the transaction, or recover damages for any loss it has suffered.

58 Cal. Rptr. at 688. Thus, the court holds that one of the requirements of the promoters' fiduciary duty is disclosure of a self-interested transaction. When a party fails to observe this duty, the corporation can bring an action for recovery. However, it is worth mentioning that not all promoter pre-incorporation contracts are actionable, even when such contracts are not disclosed. In fact, such contracts, like other insider contracts, can be "sanitized." For instance, a promoter may be able to avoid liability for a previously undisclosed transaction by demonstrating that the transaction was fair to the corporation. In other words, the promoter will not be liable if the promoter can show that a reasonable consideration was passed to the corporation.

D. Corporate Formation

Once the promoters of a corporation are ready, it does not take much for them to form an official or *de jure* corporation. To form a corporate entity, they need only file articles of incorporation, also variously known as a charter, with the appropriate state body, usually the Secretary of State. With the filing of the articles (and fee payment), the corporation is a legal entity distinct from its owners with perpetual existence by default. At its founding or shortly thereafter, the corporate entity needs to adopt by-laws that govern internal policy-making for the corporate entity and establish a board of directors that oversees the entity.

1. Articles of Incorporation

As mentioned, the corporation is formed by the filing of the articles of incorporation. Like other public foundational documents discussed in previous chapters (*e.g.*, the certificate of formation), the incorporators of a corporation are only required to include a modest amount of information in the organizing document. For instance, the Model Business Corporate Act provides that the company's articles of incorporation must only include four things—the name of the entity; the number of shares to be issued; contact information for service of process; and the name of the incorporator. *See* Model Bus. Corp. Act § 2.02 (2005).

The "incorporator" may be a promoter of the entity who might continue as a shareholder or officer or director of the corporation post-formation. Alternatively, the incorporator may be an attorney who will have no continuing obligation to the entity after the required filing. Importantly also, the articles of incorporation must include authority for the firm to issue shares. Although the corporation has discretion to issue shares for less than the amount provided in the articles, the corporation cannot issue shares not described in the articles of incorporation. Thus, the articles will routinely state a level of shares significantly above the amount that the corporation expects to issue in the near term. Later, when the board is ready to issue the remaining shares, it will sell them in a subsequent issue.

Additionally, the articles of incorporation may, but is not required to, put in other provisions. *See* Model Bus. Corp. Act § 2.02(b) (2005). For instance, the articles may provide the name of the first slate of directors or the method of their election. This way, the entity can avoid having to do this in the first organizational meeting for the entity. If the articles do not name the first board of directors, the incorporators will serve that function until a slate of directors is seated. *See, e.g.,* Del. Code Ann. tit. 8, § 107 (1999); Model Bus. Corp. Act § 2.05 (2005).

Further, the articles may include the nature of the business to be undertaken by the corporation. Such provisions appears to be a remnant of yesteryear when corporations were required to be formed only for a single, specific purpose. Now, since corporations undertake a variety of business activities, it is less useful for a corporate entity to list specific purposes beyond a purpose of pursuing legal activities broadly. Thus, under the MBCA, such additional provisions are discretionary. *See* Model Bus. Corp. Act § 2.02(b) (2005). By contrast, under Delaware law, the articles of incorporation are still required to include a purpose. Nonetheless, this requirement is of little practical consequence because Delaware law permits the incorporators to state that "the purpose of the corporation is to engage in any lawful act or activity." Del. Code Ann. tit. 8, § 102(a)(3) (1999). Moreover, the articles of incorporation can list procedures for running the corporate entity. Most such procedures will appear in the corporation's by-laws, but frequently firms will put some procedures in the articles as well.

Finally, the articles of incorporation can be used to contract around certain default rules, many of which will be discussed in greater detail in later chapters. For instance, the founders of a corporation can contract around the default rule of perpetual existence by including a time limit in the articles. *See, e.g.,* Del. Code Ann. tit. 8, § 102(b)(5) (1999); Model Bus. Corp. Act § 3.02 (2005). In addition, the articles can change the default rule for the number of votes needed to take corporate action (*see, e.g.,* Del. Code Ann. tit. 8, § 102(b)(4) (1999); Model Bus. Corp. Act § 8.24 (2005)); or the default rule that shareholders are shielded from personal liability (*see, e.g.,* Del. Code Ann. tit. 8, § 102(b)(6) (1999); Model Bus. Corp. Act § 6.22 (2005)); or reducing the fiduciary duties of corporate insiders (*see* Del. Code Ann. tit. 8, § 102(b)(7) (1999)).

2. By-Laws

The other foundational document for corporation is the entity by-laws. The by-laws spell out the procedure for business operations. For instance, the by-laws may provide the method for electing members to the board of directors. If there is a conflict between the by-laws and the articles of incorporation, the articles trump. *See, e.g.,* Del. Code Ann. tit. 8, § 109 (1999); Model Bus. Corp. Act § 2.06(b) (2005). In addition to the company by-laws, some corporations rely on other documents. For instance, some closely-held firms use shareholder agreements. *See* Model Bus. Corp. Act § 7.32 (2005). These agreements are between the shareholders (although not always all of them) and provide for such things as how shareholders are to be bought out in the case of departure, voting arrangements, and the payment of dividends.

3. Amendment of By-Laws or Articles

The articles of incorporation can only be changed by the approval of both shareholders and the board of directors. *See, e.g.,* DEL. CODE ANN. tit. 8, § 242 (1999); MODEL BUS. CORP. ACT § 10.03 (2005). Once the board of directors has approved a change or amendment to the articles, they must submit the changes to shareholders for their approval and obtain a majority of those voting on the measure. If approved, the board then submits articles of amendment to the state. By contrast, it is easier to amend the by-laws of the corporate entity. The by-laws can be amended by the shareholders or the board of directors (unless the articles provide otherwise). *See* MODEL BUS. CORP. ACT § 10.20 (2005).

E. Defective Formation

Although forming a *de jure* corporation is a straightforward process—filing of the articles of incorporation and payment of any applicable fees and taxes—frequently the incorporators fail to properly file. Some of the defects in formation are small. For instance, they may mail their articles of incorporation to the wrong state office, which may cause an unusual delay in the filing. Others are evidence of a more slipshod filing or laziness on the part of the incorporator or her lawyer. There are several consequences that result from a defective or delayed formation of a corporate entity. In addition to wasted money on stationary (as one forthcoming case shows), defective formation can also result in lawsuits against the individuals who attempted to organize the corporation, but failed to do so correctly. Further, contracts between the never-formed corporation and a third party may be void, because of the defective formation. However, even though the corporation may have never been formally organized correctly, under equitable principles courts have still frequently upheld such contracts or the limited liability shield for individuals. In particular, in many of these cases courts have found that a *de facto* corporation was formed; in others, courts have found a corporation by estoppel.

1. *De Facto* Corporations

Corporations that are defectively formed may still be corporations *vis-à-vis* third parties, although not corporations *vis-à-vis* the state. In some instances, such corporate entities have been referred to by courts as *de facto* corporations. Under case law, a *de facto* entity is formed whenever the promoters make a good faith attempt at corporate formation. If a *de facto* corporation is formed, the promoters are not individually liable for corporate debts as long as the corporation is later officially formed. For instance, courts have found that there should be no individual liability if the promoters made a correct filing with the state, which was misdirected to the wrong public office and the filing delayed. Principles of *de facto* incorporation apply broadly to cover instances affecting contracts entered into in the company's name and also torts committed while acting on behalf of the company.

Hill v. County Concrete is a darling of a case, which demonstrates the importance of the good faith requirement for establishing a *de facto* corporation. 672 A.2d 667 (Md. Ct. Spec. App. 1996). In *Hill*, two contractors decided to form a corporation that specialized in concrete construction and asked an attorney to make the necessary filings. The duo decided they would call the company "C & M Builders, Inc." They ordered stationary with the entity name, painted their trucks with company slicks, opened a bank account, and, importantly, entered into contracts for concrete supply using the entity name. Months later, their attorney informed the two entrepreneurs that the name "C & M Builders" was already registered in the state and not available. The two decided that their company would be incorporated as "H & N Construction, Inc" instead. However, they continued to use the old stationary and failed to inform their suppliers about the change in incorporation. When one of those suppliers, County Concrete, sought to collect on a large unpaid bill, the two contractors argued that they were immune from liability. They argued that, although there was no official corporation, there was a *de facto* incorporation, because their attorney had attempted to form "C & M Builders." The court rejected this argument for *de facto* incorporation. Although the two had made an attempt at incorporation, their conduct was not in good faith. Once they found out that incorporation under the former name was impossible, they acted in bad faith by not informing their suppliers and other known creditors.

To summarize, courts, like the court in *Hill*, require at least three elements to be met in order to claim protection under a theory of *de facto* incorporation: (1) authority, (2) use of corporate power, and (3) a good faith attempt at incorporation. First, in order to form a *de facto* corporation, the state must have authorized the formation of a corporation in the jurisdiction. This test is easily met, because all states authorize the corporate entity. Second, there must be some use of corporate-like power. That is, there must be a transaction in which individuals must have been acting or purporting to act on behalf of the still-to-be-formed corporate entity. In *Hill*, for example, the corporate promoters purported to do business with County Concrete on behalf of their entity, not in their individual capacities. Third, there must be a good faith attempt at incorporation. As demonstrated in *Hill*, a simple attempt is not by itself enough.

2. Corporations by Estoppel

In addition to forming a *de facto* corporation to enforce contracts with other parties, some courts have suggested that a corporation may be created under the doctrine of estoppel. Under this doctrine, contracts with a defectively formed corporate entity may still be enforceable. At the outset, it is important to note that the estoppel doctrine of incorporation is a creature of case law. As a consequence, there is far from universal agreement among state courts as to the contours of the doctrine. Some jurisdictions, like Washington, D.C., have held that there is no relief from individual liability on the basis of estoppel. *See Robertson v. Levy*, 197 A.2d 443, 446 (D.C. 1964). Other courts have held broadly that the doctrine of estoppel may apply to remedy "inequity", a malleable notion. Despite these disagreements among the states, it can be generally said that the parties are estopped from denying corporate existence if both parties believed they were dealing with a corporation and had no actual knowledge that the entity was not properly formed.

The incorporation by estoppel holdings produce two important upshots. First, in operation, the doctrine protects corporate investors from individual liability in cases where the third party understood it was dealing with a corporation. Second, in these cases the parties cannot disclaim contracts entered with the entity, even if it later turns out to be a mistaken one because of a defective or delayed filing. Put differently, under the theory of corporation by estoppel, some contracts cannot be repudiated based on a defective or delayed formation. In some cases, the entity may want to enforce a lucrative contract despite the fact that the corporation was never formed or formation was delayed. For instance, during the pre-incorporation period a promoter may be able to secure agreements for valuable product or cheap financing. If the price of the product goes up or the interest rates change, the supplier or creditor may be reluctant to perform. As a matter of ordinary contract principles, an unformed corporation cannot enter into contract and certainly not enforce them, which may create a basis for non-performance. However, the estoppel doctrine, as the next case shows, may create the basis for enforcing contracts made prior to proper corporate formation.

In *Southern-Gulf v. Camcraft*, the plaintiff contracted to purchase a large ship in the name of a corporate entity, "Southern-Gulf Marine Co. No. 9, Inc."

410 So. 2d 1181 (La. Ct. App. 1982). The sales contract suggested the buyer, Southern-Gulf, Inc., was incorporated in the state of Texas. At the time of contracting, however, it appears that the Southern Gulf was not incorporated at all. Later, while the ship was in construction, Southern Gulf was incorporated in the Cayman Islands, a British possession. Although the entity appeared willing and ready to pay the $1.3 million purchase price for the vessel, the defendant-seller balked. The defendant argued that the company did not exist at the time of contracting; thus, there was no valid consent. The court held that the defendant could not claim lack of existence of the corporation as a defense to contracting, unless the corporation's lack of incorporation somehow prejudiced the defendant's rights:

> The plaintiff relied upon the contract and secured financing. The defendant likewise relied on the contract and began construction of the vessel. We have no doubts that defendant would assert that plaintiff and D.W. Barrett were liable on the contract had they defaulted and enforcement was advantageous, but defendants refuse to recognize any rights they may have therein. In all likelihood, the true state of affairs is as represented by plaintiff's counsel: the vessel appreciated in value above the contract price between the time of the contract and the agreed delivery date. We hold the defendant estopped to deny the corporate existence of plaintiff in this regard.

410 So. 2d at 1183–84. Thus, as in *Southern-Gulf*, a party cannot disclaim a contract on the basis of a lack of proper incorporation unless the party has relied on the corporation's existence to its detriment. If it makes no difference whether the corporation exists or not, then a party will be estopped from using this as a defense to contracting. However, as the next case shows, courts have held that an important exception exists to the estoppel doctrine: That is, the doctrine does not apply if the parties have actual knowledge that the corporate entity was not properly formed.

In *American Vending Services, Inc. v. Morse*, two lawyers attempted twice to form a corporation for the purposes of buying a car wash. Both times, their articles of incorporation were rejected by the state. 881 P.2d 917 (Utah Ct. App. 1994). Finally, the third attempt at filing turned out to be the charm. Before the third time, however, the lawyers had already entered a purchase contract for the car wash in the name of their corporate entity, American Vending Services, Inc. (AVSI). The contract called on the "corporate" entity to pay part of the consideration over time. When the entity failed to make timely payment, the seller of the car wash sought to recover against the two lawyers, individually. The court considered whether the seller would be estopped from pursuing the lawyers because, at all relevant times, the sellers thought they were dealing with a corporation. The court, however, clarified the doctrine and held that it does not apply when the parties had actual knowledge of the failure to form a corporate entity. In the case at bar, the court suggested that the lawyers knew that the first two attempts at filing their articles were rejected by the state secretary and, thus, at the time of contracting knew that no corporate entity existed.

In summary, the doctrine of estoppel, although a slippery concept, frequently operates on narrow grounds. At its core, the doctrine works to protect individuals from liability when none of the parties had any reason to believe that they were dealing with anything but a corporate entity. Importantly, only parties without knowledge (or without good reason to know) that the corporate entity was not formally organized will be estopped from disclaiming the existence of the corporate entity. For instance, in *American Vending Services*, if only one of the two lawyers had no knowledge that there had been a failure to properly organize, only the ignorant lawyer is likely to be protected on estoppel grounds.

F. Dissolution

The corporate entity may be dissolved by joint effort on the part of the shareholders and the directors. *See, e.g.*, DEL. CODE ANN. tit. 8, § 275 (1999); MODEL BUS. CORP. ACT § 14.02 (2005). To begin dissolution, the board of directors makes such a recommendation to the shareholders and calls for a meeting of shareholders to vote on the recommendation. If the majority of shareholders agree with the recommendation, then to complete the dissolution the board must file articles of dissolution with the approved state office. MODEL BUS. CORP. ACT § 14.03 (2005).

As with the dissolution of other business entities, the dissolution of a corporate entity does not necessarily end the business, but instead signals the winding up of the corporation's on-going business, debts, and contracts. *See* MODEL BUS. CORP. ACT § 14.05 (2005). In fact, under Delaware law the corporate entity continues for a minimum period of three years for these purposes. *See* DEL. CODE ANN. tit. 8, § 278 (1999). The corporate entity will also want to give notice to potential claimants regarding the dissolution. If the corporation makes proper notifications to claimants but such claimants do not come forward in a timely manner, then the claimants are barred from pursuing the corporation. Under Delaware law such notice is effective if mailed to all known claimants and if published in a newspaper at least once a week for two weeks. *See* DEL. CODE ANN. tit. 8, § 280 (1999).

Like other actions, the board of directors controls corporate dissolution. As mentioned, even though the dissolution has won shareholder approval the board is under no immediate obligation to file articles of dissolution necessary for completion. Further, the board of directors can put conditions on shareholder approval. One such condition may be to give the board of directors the right to revoke articles of dissolution filing. If so, the board of directors, even after a filing of articles of dissolution, can revoke the filing. Under the MBCA, for example, in these instances the board of directors has four months to revoke a dissolution filing. *See* MODEL BUS. CORP. ACT § 14.04 (2005).

Checkpoints

- To form a corporate entity, one needs to file articles of incorporation, also variously known as a charter, with the appropriate state body, usually the Secretary of State. With the filing of the articles (and fee payment), the corporation soon becomes a legal entity distinct from its owners with perpetual existence by default.

- A promoter's liability on pre-incorporation contracts depends on three factors: the intent of parties at time of transaction, whether the corporation was ultimately formed, and whether the corporation, once formed, "accepted" the contract.

- In the event that the corporation is never formed, the promoter is individually liable under basic agency principles.

- While amending the articles of incorporation requires both shareholder and board of director approval, amending the firm bylaws may only require approval by one of the two groups.

- In order for a promoter to obtain limited liability under the theory of a *de facto* corporation, at least three elements must be met: authority, use of corporate power, and good faith attempt at incorporation.

- Corporation by estoppel creates the basis for enforcing some obligations between a private party and a defectively formed corporate entity.

Chapter 7

Corporate Characteristics, Capital Structure, and Management

Roadmap

- Transferability of Shares
- Limited Liability and "Piercing the Corporate Veil"
- Capital Structure of the Corporation
- Management of the Corporation: Officers, Board of directors, and Shareholders
- Board of Director Powers
- Shareholder Rights

Several characteristics of the corporate entity set this organizational form apart from the others discussed thus far. Some, but certainly not all, of the most intriguing attributes of the corporation are the transferability of shares, limited liability, and double taxation.

A. Transferability of Shares

Corporate shares represent both a financial interest in the corporation and limited managerial power, like the power to vote on nominees to the board of directors. One of the important characteristics of the corporate form is that shareholders are permitted to transfer or sell shares, their interest in the firm. Upon sale or transfer, the shareholder's connection to the corporation ends and the transferee receives all of the shareholder's rights and interest in the firm. The power of shareholders to transfer ownership should not be discounted. This characteristic seems to create ample incentives for managers to perform well, as other well-known commentators have noted. *See generally* Frank H. Easterbrook and Daniel R. Fischel, *Limited Liability and the Corporation*, 52 U. CHI. L. REV.

89, 95 (1985). To understand the connection of the transferability character-istic to managerial performance, consider a corporation that is poorly managed. The returns from that investment will reflect the deteriorating state of affairs. As a result, investors will sell their interest at a discount and the value of the shares of the entity will tumble. As this happens, the likelihood of another in-vestor swooping in with plans to buy up a controlling stake and sack current management increases.

The sale of an interest in the firm is arguably easiest in the corporate form. For one thing, shareholders need not obtain the consent of the other owners in order to exit, as in a general partnership. In fact, in a public corporation, the trans-fer of shares can often be accomplished with a few taps of a mouse or ring to a broker's office. By contrast, in a closely-held firm, the transfer of shares is sig-nificantly tougher to accomplish, because there is no ready market of buyers. Thus, a departing shareholder may only be able to sell to current shareholders, because they are likely to be the only ones interested in acquiring an interest in the firm. However, even in closely-held firms, shareholders almost always have the right to sell their interest in the company and exit (assuming they can find a willing buyer). Also, transfer of ownership in a corporation is relatively easy, because the transfer does not affect the existence of the corporation. The corporation continues in business, without regard to who the other owners are. Thus, re-lated to transferability, another characteristic of corporate entities is perpetual "life." DEL. CODE ANN. tit. 8, § 102(5) (1999). Regardless of transfer, the corporation continues long after its original owners have passed away.

B. Limited Liability

Second, an important advantage of the corporate form is the protection of limited liability. In the corporate form, a shareholder is not liable for the mis-deeds and misrepresentations of the corporation in which she has invested. For instance, the Model Business Corporate Act provides that (absent agree-ment to the contrary) shareholders are not personally liable for "the acts or debts of the corporation." MODEL BUS. CORP. ACT § 6.22 (2005); see also DEL. CODE ANN. tit. 8, § 102(6) (1999). This liability shield extends not only to shareholders who are individuals, but also inures to the benefit of corpora-tions-as-shareholders. In this way, when parent corporations create a wholly-owned subsidiary to conduct a particular form of business, the parent corporation is normally shielded from liability.

Thus, a party injured by the tort of an employee of a corporation may sue if she can prove the tort was committed by the employee on behalf of the corporation. However, the claimant would only be able to recover against the assets of the corporate entity. Even if the assets of the corporation are insufficient to cover the claimant's losses, the claimant cannot usually recover against investors in the corporate entity. In this way, limited liability protects investors and they only risk a loss of their investment for the unsatisfied debts and torts of the corporation. Equally, it is worth mentioning that the directors and officers of a corporation are also generally shielded from liability for their mistakes in management of the corporations. Under the doctrine of the "business judgment rule," discussed in detail later in Chapter 8, courts usually presume director good faith in decision-making and protect directors from liability.

1. Veil-Piercing

Still, from time to time, an investor will be permitted to pursue the shareholders of a corporation directly, in the same way that investors of a limited liability company can sometimes be reached. This concept, known as piercing the corporate veil, is generally available when shareholders unreasonably commingle funds, fail to follow corporate formalities, and otherwise treat the corporation as their alter ego, instead of a distinct legal entity. Generally, veil-piercing is a common-law doctrine, without specific statutory support. As mentioned, the MBCA and the DGCL provide that shareholders should generally not be liable for the acts of the corporate entity. Without elaboration, though, both the MBCA and the DGCL leave open the possibility that a shareholder may be personally liable because of their own acts or conduct. *See, e.g.,* MODEL BUS. CORP. ACT §6.22 (2005); DEL. CODE ANN. tit. 8, §102(6) (1999). This seems to have left open a small possibility that under certain circumstances the personal assets of investors could be used to satisfy a contract or tort obligation. Perhaps with this in mind, in special cases, courts have agreed that it is appropriate to pierce the so-called corporate veil and allow the claimant to reach personal assets. Not surprisingly, as the doctrine is significantly a product of case law, courts have come up with various definitions for what type of conduct might provide good reason to pierce the corporate veil.

For instance, in what the court aptly describes as a "spicy case", Sea-Land Services, a shipping company, attempted to recover for transporting Jamaican sweet peppers for Pepper Source, Inc. *Sea-Land Services, Inc. v. The Pepper Source*, 941 F.2d 519 (7th Cir. 1991). With Pepper Source a defunct and bankrupt corporate entity, the shipping company sought to recover against the entity's individual owner, Marchese. The plaintiff's theory was that that the company was nothing more than an alter ego of Marchese. In addition, not only did Sea-Land want to recover against the individual owner of Pepper Source,

Marchese, but it also pursued the other corporate entities owned by Marchese on the theory that the plaintiff should be able to "reverse pierce" those company assets as well. They were all wholly owned by Marchese, with one exception. The one exception was co-owned by Marchese and another individual. Still, with respect to the one partly owned corporation and the other entities wholly-owned by Marchese, the plaintiff argued that the limited liability shield should not be observed. In Sea-Land's view, they were all alter egos of Marchese.

The court in *Sea-Land* lays out one test for veil-piercing, which is typical of these cases. According to the court, veil-piercing will be permitted in cases in which two elements are present. First, there must be unity of ownership. In other words, in order to avoid veil-piercing, the corporate entities must be treated as separate and distinct from other corporations or the investors. Second, because veil-piercing is an equitable remedy, it is only permitted in cases where there is evidence of fraud or injustice. That is, the court in *Sea-Land* suggests that veil-piercing is only permitted when it is shown that treating the corporate entity as separate from its investors would produce fraud or would "promote injustice."

The court proceeds to address both these points. On the first point, unity of interest and ownership, the court found that the veil should be pierced in the case, because Marchese used these entities as his personal "playthings":

> During his deposition, Marchese did not remember any of these corporations ever passing articles of incorporation, bylaws, or other agreements. As for physical facilities, Marchese runs all of these corporations (including Tie-Net) out of the same, single office, with the same phone line, the same expense accounts, and the like. And how he does "run" the expense accounts! When he fancies to, Marchese "borrows" substantial sums of money from these corporations — interest free, of course. The corporations also "borrow" money from each other when need be, which left at least PS completely out of capital when the Sea-Land bills came due.

941 F.2d at 521. The court goes on to note that Marchese co-mingled personal and corporate funds. He used funds from the various entities to pay strictly personal debts, like his alimony and child support payments, car maintenance and pet care, among other expenses. The court neatly sums up his propensity to disregard personal and business accounts when it reasons that Marchese did not even have a personal bank account, because "[w]ith 'corporate accounts like these, who needs one?".

Therefore, on the unity of ownership point, cases like *Sea-Land* make clear that several factors are worth considering. To start with, a corporate entity should maintain corporate formalities in order to avoid veil-piercing. The corporation should maintain separate books and records of the corporation. Another factor that goes to the issue of unity of ownership is whether the corporation has mingled corporate funds with another corporation or another individual. Funds of one corporation should not ordinarily be used to pay the obligations of another. Still another factor that is useful in making this determination is whether the corporation has been unusually under-funded or under-capitalized or is functionally insolvent. When corporate assets have been plundered by its investors, for instance, courts have considered this a sign that the corporate entity should be disregarded.

As for the second point, the requirement that veil-piercing only be permitted to prevent a "wrong" or avoid injustice, the court noted that it would have been enough to show that the corporate entity was being used to defraud creditors or unjustly enrich Marchese:

> [W]e see that the courts that properly have pierced corporate veils to avoid "promoting injustice" have found that, unless it did so, some "wrong" beyond a creditor's inability to collect would result: the common sense rules of adverse possession would be undermined; former partners would be permitted to skirt the legal rules concerning monetary obligations; a party would be unjustly enriched; a parent corporation that caused a sub's liabilities and its inability to pay for them would escape those liabilities; or an intentional scheme to squirrel assets into a liability-free corporation while heaping liabilities upon an asset-free corporation would be successful.

941 F.2d at 524. However, the court found that there was little evidence of fraud, deception, unjust enrichment, or other wrongful conduct that would meet this element. Thus, the court in *Sea-Land* articulates a two-element test for deciding when it's appropriate to veil-pierce: unity of ownership and fraud or injustice.

Still, as mentioned, there are divergent views by courts as to which factors are most important. For instance, the next court downplays the relevance of undercapitalization as a factor. In *Walkovsky v. Carlton*, the defendants used the feature of limited liability greatly to their advantage. 223 N.E.2d 6 (N.Y. 1966). The defendants owned several taxicabs, but placed ownership in each of the taxicabs in a separate corporate entity. The corporations, which owned one or perhaps two cabs, had no other notable assets, though they did carry the minimal liability insurance. Thus, individuals who were injured by a taxicab could, absent veil-piercing, only reach the limited assets of the corporation. The plaintiff was run over by one of these separately-incorporated taxicabs. She attempted to reach the assets of the investors on the theory that the businesses operated as a unit. The investor owned ten other corporations, which each, in turn, owned one or two cabs. All of the corporations operated out of the same garage. She also argued that the organizational scheme devised by the investors in the taxicab business was an attempt to defraud customers and others, like her, who are injured by the taxicabs. The court stopped short of giving the plaintiff relief on the basis of the separate incorporations. In the court's view, so long as corporate formalities were maintained, the corporate entities should be respected.

Additionally, the court noted that corporate entities are not necessarily under-capitalized because the corporate assets might be insufficient to cover a (tort) creditor's claim:

> The corporate form may not be disregarded merely because the assets of the corporation, together with the mandatory insurance coverage of the vehicle which struck the plaintiff, are insufficient to assure him the recovery sought. If Carlton were to be held liable on those facts alone, the decision would apply equally to thousands of cabs which are owned by their individual drivers would conduct their businesses through corporations ... and carry the minimum insurance required....

233 N.E.2d at 9. According to the court, therefore, the taxicab corporations carried enough insurance to meet statutory guidelines, which was sufficient to avoid veil-piercing based on failure to fund.

In the end, investors in corporate entities are not always protected from liability, regardless of their conduct. Under the principle of veil-piercing, the investors in a corporation can be pursued in their individual capacity in some discrete cases. Interestingly, also, veil-piercing is not the only way for a claimant to reach the personal assets of investors. For one thing, in addition to liability in veil-piercing cases, shareholders are always liable for their own misconduct. Furthermore, some shareholders (particularly in close corporations) voluntarily assent to liability. Under the DGCL, for instance, the incorporators of the entity could devise articles of incorporation that provide that shareholders can be held personally liable for the firm's misconduct. DEL. CODE ANN. tit. 8, § 102(6) (1999). Similarly, the owners of the corporate entity can contract around the rule, like any other default, to accomplish a specific transaction, and they often do. For instance, consider a particular transaction, like a revolving loan, for ordinary business expenses. A shareholder may guarantee the loan's payment to the lender. In the case of smaller corporations, a lender may even demand such a guarantee. In this case, if the corporation defaults on the debt, the lender may not only pursue the assets of the entity by also of the share-holder-guarantor. Thus, the rule of limited liability, which is arguably the most important corporate characteristic, is a default rule.

2. Theory and Evidence in Veil-Piercing

Although some factors appear to be frequently present in cases in which the courts permit veil-piercing, the case law, as mentioned, is far from coherent. The point is that the factors, while important, do not provide a clear line of conduct that would warrant disregarding the corporate liability shield. As many commentators have previously observed, some courts consider factors that others do not. To fill some of the void in these cases, several observers have formulated theories about which types of cases are more likely ripe for veil-piercing. Notably, for instance, Frank Easterbrook and Dan Fischel have argued that an economic analysis can be used to sort out what courts are doing when confronted with veil-piercing cases.

The two noted scholars hypothesize that veil-piercing is more likely in close corporations than in large public corporations, which reflects the difference in costs to investors of monitoring manager conduct. In close firms, investors and managers of the entity are usually the same individuals. Thus, limited liability does not work to decrease monitoring costs. By contrast, in large public corporations, investors and managers are largely separate and, thus, veil-piercing in these cases would increase monitoring costs. In a universe of unlimited liability, that is, investors in large public firms would have to watch manager's conduct.

Additionally, Easterbrook and Fischel have argued that recovery in a veil-piercing case should be more likely when the investor is a corporate entity rather than an individual, such as the parent-subsidiary context. They theorize that veil-piercing may be more likely in these cases because in these relationships the subsidiary is more likely to be under-capitalized. The parent corporation has an incentive to deplete the subsidiary's assets in order to head off creditor claims. A third conclusion of Easterbrook and Fischel is that veil-piercing is more likely to occur in tort cases than in contract cases. The theory here is that in contract cases (at least in many of them) the creditor has an opportunity to be compensated for the risk that corporate assets might not cover the contract debt. In tort cases, however, the victims are involuntary creditors insofar as they have had not a chance to negotiate a price *ex ante* for the risk of business failure and uncompensated damages.

However, even these theories might not get one very far. After the Easterbrook and Fischel article, some interesting empirical research on veil-piercing was done by Vanderbilt's Robert Thompson. In his 1991 article, Thompson uncovers empirical evidence that flies in some of the face of some of the assumed theories about veil-piercing cases. Some of the more interesting results of the Thompson study is the finding that veil-piercing is more likely to occur in contracts cases than in tort cases. Also interesting, Thompson finds that veil-piercing is more likely to occur when the corporate investor is an individual as opposed to another corporation. Further, Thompson finds that there is an inverse relationship between the number of shareholders and the likelihood of success in a veil-piercing case. That is, the more widely-dispersed the shares are, according to Thompson, the less likely one is to be able to pierce the corporate veil. In fact, Thompson finds that among public corporations there are no successful veil-piercing cases. *See* Robert Thompson, *Piercing the Corporate Veil: An Empirical Study*, 76 CORNELL L. REV. 1036 (1991).

C. Double Taxation

A third characteristic of the corporate form is actually a disadvantage, the taxation of corporate-generated earnings. Unlike other entities discussed so far, the corporation is taxed at the entity level and at the ownership level. This so-called double taxation means that investors in a corporation may only use corporate-generated profits, first, after the corporation has paid taxes on the income and, second, after the recipient/investor also pays taxes off any gains. To put this in more concrete terms, when successful corporations generate some level of profits as earnings each year, these profits are taxed as income to the corporation. Thereafter, the corporation can use the profits to expand its operations; gobble up a competitor; re-purchase shares; or make a payment to the owners of the corporation, the shareholders. If the corporation wants to make a payment to shareholders, it may issue a cash dividend. However, the dividend, which is the after-tax profits of the corporation, will also be taxed as ordinary income to the shareholder. The level of tax to the shareholder will depend on the shareholder's income.

Nevertheless, some corporation strategies can mitigate the impact of double taxation. For instance, in smaller enterprises, the company could try to zero-out net profits at the end of each year. For example, the corporation could simply distribute earnings as bonuses to each shareholder-employer. Because payments to employees are not taxed at the entity level *per se*, the corporation could effectively avoid double taxation. This only works if all the shareholders are actually employed by the corporation. Furthermore, double-taxation does not apply to small, non-public corporations that elect to be treated like a partnership. More specifically, the I.R.S. provides that corporations with fewer than 100 shareholders can choose subchapter S status, which gives them the option to be taxed and treated either like a large public corporation or like a general partnership. In all events, much investor income generated by the corporation is taxed at more favorable rates. At the date of this writing, for instance, long-term capital gains for stock sales are taxed at 15%, compared to higher rates of taxation for ordinary income.

D. Capital Structure

The corporate form permits promoters to raise large sums of money to pursue corporate activities. The entity raises money by selling off ownership in the company in the form of shares and other securities. In addition, the corporation may raise money by borrowing.

1. Shares

One of the principal ways the corporation finances operations is by selling shares. Shareholders are paid out from the profits of the company; they are so-called residual claimants. In other words, shareholders are only paid from company revenue after all company liabilities are taken into account. Thus, the shareholders, as residual claimants, have no security claim, like banks and other lenders that the corporation is obligated to pay regardless of net profits. The corporation may issue any class of shares authorized in the articles of incorporation. The most abundant type of share that is issued by a corporation is the common share. Such shares usually give the holder the right to any profits generated by the company, if the board of directors ultimately approves a distribution. Unless otherwise agreed, corporate shares are by default common shares with equal voting rights and with equal rights to residual claims of the corporation.

However, in the articles of incorporation, the corporate entity may agree to issue more than one class of share, in addition to common stock. However, the shares must be authorized by the articles of incorporation:

> The articles of incorporation must set forth any classes of shares and series of shares within a class, and the number of shares of each class and series, that the corporation is authorized to issue. If more than one class or series of shares is authorized, the articles of incorporation must prescribe a distinguishing designation for each class or series and must describe, prior to the issuance of shares of a class or series, the terms, including the preferences, rights and limitations of that class or series.

MODEL BUS. CORP. ACT § 6.01 (2005); *see also* DEL. CODE ANN. tit. 8, § 102(4) (1999). In most of these instances, the corporation will issue preferred shares with unique rights for the holders. Holders of preferred shares usually get some right to partake in company profits not available to holders of common stock. Most importantly, holders of preferred shares are entitled to dividends *before* the company pays out dividends to common stockholders. Further, they are also entitled to a payout upon dissolution of the company before other residual claimants. However, holders of preferred stock usually have weaker voting rights than other owners. An owner of preferred stock, in fact, may have not absolute right to vote on members of the board of directors. Further, holders of preferred stock, like other stockholders, are in terms of priority behind holders of debt.

2. Options

Another type of interest that a corporation may issue is an option. Options operate similar to shares, in the sense that an investor only has a residual claim. Options, like shares, are routinely issued by corporations to their employees. Options are much easier to tie to the employee's performance, because the value of the option is based on the value of the company's shares. In so doing, a corporation is able to align the interests of its employees with those of the shareholders. Because the value of the option is tied to the shares, high-level employees will have an incentive to behave in a way that increases the company's share price.

More specifically, the value of the option is derived from the value of the shares. Options are perhaps the simplest variant of a broad array of securities today called "derivatives." The two most of common types of options, for instance, are "call" options and "put" options. A call option gives the holder of the option a right to buy at a particular price. In a typical call option scenario, an investor may purchase an option to buy several thousand shares of Company X at $5, the exercise price. The option contract will also state the period of time that the investor has to decide whether to purchase the stock, the exercise period. Of course, if Company X's stock never reaches $5/share, the investor will not exercise her option. In this case, the stock is said to be "out of the money." Only if the stock soars past $5 will the investor use the option. If the stock passes the strike price, then it is said to be "in the money." A put option, by contrast, give the holder of the put option the right to sell. Here, an investor may anticipate that the shares of Company Y may be headed for a slump. Assume she holds stock in Company Y, which is currently trading at $6.50 a share. Her option will give her the right to sell her stock at, say, $5. If the stock falls below $5, the option holder is in-the-money. He sells and makes a profit, since he can sell at $5 per share and re-buy the same stock at its current trading price. However, if the stock continues to trade at or above $6.50 a share, the option is not exercised; the option holder is out-of-the-money.

3. Debt

Lastly, the company also raises money by issuing debt. The corporate entity may borrow money from traditional institutional lenders, like banks. Furthermore, the corporation may borrow from smaller investors by issuing bonds or debentures. The bonds are secured by company assets and promise the holder a certain rate of return as interest. Holders of debt have little say-so in the operation of the company and cannot, for instance, vote on company directors. However, the advantage of holding debt is that these obligations are not dependent on company profits. Regardless of the corporation's success, debt holders are promised a guaranteed rate of return. Further, in the event of dissolution of the company, debt holders are paid out first.

E. Introduction to Corporate Management

Corporations are usually large entities with countless decisions that need to be made. If every investor in the corporate entity could play a role in decision-making the corporation would get very little done and routinely face deadlock. To avoid these large coordination problems, the management of the corporation is centralized in the board of directors, but really several additional bodies have management authority. For instance, much of the routine management of the firm begins with the executives and other officers. At the same time, shareholders have some authority, albeit limited, to veto fundamental corporate decisions.

F. Corporate Officers

The corporate officers attend to the day-to-day operations of the corporate entity. These individuals are expected to execute firm policy, set prices, hire and fire underlings, and make decisions on which markets to enter, among other duties. In addition, however, federal law provides that some corporate officers have specific duties. For instance, Sarbanes-Oxley provides that the CEO and CFO must certify company financial statements. The officers are agents of the corporation. Thus, the limits of authority of officers of the corporation are a function of common law principles of agency, like apparent authority and actual authority. As agents, officers may enter into contracts in the usual course of operations, as the next case shows.

In *Lee v. Jenkins Brothers*, the president of a corporate entity made a generous pension promise to one of his employees, even though it was not clear whether the president had the authority to make the promise. 268 F.2d 357 (2d Cir. 1959). According to Lee's testimony, the promise by the company president was that the pension benefits would be paid "regardless of what happened." The court noted that the president had no actual authority to enter into such a contract under the company charter or its by-laws. Without that kind of proof of actual authority, however, the agreement might still be binding on the corporation under principles of apparent authority. The president's apparent authority, the court reasoned, would turn on the extent the pension promise was an extraordinary one or one that fell within the usual confines of business operations. If too unusual, the court noted that there would not be apparent authority to bind the company to the agreement. The court notes, for instance, that an agreement for lifetime employment would be unusual. However, the court held that alleged lifetime pension promise was different and, thus, may be enforceable under apparent authority.

The point is that the scope of the powers of corporate officers comes down to agency principles in many instances. As in agency cases, corporate officers can, of course, form enforceable contracts on behalf of the entity, if they have authority to do so. Actual authority to act might be evidenced by the corporation's articles of incorporation, by-laws, or board resolution, for instance. Further, corporate officers have apparent authority to take decisions in the ordinary course of business operations. If this were not the case, the board of directors could strategically disclaim obligations of the corporation on the ground that the agent had no authority. This would create an injustice and put in jeopardy the dealings between the corporations and its suppliers, customers, or any other unwary souls who do business with the corporation through its agents.

However, despite agency principles, the officers of the corporation have limits to their actions, as *Grimes v. Alteon* shows. In this case, the president of a small pharmaceutical concern made a promise to one of the company's early backers that it would sell the investor 10% of any private share offering. 804 A.2d 256 (Del. 2002). The promise was made orally and was not approved by the board. At the time of the promise, the investor, Grimes owned close to 10% of the company. A subsequent offering would threaten to dilute his ownership. As a result, the company president merely made the promise in order to assure its investor that it would have an opportunity to ensure that its current holdings would not be diluted if more shares were issued. However, when Alteon did privately place shares, it did not permit Grimes to participate. The court in the case had to consider whether the president of the corporation had the power to make a promise relating to the company's capital structure. The answer was a resounding no. The court held that the promise was not enforceable, because the right to make stock commitments was exclusively within the purview of the board of directors. Further, the promise to Grimes was unenforceable, the court reasoned, because promises regarding stock issuances have to be in writing. In sum, therefore, the court held that the right to manage the capital structure of the firm is exclusively vested with the board of directors, not officers.

G. Board of Directors

The board of directors is the nucleus of the operation. In fact, state corporate law mandates that this be the case. The DGCL provides that the "business and affairs of every corporation … shall be managed by and under the direction" of the board of directors. DEL. CODE ANN. tit. 8, § 141(a) (1999). Similarly, the MBCA provides that "all corporate powers shall be exercised by … the board of directors" and that "the business and affairs of the corporation shall be managed by … its board of directors." MODEL BUS. CORP. ACT § 8.01(b) (2005).

By default, the members of the board are elected by all shareholders at the company's annual meeting. However, the articles of incorporation may provide for alternative arrangements for election of directors. Some corporations stagger the election of the board. If the elections are staggered, only a portion of directors (usually one-third) comes up for election at the annual meeting:

> The directors of any corporation organized under this chapter may, by the certificate of incorporation or by an initial bylaw, or by a bylaw adopted by a vote of the stockholders, be divided into 1, 2, or 3 classes: the term of office of those of the first class to expire at the first annual meeting held after such classification becomes effective; of the second class 1 year thereafter; of the third class 2 years thereafter; and at each annual election held after such classification becomes effective, directors shall be chosen for a full term, as the case may be, to succeed those whose terms expire.

DEL. CODE ANN. tit. 8, § 141(d) (1999). Provisions to stagger ensure that there is some stability and institutional experience among the board. This also means that shareholders cannot unilaterally change the entire board in one swoop. Thus, in the event of takeover by another company or group of investors, the staggered board would be a significant impediment.

Although there is no particular set of directors required, boards are usually comprised of small, workable number of directors, perhaps between 7 and 9 members. The organizing documents of a corporation may, but need not, provide some qualifications for membership on the board of directors. In any event, the board members are often selected because they have some core competency that the corporation needs or because they are amongst the largest shareholders of the entity. Also, frequently, directors are "insiders" or executives of the firm. These individuals, like the company's president or CEO, have the most intimate and up-to-date knowledge about the on-going firm activities. At the same time, larger firms also usually retain several "outside" directors. Outside directors are individuals who do not work full-time at the corporate entity. These individuals are usually drawn from the ranks of chief executives and other high-level officers at other companies.

Board members are usually compensated for the service. Interestingly, the pay for service of the board of directors is, by default, a power reserved for the board of directors. *See, e.g.*, DEL. CODE ANN. tit. 8, §141(h) (1999). (Of course, corporations can contract around this rule by changing the corporate by-laws or, if necessary, the articles of incorporation.) In addition to cash compensation, firms usually provide insurance for board members, in the event they are sued for work in their official capacity. Firms that do not insure directors *ex ante* are compelled to indemnify directors *ex post* who are found in court (or other proceeding) to have participated in no wrongdoing. MODEL BUS. CORP. ACT §8.51 (2005).

Board members have no power to act except as a unified group at an official meeting of the board. Thus, in contrast to some corporate officers, individual board members are not agents of the corporation. They act as a united body by resolution at a meeting of the directors. With only two exceptions, the board may only act by physically meeting as a board. First, the board of directors may act without a meeting by written consent, but only if all board members agree. *See, e.g.*, DEL. CODE ANN. tit. 8, §141(f) (1999). Second, the board may act without physically meeting if members are available by phone or similar device.

Unless the articles provide otherwise, in order to transact business in an official meeting of the board of directors, a quorum must be present, which by default means half of the members of the board. *See, e.g.*, DEL. CODE ANN. tit. 8, §141 (1999). Thus, a corporation could require a lower number of members be present in order to transact business. In Delaware, the articles of incorporation could provide that as few as a third of board members is sufficient to constitute a quorum. Decisions are made by a majority vote of those present at the meeting. This rule is largely immutable. In other words, while the articles of incorporation can provide for a greater number of affirmative votes, there must at least be a majority.

1. Introduction to the Powers of the Board of Directors

The board of directors has far-reaching powers to run the operations of the company however it sees fit. But, this was not always the case. In early days of incorporations, corporations were mistrusted, because they could generate large concentrations of wealth. As a result, legislators required corporations to pursue a very narrow purpose. Further, corporate entities would have to be single-minded about strategy of generating profits for shareholders. In these days, corporate entities (and by consequence their boards) were forbidden from taking on decisions that were at odds with a narrow corporate purposes. If they did, those actions would be void as *ultra vires*.

Even today, there are limitations on the authority of the board of directors. Certainly, the board of directors has no authority to use its power to engage in self-dealing transaction, violate the law, or commit fraud. Furthermore, though, the board of directors cannot distribute firm assets, if the distribution would effectively make the firm functionally insolvent. The MBCA provides, for instance, that if the distribution would make firm liabilities exceed firm assets—*i.e.*, balance sheet insolvency—the distribution is prohibited. MODEL BUS. CORP. ACT §6.40 (2005). Further, the board of directors is limited by their fiduciary duty and obligations to the corporation, each of which will be discussed in more detail later. Suffices to say for now, directors have an obligation of good faith and fair dealing and a fiduciary duty not to waste corporate assets, a duty of care, and a duty of loyalty.

Still, today's board has much greater leeway to make decisions and, as mentioned, delegate authority to make decisions to others. The board is no longer hamstrung by a purpose requirement. Further, many state statutes, so-called constituency statutes, have liberated boards of directors such that they no longer have to be concerned exclusively with shareholder profits. Under these statutes, directors may not only consider the impact of their business activity on those holding shares, but may also consider the interests of other stakeholders in the community, including workers and communities.

2. Power over Internal Operations

Importantly, as the next case shows, the board of directors has the power to devise strategy about the direction of the business.

In *Shlensky v. Wrigley*, the board of directors of the Chicago Cubs decided that the team would not follow the trend of other major league ball clubs and affix lights to the revered Wrigley Stadium, the Cubs' arena. 237 N.E.2d 776 (Ill. App. Ct. 1968). The majority shareholder and President of the Corporation that owned the cubs, Phillip Wrigley, thought that lights were a terrible idea in baseball, even though every other team, including cross-town rival the Chicago White Sox, had installed lights. Baseball, he is quoted as saying, is a "daytime sport." Further, Wrigley thought lights would have a "deteriorating effect" on the neighborhood were the stadium set. The board of directors agreed with Wrigley. However, a minority shareholder challenged the board's decision against lights. In his view, the lights would help the team increase attendance, because with lights the team can hold night games that families could attend after work. This change, the shareholder argued, would drive up profits. Evidence was introduced to show that the Cubs had suffered losses on baseball operations for the last five years.

The court implicitly acknowledges that lights might increase revenues for the club. However, the court reasoned that the board of directors was empowered to consider the interests of the corporation more broadly than as simply the immediate financial interest of the shareholders. The court stated that the board of directors could consider, for instance, the "long run interest of the corporation in its property value at Wrigley Field". Thus, decision-making regarding the internal operations of the entity are left to the board of directors. Even if shareholders have ideas that might generate profits for the enterprise, it is up to the board of directors to decide whether to adopt the strategy or not. Courts will not ordinarily upset board power by second-guessing corporate decisions.

3. Power to Distribute Earnings

Furthermore, the Board has the power to decide on how the profits of the enterprise are to be used. Traditionally, profits generated from the enterprise are plowed back in to the business to fund expansion or returned to shareholders as the owners of the enterprise. But, the board of directors' authority to decide how earnings are used, as the next case abundantly shows, goes far beyond deciding between even those two options.

Specifically, in *A.P. Smith v. Barlow* the board of directors of a for-profit corporation elected to use a portion of earnings to make a charitable donation. 98 A.2d 581 (N.J. 1953). In that case, the board of a manufacturing company approved a $1,500 donation to Princeton University. Today corporations frequently make donations to charities or local interests without creating so much as a stir. Theoretically, however, such a decision is beside the core point of the corporate entity, which is to make money for shareholders, not to give it away. When the company made the gift, some shareholders grumbled, though the corporation had made other donations to local interests in the past. Thus, the board asked the court for a declaratory judgment to determine whether the board could take such action. The board argued that the action was in the interest of the corporate entity, broadly speaking. The donation created goodwill among locals, helped promote liberal education, and created a "favorable environment" for business, among other positives. The contrary view was that the articles of incorporation did not permit this type of activity. The court held that the donation was a valid exercise of authority.

4. Power to Delegate

Lastly, but as important as any other power, the board of directors has the power to delegate authority. As a result, the board's oversight of company operations is frequently from afar. Thus, the corporate board of directors may be split into sub-boards to handle function-specific tasks. In larger corporations, there is usually compensation or audit committees, for example, which are both sub-committees of the larger board of directors. More importantly, the board hires the company CEO and, through the CEO, can direct day-to-day corporate operations. The CEO then appoints other employees and makes recommendations to the firm for other important positions. In fact, the board of directors frequently delegates to others various company functions. This power of the board to delegate authority to underlings usually goes without question; after all, the board of directors is usually comprised of individuals who have limited time themselves to directly manage internal corporation operations. The board is often comprised of individuals, CEOs or other high-level executives, with full-time jobs and responsibilities at other companies. However, in some cases, like the next one, the question arises as to whether the board of directors has inappropriately delegated its authority.

In *Grimes v. Donald*, a shareholder brought a suit arguing that the corporate entity had abdicated to the company CEO ultimate decision-making power. 673 A.2d 1207 (Del. 1996). The plaintiff in that case pointed to the employment agreement between the company and the CEO, which gave to the CEO "the general management of the affairs of the company" without "unreasonable interference" from the board of directors. In fact, under the agreement, the CEO could claim a constructive termination of the contract if the board of directors interfered too much with his management of the company. In this event, the CEO would get a generous severance package, including his then-existing salary, bonuses, and medical/retirement benefits, worth according to the plaintiff $20 million. The court below dismissed the plaintiff's claims, but attacked the lop-sided agreement as "foolish" and "ill-conceived."

Importantly, on appeal, the court conceded that a board could be hauled into court for an absolute and complete abdication of their authority. However, the relatively large severance package, which might be costly to the firm, did not negate the fact that ultimate power still rested with the board:

> In a world of scarcity, a decision to do one thing will commit a board to a certain course of action and make it costly and difficult (indeed, sometimes impossible) to change course and do another. This is an inevitable fact of life and is not an abdication of directorial duty.... The Board of DSC retains the ultimate freedom to direct the strategy and affairs of the Company. If Donald disagrees with the Board, the Company may or may not (depending on the circumstances) be required to pay him a substantial sum of money in order to pursue its chosen course of action. So far, we have only a rather unusual contract, but not a case of abdication.

673 A.2d at 1220. Thus, *Grimes* reinforces the notion that the ultimate responsibility for the operations of the entity, regardless of board appointments, rests with the board of directors. Still, the board of directors may not enter into contracts that vest another party or entity with complete Board power. For instance, recall that the Board of directors cannot delegate to another—*e.g.*, the company president—the power to regulate the firm's capital structure. However, the board of directors may delegate to others operational authority. And, though there are limitations, this authority to delegate is extremely expansive. As *Grimes* shows, even in cases in which the delegation may be foolhardy or unusually costly to the firm, the board still has the inherent power to delegate authority to another. This is also a good time to mention one limitation on the board's power to act by delegating. That is, some actions must be considered by the entire board, not merely a sub-set of the board or board committee. For instance, the MBCA provides that subcommittees do not have the power to change by-laws or fill vacancies on the board of directors or make unilateral decisions regarding distributions. *See* MODEL BUS. CORP. ACT § 8.25 (2005).

H. Shareholders

Shareholders have limited managerial rights, since most of the authority for decision-making in the corporate context lay with the board of directors and, by extension, the officers the board chooses. Still, shareholders are able to exert some influence over some decisions of the board of directors and may be able to affect the make-up of the board. As discussed fully in Chapter 10, shareholders have the power to elect and remove the members of the board. Further, shareholders have the power to veto transactions taken that would dispose of a substantial portion of corporate assets. As for the officers of the corporation, the shareholders' ability to control their day-to-day conduct is remote.

I. Dual Managerial Responsibilities

Despite the distinct roles and accompanying powers, in perhaps most corporate entities there is tremendous overlapping of responsibilities. For instance, the CEO frequently serves on the board of directors of the corporate entity. Frequently, she is the chairman. Further, directors and officers of the corporation are almost always shareholders in the entity, sometimes these individuals are the largest shareholder. Lastly, by holding other capacities, a few powerful shareholders might also end up with effective control of the corporation. For instance, relatively large shareholders may be elected to the board of directors, where they can exert authority. Of course, this creates all sorts of agency and incentive problems. For instance, it smacks as strange, to say the least, to have the company CEO participate, as a member of the board of directors, in setting policy for the hiring and firing of the CEO. Of course, there are mechanisms for off-setting obvious conflicts when participants wear multiple hats. For instance, policy respecting the CEO can always be decided by a sub-committee of independent directors that does not include the CEO or other officers. Still, other challenges remain.

Checkpoints

- While shareholders are not liable for the misdeeds and misrepresentations of the corporation, they may be personally liable for their own acts or misconduct and in rare cases of so-called veil-piercing.

- While the courts differ in their views of veil-piercing, factors that may be considered are commingling of personal and corporate funds, under-funding the entity, plundering of assets by investors, and using funds of one corporation to pay obligations of another.

- Unless otherwise stated in the articles of incorporation, corporate shares have equal voting rights and equal rights to residual claims on corporate assets.

- The board of directors of a corporation is at the nucleus of firm operations. The board has the power to determine the firm's capital structure, delegate responsibility to others, hire or fire the firm CEO, and otherwise manage the firm.

- While shareholders have limited managerial rights, they do have the power to elect and remove the directors and to veto transactions proposed by the board.

Chapter 8

Fiduciary Duty of Care

Roadmap

- Fiduciary Duty of Care
- Introduction to Business Judgment Rule (BJR)
- Standard of Care versus Standard of Review
- Rationales for the BJR
- Additional Statutory Protections for Directors
- Exceptions to the BJR
- Obligation of Good Faith

The board of directors, the nucleus of corporate operations, is judged by its ability to make careful and well-founded decisions for the firm. Among other important decisions, good boards of directors hire a levelheaded, seasoned chief executive and quickly sack a leader who fails to meet firm objectives. The board keeps informed of economic conditions and taps capital markets to expand the business at the most opportune times. The board decides when to divest or sell company assets, always making a sober judgment about how much such assets should fetch in an arms-length transaction.

The board, unfortunately, is fallible and its decisions sometimes go cock-eyed. Directors' decision to make an offering of company shares, for instance, may be mistimed for when capital markets are tightening. Business leaders with stellar resumes may prove incapable to rally the rank-and-file. Mergers go south and disparate business units never cohere. Mistakes are costly and raise the ire of shareholders and other stakeholders in the firms. Invariably, some of these stakeholders will lay blame at the feet of the board of directors, the ultimate decision-makers. When decisions turn out badly, therefore, directors may be susceptible to protracted litigation, which begs the question of what legal duty, if any, does a director owe to the firm in decision-making?

Generally, directors have at least two legal duties with respect to decisions to act (or not act). First, and of primary importance, a director has a fiduciary duty of care to the corporate entity. According to some corporate statutes, the fiduciary duty of care requires directors to make decisions that are "reasonable" under the circumstances. Instead, as will be explained more fully, directors of a firm are never held to a standard of reasonableness in decision-making. Directors are insulated from liability for error in decision-making, even negligent decision-making. Second, directors appear to have an obligation to take decisions in good faith. Although the concept is somewhat amorphous, recent court decisions suggest that the obligation of good faith is not one that should be ignored or discounted.

A. Introduction to the Business Judgment Rule

Some legal sources on director duty in decision-making and court review of director decisions are, in a way, at tension. On the one hand, a review of the applicable sources of legal principles regarding the duty that directors owe the firm in decision-making suggests that the fiduciary duty of care, the standard of *care*, is a high one. Legal sources, on their face, equate a director's duty of care in decision-making to a negligence standard. Consider, for instance, the American Law Institute (ALI), which publishes the well-known restatements of law. The organization has also published an advisory tome for corporate law known as the *Principles of Corporate Governance*. According to the ALI's *Principles*, directors have a duty to make decisions "with the care that an ordinarily prudent person would reasonably be expected to exercise in a like position and under similar circumstances." AMERICAN LAW INSTITUTE, PRINCIPLES OF CORPORATE GOVERNANCE § 4.01(a) (1994). Furthermore, the Model Business Corporation Act, which several states have used as the model to draft their own corporate codes, provides that directors shall discharge their duties in "good faith" and, what's more, "in a manner the director reasonably believes to be in the best interest of the corporation." MODEL BUS. CORP. ACT § 8.30(a) (2005). Such statements make it seem that directors will be responsible for any negligent decision.

However, on the other hand, though it is theoretically possible for a director to be held liable for negligent decision-making, the chances of such a result are extremely remote. In contrast to the standard of care, the standard of *review* by courts relevant to director decision-making is a low one. Under the so-called business judgment rule, the standard of review of managerial decision-making is remarkably deferential to managers and directors. This business judgment rule is largely judge-made law. Judges, that is, presume that directors have acted with due care in making their decision. As former Yale Law Professor (now Second Circuit Judge) Ralph Winter put it:

While it is often stated that corporate directors and officers will be liable for negligence in carrying out their corporate duties, all seem agreed that such a statement is misleading. Whereas an automobile driver who makes a mistake in judgment as to speed or distance injuring a pedestrian will likely be called upon to respond in damages, a corporate [director or] officer who makes a mistake in judgment as to economic conditions, consumer tastes or production line efficiency will rarely, if ever, be found liable for damages suffered by the corporation. Whatever the terminology, the fact is that liability is rarely imposed upon corporate directors or officers simply for bad judgment and this reluctance to impose liability for unsuccessful business decisions has been doctrinally labeled the business judgment rule.

Joy v. North, 692 F.2d 880, 885 (2d Cir. 1982). This assumption of business judgment is not without exception, but successful rebuttals of the presumption of reasonable care and prudence that attaches to director decision-making are unusual. In fact, recent research suggests that directors have only been individually liable in cases of poor decision-making, by itself, in only a handful of cases.

Moreover, whether the director is entitled to the presumption of reasonable care under the business judgment rule will almost never turn on the substance of the decision. Courts would thus not normally make inquiry into, say, how the board missed important signs that the CEO they were considering would be a poor fit. Instead, the only important question for reviewing courts is whether the board of directors had created a reasonable process for evaluating its options. In the case of hiring the leader of the firm, courts might only look to whether the board has considered several applicants. In other decisions, courts have evaluated decision-making by taking a cursory check of whether the directors met regularly, reviewed financial reports, and were given sufficient time to review information important to the corporate activities. Under the business judgment rule, if the board has established a rational process for decision-making, the content of the decision reached will not be second-guessed by the courts.

1. Reasons for the Business Judgment Rule

Several justifications support the business judgment rule, which as mentioned protects the vast majority of director decisions from courtroom review. First, compared to directors, judges (and juries) are in a worse position to decide whether a decision is made in the interests of the firm. This is particularly true in states where questions of prudent business judgment are factual matters to be decided by a jury, which may be composed of ordinary citizens with little business experience. Judges, too, may not be competent to evaluate business strategy. Judges are not necessarily trained business leaders. Many judges are drawn from the rank of government and academia, not commercial industry. Further, even in cases where the judges who decide have substantial business experience from a prior career, it seems reasonable to suspect that many judges have little relevant *judicial* experience. With the exceptions of Delaware judges, for instance, it is unlikely that many judges have presided over complicated derivative suits by shareholders of public companies.

On the other hand, directors tend to be sophisticated, successful business men and women. They traditionally have long experience with the company as a day-to-day manager or experiences from working in the industry. Furthermore, directors, executives, and other corporate insiders probably have better information about intimate details of the company that informs their decision-making. Although courts may learn about firm details through discovery, hearings and a trial, these methods of information-gathering are far less superior to directors' direct access to information through their day-to-day involvement of the firm. Because of their comparative advantage in terms of experience and insider information, it stands to reason that directors have a better sense of what decisions will maximize firm value.

Second, the business judgment rule counterbalances human psychology. Without the business judgment rule, judges (and justice) are put in an untenable position. They are forced to look backwards in time and evaluate the full range of options the board faced under time, budget, and information constraints. In these circumstances, no doubt, some courts might impose liability too frequently if they did not defer to management. For instance, with the benefit of hindsight, they might be inclined too often to confuse a decision that turns out to be unprofitable as obviously the wrong one. The problem, again, is that managers face a wide range of options, many of which appear to be reasonable at the time. Thus, the question judges would be forced to answer in these cases is not what would have maximized profits *ex post*. Rather, it's an inquiry into whether at time of the decision managers gave each of their options a fair and balanced appraisal. For judges, as for anyone, this is hard to do.

Third, if courts were to intervene in decision-making, it might have a destabilizing effect on business. By filing lawsuits, shareholders (and other stakeholders) would be able to easily second-guess corporate decisions that turn out awry. As a result, directors in a world without business judgment protection would be hesitant to act for fear of suit. In the case of a risky decision, in particular, the chances for failure are heightened. If failure does occur, shareholder dissatisfaction predictably follows. Thus, directors would be extremely leery to take risky decisions with significant downside potential. One could argue that directors should be hesitant when it comes to risky decisions that might reduce firm value. However, shareholders, by making a decision to invest in a particular company by buying shares when more conservative options are available, have in effect affirmed their preference for some level of risk-taking. For such shareholders, such ventures, if successful, might produce outsized gains. The point is that without the business judgment rule, directors might be over-deterred and might avoid a fair amount of risks. Without protection, directors would be hesitant to take decisions that have the potential of generating losses for the company, since they do not fully realize the benefits of any gains but do realize extraordinary costs—e.g., defending against a lawsuit—should the decision turn out poorly. Shortly, in a world without the business judgment rule protections, directors would be hesitant to take any chances, even though that is precisely what shareholders want.

A fourth and related effect is that without the protection of the business judgment rule potential directors would balk at taking board positions in the first place. For some directors, the expected costs of liability should a shareholder suit arise far exceeds the monetary benefits of the directorship, salary and limited stock options. Without this protection, the type of individuals who agree to serve as directors may be significantly poorer in credentials. For instance, one might expect that without business judgment protection the directors who ultimately serve may be either more unusually risk-seeking or have few assets at stake should they make a decision that exposes them to liability. In either event, board decision-making would likely be compromised. The business judgment rule makes it possible for firms to recruit the best directors possible, because there is only a small chance that there decisions will be second-guessed by courts. Thus, the business judgment rule helps ensure that individuals with the best set of experiences are not unusually deterred from taking board positions.

2. Applications of the Business Judgment Rule

Although the business judgment rule is largely the product of common law, statutory support also exists for insulating directors from errant decision-making. For instance, the MBCA advises as follows:

> A director shall not be liable to the corporation or its shareholders for any decision to take or not to take action ... unless [the claimant] establishes that ... the director did not reasonably believe [the decision] to be in the best interests of the corporation, or ... the director was

not informed to an extent the director reasonably believed appropriate in the circumstances, or a sustained failure of the director to devote attention to ongoing oversight of the business and affairs of the corporation....

Model Bus. Corp. Act § 8.31(a) (2005). Importantly, as the above suggests, the relevant inquiry is based on subjective evidence, not an objective or a reasonable person standard of stewardship. However, as a common law rule, the parameters of business judgment are still evolving as courts take new cases and adopt novel reasoning. Suffice it to say for now though, the business judgment rule insulates even the most troubling decisions taken by a board of directors. The next case, *Kamin*, is famous as illustrative of the broad discretion afforded directors to take decisions, even silly ones, without fear of liability.

In particular, in *Kamin v. American Express*, the directors adopted a decision which they all knew (or should have known) would cause the company to lose valuable tax savings. 383 N.Y.S.2d 807 (N.Y. Sup. Ct. 1976). Even in this case, however, the court held that directors have discretion to make such decisions. In the case, American Express held a large position of stock in DLJ, an investment firm. When American Express acquired the stock in 1972, the investment cost over $29 million. By the time American Express decided to dispose of the stock, three years later, the stock (and the company) had tanked. American Express' position was worth only around $4 million, when the board of American Express decided to distribute it as an in-kind dividend to their shareholders. In American Express' view, by distributing the under-performing stock to shareholders, the company would avoid having to show a $25 million loss on financial statements. If they had sold the stock at a loss, the loss would have appeared on the financial statements and it would have reduced the company's booked earnings for the year by $25 million. These financial statements are public information and a large publicly-reported loss could create an incentive to unload American Express stock. That is, because the loss would have a negative effect on the price of American Express' booked earnings per share, the belief was that some shareholders would sell American Express stock and the price of the company's stock would fall.

The shareholders argued, rightly, that American Express could just sell the DLJ stock and use the capital gain loss to offset other taxable income. Such tax savings had real value. The tax savings, they submitted, would be worth millions to the company, which had significant taxable income. It was plain that the shareholders were largely right on the tax savings point. Further, American Express' losses related to its holding in DLJ were probably already capitalized into the price of the stock. In other words, the current stock price reflects all relevant public information. The rapid decline of DLJ's stock price was public information. Investors in American Express, therefore, would have already accounted for this decline when pricing how much they would pay for its stock. Thus, it is not obvious why reporting the losses on their financial report would be viewed as anything but old information for shareholders and potential buyers of the American Express stock.

Nevertheless, the court rejected the shareholders' plea. In the court's view, decisions made by directors are normally protected under the business judgment rule. The decision by American Express may have been a bad one, but the directors could show some, albeit faulty, rationale. That is enough. The American Express board held a special meeting to weigh a potential distribution versus selling the stock at a loss and concluded the former would be the better course. Under the business judgment rule, courts do not inquire into whether a decision was substantively a good one or not. Regardless of American Express' potentially faulty reasoning, the court only looked to the process of the decision and American Express appeared to consider all of its options. Thus, the most important feature of BJR review is a review of process or procedure. If the process the board of directors took to arrive at the decision was a reasonable one or taken in good faith, then the decision is protected by the business judgment rule.

B. Statutory Director Protections

Operating along side the business judgment rule, directors are also protected by several state statutes. The problem in the view of some state legislatures is that the business judgment rule is largely a product of judge-made common law. Sure, as mentioned, some state legislatures have tried to codify the business judgment rule by statute. However, most of the relevant interpretations have read such statutes as supplementing, rather than supplanting, the common law rule of BJR.

As a consequence perhaps, in addition to the protection that the common law BJR affords directors, states have enacted a series of other statutory protections that insulate directors from liability for their decisions. For instance, corporate codes protect directors who make uninformed decisions, if in making such decisions it could be shown that the directors relied on reports of experts. Additionally, state corporate law provides that the firm may purchase insurance that protects director decision-making and may indemnify directors in certain cases of alleged errant decision-making. Lastly, in keeping with the notion that corporate law is a set of default rules that stakeholders can contract around, some state statute provides that firms can privately modify the directors' obligation under the duty of care.

1. Expert Reports

First, in Delaware and other states, the corporate code provides that directors are "fully protected" for decision-making in which they rely on expert reports. DEL. CODE ANN. tit. 8, § 141(e) (1999). Similarly, under the Model Business Corporation Act, directors are protected in cases in which they rely on the "reports" of experts. MODEL BUS. CORP. ACT § 8.30(f) (2005). In pertinent part, Delaware's code provides that ignorant directors may still retain business judgment rule protection if they rely on expert reports:

> A member of the board of directors, or a member of any committee designated by the board of directors, shall, in the performance of such member's duties, be fully protected in relying in good faith upon the records of the corporation and upon such information, opinions, reports or statements presented to the corporation by any of the corporation's officers or employees, or committees of the board of directors, or by any other person as to matters the member reasonably believes are within such other person's professional or expert competence and who has been selected with reasonable care by or on behalf of the corporation.

DEL. CODE ANN. tit. 8, § 141(e) (1999).

For background, consider that in many cases the board makes decisions on matters that no member of the board has the competence to address without aid. The board may be called on to decide whether to transfer taxable assets off shore even though no member of the board has legal training, for instance. Or, the board may have to decide how much to pay a new chief executive even though no board members has superior knowledge of current CEO salaries. Even in cases where the board decision seems to be completely devoid of serious thinking, the business judgment rule may still operate to protect director decisions if the board relies on an expert to reach its decision. In the examples just mentioned, for instance, the board might qualify for protection by retaining a tax attorney to draft an opinion of the legality of the off-shoring or a compensation expert to opine on a reasonable salary-benefit package. Thus, business judgment rule protection, as the next case shows, extends to cases in which the board takes a decision in reliance on a report created by an outside expert. Further, the board can also reasonably rely on reports generated internally by managers or other executives.

In *Brehm v. Eisner*, one of the early shots in a series of cases about the same events, shareholders exploded when Disney paid out the equivalent of $140 million in severance to its disaffected former company President, Michael Ovitz. 746 A.2d 244 (Del. 2000). The litigation would span many years and create more than one important Delaware Supreme Court precedent.

The severance package was part of a 5-year employment agreement that Disney negotiated with Mr. Ovitz. Among other provisions, the agreement provided that Disney could only avoid triggering a payout under the severance agreement if Ovitz committed "gross negligence." In particular, in the event of a "no-fault" termination, Ovitz would receive his full five-year salary, three million shares of Disney at a discount price, and $7.5 million per year remaining under the employment term. Not only was the package rich in compensation, the terms of the compensation were also unusually lop-sided. Under the terms of the agreement, Mr. Ovitz would get severance regardless of the terms of his departure and without regard to how long he was employed by Disney.

As it turns out, Ovitz was a poor fit for Disney. According to the plaintiff's complaint, before Ovitz was at the company for even a year he had circulated a letter to Disney's mercurial CEO, Michael Eisner, noting his intent to leave the company. Eisner recommended to the board that Ovitz be terminated without fault and thus be eligible for the severance package. Angered, the shareholders argued that Disney's board set the stage for Ovitz to find a way to get terminated and trigger the severance payout. In their view, the employment agreement set up a perverse scenario where Ovitz would receive significantly more compensation from not working for Disney than from working for the firm. Among their allegations, the shareholders complained that the Disney board had made an uninformed decision, because they failed to make several simple calculations that would have made them aware of the extravagant payout to Ovitz. More importantly, the court suggested that even if the board was uninformed about the unusual nature of the severance provision, they would still be entitled to protection under the business judgment rule, because the board retained a compensation expert and sought advice. The court agreed that the board was justified in relying on the expert's advice and that it was the expert, not the board, who failed to make the relevant calculations.

Thus, as in Delaware, several states have provided explicit director protections when there is evidence that they relied on the advice of an expert. This is a rather broad protection, as the board can rely on reports of both outsider experts, like the compensation consultant in *Disney*, and insiders who are experts, like the CFO of the firm who from time to time may present financial reports to the board. In some sense, this statutory protection may be costly on the firm, without always resulting in a commensurate benefit. For instance, some expert opinions may be suspect, particularly if the expert desires a long-term relationship with the firm. Keep in mind also that outside experts cost money. Because directors are insulated when they rely on expert reports and the directors do not directly pay for these experts themselves, they may be inclined to over-hire experts. In fact, the board may make some hires to opine on matters that are not necessarily outside of the board's own expertise. In these cases, the expert reports merely reaffirm what the board of directors had already decided.

Still, even in cases in which the board relies on a so-called expert report, such reliance may be unwarranted and unreasonable. In these cases, the board will not be able to claim protection on the basis of expert advice. More specifically, consider Delaware's expert report protection statute, which limits reliance to cases in which the director "reasonably believes [it is] within such other person's professional or expert competence and who has been selected with reasonable care by or on behalf of the corporation." DEL. CODE ANN. tit. 8, § 141(e) (1999). Thus, these cases usually come down to two important issues related to the reliance on expert advice in a case of alleged director liability: (1) whether the selection of the expert is reasonable and (2) whether it is inappropriate for the board to rely on the advice of an expert if the advice is not within the expert's field.

2. Indemnification and Insurance

Second, state corporate codes provide that the corporation may offer to insure and indemnify its directors in the event of a suit for errant decision-making. *See, e.g.,* DEL. CODE ANN. tit. 8, § 145(a)-(b) (1999). For starters, state statutes provide that corporations may (and, in some cases, *must*) give director indemnification or reimbursements for reasonable expenses in defending some suits. As alluded, some indemnification protections corporations are mandatory. For instance, under Delaware law and the MBCA, corporations are required to reimburse directors for expenses incurred in defending a lawsuit, if the director is "wholly" successful on the merits or other procedural basis. DEL. CODE ANN. tit. 8, § 145(c) (1999); MODEL BUS. CORP. ACT § 8.52 (2005). Additionally, state statutes contemplate voluntary indemnification. If the corporation promises to voluntarily indemnify, it will pay the legal fees for officer acts, if such acts were on behalf of the corporation. Here, though, there are exceptions to the firm's ability to voluntarily indemnify. Significantly, for instance, in Delaware the board may only indemnify if the director has "acted in good faith and in a manner ... reasonably believe[d] to be ... in the interests of the corporation." *See, e.g.,* DEL. CODE ANN. tit. 8, § 145(a)-(b) (1999). Under the MBCA, voluntary indemnification is not available if the director has intentionally misled the corporation. *See* MODEL BUS. CORP. ACT § 2.02(b)(5) (2005).

Additionally, state statutes provide that corporations may protect directors prospectively from the specter of suits by buying insurance on the director's behalf. In this case, the corporate entity agrees to pay the premiums for directors' and officers' insurance, which would protect directors in the event of a suit for liability. All told, this protection from liability also, it stands to reason, encourages risk-taking by members of the board of directors. That is, directors are insulated from the hazards of suit. Normally, because insurance premiums are function of the insurers' belief of future misconduct, it is likely that rising insurance premiums would deter overly risky behavior. However, as directors do not pay the insurance premiums themselves, rising premiums might do little to check overly risky behavior. Further, other research shows that insurance companies do little to police potential corporate misconduct and firm governance practices. *See* Tom Baker & Sean Griffith, *The Missing Monitor in Corporate Governance: The Directors' & Officers' Liability Insurer*, 95 GEO. L.J. 1795, 1798–99 (2007).

The right to buy director and officer insurance (D & O insurance) to protect directors is more expansive than the power to indemnify:

> A corporation shall have the power to purchase and maintain insurance on behalf of any person who is or was a director, officer, employee or agent of the corporation … against any liability asserted against such person and incurred by such person in any such capacity, arising out of such person's status as such, *whether or not the corporation would have the power to indemnify* such person against such liability under this section.

DEL. CODE ANN. tit. 8, § 145(g) (1999) (emphasis supplied). The analogous provision under the MBCA is virtually identical. Thus, depending on the insurance policy, corporate-purchased D & O insurance might protect the directors regardless of whether they acted in good faith. The point is that corporations have sweeping power under state statute to buy director and officer insurance on their fiduciaries' behalf. As a consequence perhaps, the vast majority of firms, according to recent research, have D & O Insurance for their directors. *See* Baker & Griffith, *supra* at 1821. Because of insurance or indemnification, directors would rarely pay their own expenses to defend against a suit for an errant decision.

3. Exculpatory Charter Provisions

Third, some state statutes provide that corporations can modify their charter such that directors are not liable for misjudgments in breach of fiduciary duty of care. Thus, corporations in these states can "opt out" or modify by affirmative act the common law fiduciary duty of care to fit their institutional preferences. In particular, a year after *Van Gorkom* (discussed *infra*), the Delaware legislature enacted 102(b)(7), which permitted corporations to adopt charter provisions absolving directors of liability:

> A provision eliminating or limiting the personal liability of a director to the corporation or its stockholders for monetary damages for breach of fiduciary duty as a director, provided that such provision shall not eliminate or limit the liability of a director: (i) for any breach of the directors' duty of loyalty to the corporation or its stockholders; (ii) for acts or omissions not in good faith or which involve intentional misconduct or a knowing violation of law; (iii) under section 174 of this title; or (iv) for any transaction from which the director derived an improper personal benefit.

DEL. CODE ANN. tit. 8, § 102(b)(7) (1999). However, corporate stakeholders are not completely without legal recourse for director error. Interestingly, for instance, these provisions appear only to apply to claims for damages. Shareholders can still bring suit to enjoin decisions, even when the corporate entity has passed a liability waiver. Further, Delaware's exculpatory provision does not eliminate violations of the duty of loyalty or the obligation of good faith. Because the duty of loyalty and good faith are matters largely determined on a case-by-case basis, these exceptions are significant. In this way, the Delaware state legislature has implicitly given Delaware courts room to continue to police a wide range of behaviors.

The comparable provision under the MBCA is even stronger in favor of protecting board members. It provides that firms may adopt a charter provision that eliminates liability, excepting only circumstances of theft and intentional misconduct:

> [The corporate articles may include] a provision eliminating or limiting liability of a director the corporation or its shareholders for money damages for any action taken, or any failure to take any action, as a director, except liability for (A) the amount of a financial benefit received by a director to which he is not entitled; (B) an intentional infliction of harm on the corporation or the shareholders; (C) a violation of section 8.33; or (D) an intentional violation of criminal law....

MODEL BUS. CORP. ACT § 2.02(4) (2005).

Following Delaware's lead, and frequently the MBCA template, the vast majority of states also have provisions permitting the corporate entity to eliminate or modify the director's duty of care. A few states have gone even further than the protections provided by Delaware and the MBCA. In some of these states, statutes provide that directors are automatically protected in cases of mistakes. Director liability is only possible if the corporation elects to "opt in." Thus, in these states, liability for slipshod decision-making would only be possible if the corporate charter explicitly provided so. For instance, compare the structure of the relevant statute from Ohio:

> A director shall be liable in damages for any action that the director takes or fails to take as a director only if it is proved by clear and convincing evidence in a court of competent jurisdiction that the director's action or failure to act involved an act or omission undertaken with deliberate intent to cause injury to the corporation or undertaken with reckless disregard for the best interests of the corporation.... This division does not apply if, and only to the extent that, at the time of a director's act or omission that is the subject of the complaint, the articles or the regulations of the corporation state by specific reference to this division that the provisions of this division do not apply to the corporation.

OHIO REV. CODE ANN. § 1701.59(D) (2008). Thus, in Ohio, directors are exempted for liability for misjudgment unless they deliberately attempted to create losses for the corporate entity. Corporations desiring a higher standard would have to contract around Ohio's rule.

C. Exceptions to the Business Judgment Rule

Thus, as has been shown, directors are insulated from liability by a wide-range of protections, from the common law business judgment rule to a phalanx of additional state statutory protections. However, the common law BJR protection is not without exceptions. First, in some cases directors have been liable for failing to establish some modicum of oversight to prevent insider misconduct. Second, the business judgment rule does not apply when directors fail to make an attempt to inform themselves before making critical decisions for the firm. Third, the directors may not be protected under BJR if their decision was irrational or wasteful. Fourth, the business judgment rule protection might not apply in cases in which the directors have encouraged unlawful activity. *See, e.g.*, AMERICAN LAW INSTITUTE, *supra* § 4.01(c). In cases in which one of the aforementioned exception applies, the presumption of good faith and informed decision-making that arises under the BJR is shattered.

1. Failure of Oversight

First, if the board wants to rely on BJR protection, the board of directors should create some mechanism for overseeing the firm's operations. *See, e.g.,* Model Bus. Corp. Act §8.31(a)(2)(iv) (2005). Depending on the size of the firm and the complexity of its operation, the system of oversight need not necessarily be elaborate. But, the point is the board cannot shrug off its duty to monitor on-goings at the firm. The theory here is that if a system of oversight is in place, even if it is a very rudimentary one, wrongdoing can be reported up-the-chain to management and, ultimately, to the board. Significantly though, establishing a mechanism for oversight, by itself, is not enough to warrant BJR protection. In addition, directors have to act when they uncover reasonable grounds to suspect misconduct. When directors fail to exercise any oversight, as in *Francis v. United Jersey Bank*, they are not protected by the business judgment rule.

In *Francis*, two directors of a family-held re-insurance brokerage had "loaned" themselves more than $12 million of corporate funds. 432 A.2d 814 (N.J. 1981). The third director, Pritchard, had no idea about the misdirected funds. When the company became insolvent, several of its creditors argued that they should be able to recover against Ms. Pritchard for her failure to monitor the other directors, who were also her sons. It turns out that Ms. Pritchard was a director in name only. She had inherited her stake in the company from her husband. But, she read none of the company's financial reports and had little idea what the company did. More troubling perhaps, her late husband had warned her about her cunning sons. According to the court, directors have a duty to monitor, broadly speaking, the activities of the firms on whose boards they sit:

> Directors may not shut their eyes to corporate misconduct and then claim that because they did not see the misconduct, they did not have a duty to look. The sentinel asleep at his post contributes nothing to the enterprise he is charged to protect.

432 A.2d at 822. The court in *Francis* makes three practical points regarding liability for directors of corporations.

First, recall that in *Francis* the court is troubled by the fact that the derelict director failed to review financial reports of the company, which would have put her on notice of the wrongdoing. As a preliminary matter, therefore, the case seems to stand for the proposition that directors must regularly review financial statements and stay reasonably informed of firm activities. The ALI's *Principles of Corporate Governance* back this up, providing that a director has fulfilled the obligation of due care only if such manager is "informed with respect to the subject of the business judgment to the extent the director or officer reasonably believes to be appropriate under the circumstances ..." AMERICAN LAW INSTITUTE, *supra* § 4.01(c)(2). Directors should have a rudimentary understanding of the activities undertaken by the company. In *Francis*, the director had little idea of the nature of the re-insurance business.

Second, according to the court in *Francis*, the misconduct should be a "substantial factor in producing the harm." 432 A.2d at 829. Thus, another important practical point of the case is that, as in any damages case, even when the business judgment rule does not apply, directors would only be liable if their conduct created ascertainable losses for the firm. Director decisions not entitled to the business judgment rule do not always or necessarily create such losses. The director's action would have to be the proximate cause of such damages. *See, e.g.*, MODEL BUS. CORP. ACT § 8.31(b) (2005).

Most importantly though is the third takeaway from the opinion in *Francis*, the obligation not only to just monitor, but also to police. The final point covers the board's duty to monitor and exercise some policing functions over operations if they discover that something is amiss. For instance, in *Francis*, if something is awry in those statements, the court suggests that directors have a duty to make further inquiry, to object to any discovered misconduct, to attempt to prevent the misconduct, and perhaps even resign in protest. The court found that Ms. Pritchard would have easily discovered the misconduct if she had reviewed the financial statements. Thus, according to the court, she could have stopped the theft and, because she did not, she breached her duty:

> When financial statements demonstrate that insiders are bleeding a corporation to death, a director should notice and try to stanch the flow of blood ... [Ms. Pritchard's] obligation included reading and understanding financial statements, and making reasonable attempts at detection and prevention of the illegal conduct of other officers and directors.

432 A.2d at 826. This oversight function is not just an obligation of smaller firms, like the closely-held family business described in *Francis*. As the opinion in the next case shows, even in large and complex corporations, directors have a similar obligation.

Although the directors were not found to be personally liable, *In Re Caremark* has also been read to stand for a similar proposition that the duty of care requires directors to monitor (or establish a mechanism for monitoring) the firm's operations for misconduct. In that case, several employees of the large, 7,000-employee health care company violated several federal and state laws. 698 A.2d 959 (Del. Ch. 1996). Many of Caremark's patients were insured by

Medicare and Medicaid. The employees, in short, contracted with physicians and other healthcare providers to provide patient referrals to the company. In exchange the providers were given lucrative "consulting" agreements with the company. The government alleged that the arrangement was a kick-back scheme in violation of the anti-referral payments law under Medicare. As a result of the misconduct, Caremark ultimately paid $250 million in fines penalties to regulators and other injured parties. The shareholders filed suit arguing that the board of directors breached their fiduciary duty of care by letting the lawbreaking go on unchecked. The shareholders in *Caremark* submitted that the directors had failed to act to staunch the criminal activity and as a result the company was forced to pay fines. The parties settled and the court approved the settlement.

More important though, the *Caremark* court articulated the standard for recovery against the individual board of directors in a case of the board's failure of oversight and follow-up inquiry. According to the court, directors (and other officers) are only liable in cases in which they have reason to suspect wrong-doing and fail to act. However, the court also notes that directors cannot stick their head in the sand. Rather, directors have to erect reasonable procedures for reporting wrong-doing or receiving information that would put one on awares of wrongdoing. At one point, the court asks and immediately answers its own rhetorical call for board monitoring procedures:

> Can it be said today that, absent some ground giving rise to suspicion of violation of law, corporate directors have no duty to assure that a corporate information gathering and reporting system exists which represents a good faith attempt to provide senior management and the Board with information respecting material acts, events or conditions within the corporation, including compliance with applicable statutes and regulations? I certainly do not believe so.

698 A.2d at 969.

In summary, directors must exert some reasonable effort to monitor the activities of the corporation and put them in a position to learn of wrongdoing. This oversight function does not require directors to uncover every potential infraction. However, to fulfill the oversight function properly, directors that uncover wrongdoing (or reason to suspect wrongdoing) must attempt to make inquiry and, possibly, see that the misconduct ends. For instance, the ALI *Principles of Corporate Governance* makes the point that the duty of care's obligation to monitor requires that directors have, as some scholars have put it, a "duty of inquiry":

The duty [of care] includes the obligation to make, or cause to be made, an inquiry when, but only when, the circumstances would alert a reasonable director or officer to the need therefore. The extent of such an inquiry shall be such as the director or officer reasonably believes to be necessary.

AMERICAN LAW INSTITUTE, *supra* § 4.01(a)(1); *see also, e.g.*, Melvin Eisenberg, *The Divergence of Standards of Conduct and Standards of Review in Corporate Law*, 62 FORDHAM L. REV. 437, 440 (1993). It is conceivable that if a director cannot end the misconduct, she might have no other reasonable choice but to resign her directorship.

This exception for failure of oversight might create positive incentives for members of the board of directors to curb misconduct by their underlings at the firm. That is, the exception seems to give plaintiffs an avenue to go directly after the members of the board in instances when the board fails to uncover obvious wrongdoing. This likely has some affect on governance structures, at least at bigger firms. Although directors at the larger firms are almost certainly protected by D & O insurance, there is still the prospect, no matter how small, that a lawsuit could exceed the policy limits. As a result, directors at these firms may at least set up the pretense of legal compliance programs in order to head-off wrongdoing and avoid this exception. At smaller firms, particularly those without expansive D & O insurance, the exception for failure of oversight might, again, encourage positive behavior and good corporate governance. At smaller firms, a sophisticated legal compliance program may be infeasible, but board members at these firms may still have good incentives to take a careful eye to financial reports and signs of wrongdoing.

2. Uninformed Decision-Making

Second, in rare cases courts have held that a decision was so hastily made and ungrounded in facts that it does not deserve BJR protection. However, the standard of proof that plaintiffs are required to meet for showing that the director has failed to adequately inform herself is a high one. Furthermore, courts and state legislatures have retreated significantly from imposing liability under this exception. Nevertheless, directors do have a duty to have at least a reasonable amount of information prior to making a decision, as the next case shows.

Among many corporate law scholars, *Smith v. Van Gorkom* is one of the most reviled court opinions. 488 A.2d 858 (Del. 1985). Perhaps because of the revulsion it engenders, the case is also one of the most widely-discussed analysis of the duty of care in corporate law. In the case, shareholders sued the directors after they had agreed to sell the company, a rail car leasing concern. The shareholder-defendants accused the directors of acting rashly, failing to make an informed decision, and selling the firm on the cheap.

As it turns out the deal to sell Trans Union was done relatively quickly, though not quite on the back of an envelope. The CEO and Board Chairman of Trans Union, Jerome Van Gorkom and other executives contemplated selling the company in a leveraged buy-out. He contacted a personal friend Jay Pritzker who is described as a "well-known takeover specialist" regarding the sale of the company. Although he had not met with most of the members of the board, Van Gorkom offered to sell the company to Pritzker for $55/share or $690 million. A mere five days later, Pritzker had agreed to buy the company at $55 a share. The sale of the company hinged on obtaining board approval. Thus, Pritzker's offer to buy would stay open three days to get the necessary approval from the board. Senior management objected to the sale.

At the meeting, the board received no information about how the $55 a share figure was determined. Yet, the board of Trans Union, after a brief, twenty minute presentation by Van Gorkom and without reviewing any merger documents, agreed to sell the company. The only caveat was that the firm would have 90 days to shop for a better offer. The merger agreement was signed, although neither Van Gorkom "nor any other director read the agreement prior to its signing and delivery to Pritzker." 488 A.2d at 869.

In a sweeping decision, the court held that the directors were not entitled to protection under the business judgment rule. According to the court, the board's acceptance of the offer of $55 a share without gathering more information was "at a minimum" grossly negligent:

> As has been noted, the Board based its September 20 decision to approve the cash-out merger primarily on Van Gorkom's representations. None of the directors, other than Van Gorkom and Chelberg, had any prior knowledge that the purpose of the meeting was to propose a cash-out merger of Trans Union. No members of Senior Management were present other than Chelberg, Romans and Peterson; and the latter two had only learned of the proposed sale an hour earlier....

488 A.2d at 874. The court goes on to say the following:

> Without any documents before them concerning the proposed transaction, the members of the Board were required to rely entirely upon Van Gorkom's 20-minute oral presentation of the proposal. No written summary of the terms of the merger was presented; the directors

were given no documentation to support the adequacy of the $55 price per share for sale of the Company; and the Board had before it nothing more than Van Gorkom's statement of his understanding of the substance of an agreement which he admittedly had never read, nor which any member of the Board had ever seen.

Id. Furthermore, the court found incredulous the notion that Van Gorkom's oral presentation was the equivalent of a "report" that the directors were entitled to rely on. Van Gorkom's presentation, according to the court, was not based on any substantive study of the value of the company or the terms of the sale. Thus, in the court's view the decision was taken too quickly without the directors having access or requesting access to all relevant information.

Thus, the holding in *Van Gorkom* (and some other cases), can be read to suggest that directors are not entitled to the business judgment rule, unless there is some evidence that they were reasonably informed prior to taking the decision in question. Further, in cases where the directors were uninformed, the directors are liable for gross negligence:

> The directors (1) did not adequately inform themselves as to Van Gorkom's role in forcing the "sale" of the Company and in establishing the per share purchase price; (2) were uninformed as to the intrinsic value of the Company; and (3) given these circumstances, at a minimum, were grossly negligent in approving the "sale" of the Company upon two hours consideration, without prior notice, and without the exigency of a crisis or emergency.

488 A.2d at 874. Unsurprisingly, one of the effects of the *Van Gorkom* decision was to increase the legal and professional fees that firms could expect to pay in an end-of-period transaction (*e.g.*, sales of company assets or statutory merger). After *Van Gorkom*, board of directors made sure to give the appearance, if not the substance, of making an informed decision, even if appearances are costly to the corporate treasury. For instance, after *Van Gorkom*, firms were likely advised to hold longer board meetings to consider all options, in contrast to the short presentation noted in *Van Gorkom*. No doubt, these longer board meetings left the firm with larger legal fees for counsel support at these meetings, in addition to support staff, director fees, and other related costs. Further, after the decision in *Van Gorkom*, firms were more likely to retain investment banks and other valuation experts to render an opinion on value, so as to avoid the appearance (and perhaps reality) that the decision was made in haste.

As can be expected, the decision in *Van Gorkom* spawned significant legislative action and a flood of writing, much of it irritated by the court's reasoning. As a result of *Van Gorkom* the Delaware legislature passed legislation that permitted firms to include exculpatory provisions, which effectively gave the firms the opportunity to modify privately the duty of care expected of directors. Nevertheless, the *Van Gorkom* precedent is still routinely used by plaintiffs to avoid BJR protection on the grounds that the board took an uninformed decision.

3. Irrational and Wasteful Decisions

A waning third exception to the business judgment rule occurs in cases in which the board of director's decision can be shown to have no relationship to the firm's interest. Such decisions are wasteful, irrational, or otherwise outside of the firm's interests. According to one Delaware court, there is a breach of the duty of care when the directors enter into "an exchange that is so one-sided that no business person of ordinary, sound judgment could conclude that the corporation has received adequate consideration." *In re Walt Disney Co. Derivative Litig.*, 731 A.2d 342, 362 (Del. Ch. 1998). Thus, transactions that are particularly one-sided and wasteful might breach the director's duty of care. However, only in cases where the directors have essentially given away firm assets or the transaction is utterly unconscionable will the shareholder be able to chink business judgment rule protection.

Consider the following hypothetical: The directors approve a decision to donate anonymously a significant portion of the firm's assets to charity. Such a decision may not have the protection of the business judgment rule, unless it can be shown to have at least a marginal relationship with the interest of the firm. According to the vast majority of courts, a director's decision is protected by the business judgment rule, if the decision has a rational basis. Courts have routinely held that a rational basis can be almost any reason. But, yet, there must be *some* reason connected to an interest of the firm. Decision-makers cannot give away firm assets or take decisions that are not remotely in the firm's interests. Significantly, for example, the ALI *Principles* provide that a decision should only be protected under the business judgment rule if the manager "rationally believes [the decision] is in the best interest of the corporation." AMERICAN LAW INSTITUTE, *supra* § 4.01(a). Thus, although unlikely, directors can be held accountable when the decision bears no relationship to firm interests.

Such cases, however, are few and far between. Like with other concepts, it is very difficult for a decision to be overturned because it failed this rational basis test. Thus, this showing is almost impossible to make, since the vast majority of decisions can be linked to some corporate interest. Recall *Brehm*, the case where shareholders complained after the company agreed to a large severance package for the under-performing company president, Ovitz. The shareholders in that case also claimed that the decision of the board should not be protected because it was wasteful and not rationally related to an interest of Disney. In typical fashion in cases alleging waste, however, the court refused to adopt the shareholder's view. According to the court in *Brehm*, there was at least some basis for the extravagant pay package: competition for hot Hollywood talent at the time of the hiring decision. More to the point, the court noted the strong presumption in favor of protecting board decision under the business judgment rule. According to the court, director deference is paramount: "Courts do not measure, weigh, or quantify directors' judgment. We do not even decide if they are reasonable in this context ... Irrationality is the outer limit of the business judgment rule." 746 A.2d at 264. Thus, even in cases likely *Brehm*, defendants can always come up with some basis for their decision and courts are unlikely to find waste or irrationality.

Additionally, what types of decisions are in the firm's interest has been broadly defined by other state statutes. For instance, the vast majority of the states have "stakeholder" or "constituency" statutes that expressly permit the board of directors to consider the consequences of their decisions on other interest groups, like employees, communities, and others with a stake in the corporation. *See, e.g.,* N.Y. BUS. CORP. LAW §717(b) (2003). In states that have adopted stakeholder statutes, like New York, the board still retains business judgment rule protection, even though the decision might be taken with an eye toward helping one of the enumerated classes of non-shareholder stakeholders. Notably, though, Delaware, the site of a significant number of incorporations, has not approved a stakeholder statute.

Nevertheless, in extremely rare cases, in theory it is possible that complainants will be able make this showing. While the complaining shareholders in the next case do not go after the directors directly, it is still as good of an example as any of the type of scenario where a court discusses what kind of board decisions are not related to the firm's interest. As will be seen, it helps a great deal if the decision-makers themselves admit that the decision is motivated by interests not related to the business enterprise.

In the early part of the twentieth century, the Dodge brothers would found an automobile company that today still represents an important brand. *Dodge v. Ford Motor*, 170 N.W. 668 (Mich. 1919). But, before their company would get off the ground they were among the earliest investors in the Ford Motor Company, founded by that company's namesake, Henry Ford. Henry Ford's manufacturing genius set the stage for a company that was able to generate terrific profits for himself and his earliest investors, like the Dodge Brothers. During the relevant period, Ford had made regular distributions of several million dollars and was sitting on a chest of more than $50 million cash. However, Ford, it turns out was as generous as he was business-savvy. In 1916, Ford, the majority shareholder, decreed that company profits should be plowed back into the company operations, not distributed to shareholders. His reasoning appeared to be that he wanted to build a new manufacturing plant and, more important, lower the price of vehicles, so that all could enjoy the thrill and convenience of driving the company product. Mr. Ford is reported as saying, for instance, that "[m]y ambition ... is to employ still more men, to spread the benefits of this industrial system to the greatest possible number, to help them build up their lives and their homes. To do this we are putting the greatest share of our profits back into the business." 170 N.W. at 671. Dividends to shareholders would be drastically reduced, according to Mr. Ford, indefinitely.

Ford's munificence ran aground when the Dodge Brothers, who owned 10% of the common stock, demanded that profits be distributed to investors, not passed around to others. The Dodge Brothers sued. The court did not agree that it should second-guess the decision of the board to expand its operations by building the plant. However, the court held that in light of Henry Ford comments, the company could not withhold profits strictly to enrich the lives of others. Although the court agreed that a company can take on charitable objectives, it cannot completely supplant its business objectives for charitable ones:

> The difference between an incidental humanitarian expenditure of corporate funds for the benefit of the employees, like the building of a hospital for their use and the employment of agencies for the betterment of their condition, and a general purpose and plan to benefit mankind at the expense of others, is obvious. There should be no confusion (of which there is evidence) of the duties which Mr. Ford conceives that he and the stockholders owe to the general public and the duties which in law he and his codirectors owe to protecting minority stockholders. A business corporation is organized and carried on primarily for the profit of the stockholders. The powers of the directors are to be employed for that end. The discretion of directors is to be exercised in the choice of means to attain that end, and does not extend to a change in the end itself, to the reduction of profits, or to the nondistribution of profits among stockholders in order to devote them to other purposes.

170 N.W. at 684. Notably, the court in *Dodge* held that the objective of corporations is to generate profits for its shareholders. Thus, on the one hand, the decision in *Dodge* can be viewed as an expansion of the business judgment rule. That is, the court appears to reach the substance of Ford's decision not

to make a dividend, new ground under the traditional common law rules of deference. However, probably a fairer read of the case is that it creates a narrow exception to the presumption of integrity in director decision-making for cases in which the decision-makers refuse to evaluate the range of options and take an irrational decision, which they admitted had no business purpose whatsoever. These cases are few and far between, to say the least. Even in *Dodge*, the language of the opinion would likely have been markedly different, if the case were decided today, after the advent of stakeholder statutes that broadly define firm interest.

4. Law-Breaking

Fourth, a director may forfeit business judgment protection if she takes a decision that violates the law. For instance, under Delaware statutes and the MBCA, a corporation cannot agree to modify the duty of care to exclude law-breaking or intentional misconduct. *See, e.g.*, DEL. CODE ANN. tit. C (1999); MODEL BUS. CORP. ACT § 2.02(b)(5) (2005). Such a rule makes sense because the exception permits shareholders to act as private law enforcers and bring suit in cases in which the directors break laws. This type of shareholder activity serves both a private and public interest. Shareholder suits against directors might stop shenanigans that could get the firm into jeopardy with public authorities that might exact fines and create devastating negative publicity regarding the misconduct. Shareholder suits to stop law-breaking, of course, also serve a public function in ensuring that directors follow the rule of the law.

In *Miller v. AT&T*, for instance, shareholders brought suit claiming that AT&T's directors had been derelict in failing to collect on a large unpaid account of the Democratic National Committee (DNC). 507 F.2d 759 (3d Cir. 1974). As it turns out, AT&T had provided $1.5 million in phone services for the DNC during the 1968 Democratic convention. At the time of the complaint, the bill was over 4 years old and the plaintiffs alleged that the failure to collect amounted to an illegal contribution to a political entity. The court noted that normally a decision on whether to collect on an account is presumed to be within director discretion under the business judgment rule. However, the court opined that such protections have no currency in cases in which the decision is alleged to be unlawful, as the plaintiff complained AT&T's "donation" to the DNC might have been. In the end, this exception is not as broad-sweeping as it might appear on its face. For instance, under both Delaware's codes and the MBCA, directors are only liable if they *knowingly* or *intentionally* violate the law. This means that directors can have a good faith belief that their decisions are lawful and this exception would not apply.

D. Obligation of Good Faith

Finally, it appears from recent cases and a reasonable parsing of corporate statutes that directors may have an obligation, of emerging importance, to perform their duties in good faith. The contours of the duty of good faith are still largely inchoate. For instance, a Delaware court has aptly observed that the duty of good faith is "shrouded in the fog of ... hazy jurisprudence." *See In re Walt Disney Co. Derivative Litig.* (*Disney IV*), 907 A.2d 693, 754 (Del. Ch. 2005). Still, courts have periodically referred to a "triad" of duties that a director owes, which in addition to the duty of loyalty would include duties of care and an obligation of good faith. Thus, directors' decisions that would ordinarily appear to be violations of the duty of care may also be violations of the obligation of good faith.

In Delaware and other states, the statutory basis for the obligation of good faith is somewhat shaky and fledgling. For instance, in Delaware, no corporate statute explicitly provides stakeholders an avenue to sue directors for bad faith conduct. Yet, a review of many of the most important corporate statutes, particularly Delaware statutes, reveals a tendency for state legislatures to carve out a good faith exception. Recall that under Delaware law the corporate charter can eliminate the director's duty of care, but not eliminate liability for "acts or omissions" taken in bad faith. Further, the indemnification and insurance provisions also provide that a firm cannot insure for acts taken in bad faith. *See* DEL. CODE ANN. tit. 8, § 145 (1999).

In states that have adopted the MBCA, there seems to be even a stronger statutory basis for an action based on bad faith conduct. For one thing, although the MBCA exculpatory provision does not have a similar exception for acts taken in bad faith, the act does provide that directors shall continuously be liable for intentional misconduct. *See* MODEL BUS. CORP. ACT § 2.02(b)(5) (2005). Intentional misconduct, as interpreted by several courts, is virtually synonymous with bad faith. Also, undeer the MBCA directors are only allowed to rely on expert reports in "good faith." MODEL BUS. CORP. ACT § 8.30(a),(c),(e)(ii) (2005). Finally, if the corporate charter does not include an exculpatory provision, the MBCA provides expressly that directors are liable for breaches of bad faith. MODEL BUS. CORP. ACT § 8.31(a)(2)(i) (2005).

The *Disney* cases provide a good place to begin discussion of this obligation to make decisions in good faith. In the most recent litigation over Disney's termination and severance package for the company's former president, Ovitz, the Delaware court expounds that director decisions must also comport with the obligation of good faith. *See, e.g., Brehm v. Eisner* (*Disney V*), 906 A.2d 27 (Del. 2006); *In re Walt Disney Co. Derivative Litig.* (*Disney IV*),

906 A.2d 693 (Del. 2006). The Delaware Supreme Court in the *Disney* cases agreed with the view that directors can be liable for decision-making in bad faith.

First, the court discusses the easy case of bad faith, intentional misconduct. According to the court, bad faith conduct is manifested in cases in which the director deliberately or intentionally acts to undermine corporate interests. *Disney IV*, 907 A.2d at 755. Second, the court advises that bad faith conduct is inaction by directors in the face of a duty to act. The "conscious disregard for one's responsibilities," says the Delaware court in another *Disney* case. *Disney IV*, 907 A.2d at 755. Third, it appears from the *Disney* cases (and others) that a director's violation of the obligation of good faith is determined under a subjective standard. It is an inquiry into the directors' motivation for the decision to act or fail to act, not an objective standard. If the director believes that the decision is in the corporate interest, the act is said to be taken in good faith, regardless of whether the director's belief is objectively reasonable. For instance, imagine an unruly board with factions that are at odds with one another. If the director makes a grossly negligent decision because she is motivated by a desire to harm another faction of the board (and, thus, likely cause harm to the corporate entity), such conduct might violate the obligation.

Also important to mastering the nascent obligation of duty of good faith is the Delaware's Supreme Court opinion in *Stone v. Ritter*. 911 A.2d 362 (Del. 2006). In *Stone*, shareholders brought suit against the individual directors of a large bank for failing to prevent a money laundering scheme. The court ruled in favor of the directors. More importantly though, the *Stone* court confirmed that a director could be liable for breach of the duty of good faith. Consistent with the *Disney* cases, the court held that a director breaches the obligation of good faith anytime such director consciously disregards her obligations:

> [I]mposition of liability requires a showing that the directors knew that they were not discharging their fiduciary obligation. Where directors fail to act in the face of a known duty to act, thereby demonstrating a conscious disregard for their responsibilities, they breach their duty of loyalty by failing to discharge that fiduciary obligation in good faith.

911 A.2d at 370. Interestingly though, in *Stone* the court suggests that a breach of good faith is merely a subspecies of the duty of loyalty. As will be discussed in later chapters, usually the duty of loyalty describes activities that produce a conflict of interest (*see* Chapter 9). According to the court, to act in bad faith is tantamount to an act of disloyalty. Additionally, the *Stone* court notes recovery for bad faith would be "indirect." In other words, violations of the obligation of good faith do not appear to provide an independent basis for recovery. Instead, conduct inconsistent with the obligation of good faith might be used

in combination with a claim that a director has violated a core fiduciary duty, like, notably, the duty of loyalty. In sum, directors are also subject to an obligation of good faith. Importantly, liability for the violation of the obligation of good faith appears to be less strong than claims arising out of breach of other duties, which create an independent basis for recovery. However, the standard of conduct required under the obligation of good faith continues to evolve as courts continue to define the contours of bad faith conduct.

Checkpoints

- The standard of review of director decision-making is normally referred to as the business judgment rule, the notion that courts should not second-guess director decision, absent exceptional circumstances.

- Under the business judgment rule, one of the most important factors for reviewing courts is whether or not the board of directors has created a rational process for evaluating the various options. If so, the board's decision is almost always protected by the BJR.

- While courts defer to the decisions of the board under the business judgment rule, there are exceptions to the rule for directors who fail to provide some oversight to prevent misconduct, who fail to inform themselves before making decisions, and who make irrational or unlawful decisions.

- In addition to the presumption of deference under the business judgment rule, many states have adopted various statutes that create additional protections for board members.

- Although many of the finer nuances of the obligation of good faith are hazy, it appears from the cases that directors are subject to an obligation of good faith. Director decisions that are taken in bad faith can expose the director to liability.

Chapter 9

Fiduciary Duty of Loyalty

Roadmap

- Introduction to Duty of Loyalty
- Corporate Opportunities
- Self-Interested Transactions
- Ratification of a Self-Interested Transaction
- Rule of Entire Fairness
- Limits of the Duty of Loyalty

Directors, executives and other insiders have a duty to put the interest of the corporation above their own. A loyal director, for instance, discloses conflicts of interest, avoids competition with the firm, and uses corporate property for the firm's interests only. If an insider is on both sides of a transaction—perhaps in a role as both buyer and seller—the firm's interest might be compromised. In these instances, the insider might be tempted to pursue her own interest at the expense of the firm's. A director may fail to negotiate firmly on behalf of the firm-as-buyer in a transaction in which she has a personal interest as seller. As a result, early common law corporate cases suggest that some insiders could not enter into contracts with the corporation. Two rationales might explain this outright prohibition. Perhaps judges thought the chances that such insiders would redirect firm resources for their on private benefit too great or they thought the costs of monitoring such activity too high.

Over time, however, such transactions were permitted so long as the transaction was fair to the corporation or otherwise approved by an informed, neutral body. As a consequence, today transactions where insiders have a significant stake, so-called self-interested transactions, do not necessarily create a violation of fiduciary duty under modern corporate law. In a way, this evolution in corporate law in cases of conflicts of interest catches up with the economic realities of firm operations. That is, some interested director transactions help the firm improve value for all shareholders. For instance, directors or other insiders may have an asset, like real property, that would be advantageous for the firm to utilize. A director may own a building in a prime downtown location, which the firm could lease for retail space. Under yesteryear's rules, a firm would be effectively precluded from entering into a lease contract with its director, regardless of whether the contract may have been a lucrative one for all involved. The consequences of the old rule prohibiting insider contracting with the firm, thus, put some firms (particularly smaller firms, which relied on their insider's assets and contacts) at a disadvantage and potentially squandered opportunities to increase value to the firm.

Therefore, gradually, the question became not whether the transaction created a conflict of interest, but, rather, whether the transaction was entirely fair to the firm and its shareholders. Fairness, as always, is a tough legal nut to crack. Corporate law is no different, but legislators and courts have come up with good short-hand rules for ascertaining fairness. Briefly, the transaction is presumed to be entirely fair if approved by neutral decision-makers or otherwise shown to be fair in terms of both process and substance.

A. Introduction to Duty of Loyalty

Generally, there are two types of transactions that implicate the fiduciary duty of loyalty. First, a director could potentially violate the duty of loyalty by usurping an opportunity (called a 'corporate opportunity') that properly belongs to the firm. In these cases, the director *takes from* the firm. Accordingly, directors should not normally capitalize on lucrative opportunities that are presented to them as officials of the firm. Instead, such opportunities should be turned over to the firm, as will be discussed below. Second, a duty of loyalty violation may occur in situations where the director is on both sides of a transaction. In these cases, the director *does business with* the firm. For instance, the second type of conflict of interest occurs if a director is the controlling shareholder of a manufacturing company that supplies products to the firm for which she serves on the board of directors. The director, in the case just mentioned, is operating both as a seller and representative of the buyer.

B. Corporate Opportunities

The first type of conduct that creates potential violations of the duty of loyalty surrounds corporate opportunities. The duty of loyalty bars directors and officers of the firm from taking advantage of such opportunities, if the firm is inclined to exploit them. How such opportunities are determined is somewhat muddled. Generally, however, a corporate opportunity for which the duty of loyalty would come into play is usually defined as one that the director or senior executive only realizes because of his position on the board of directors or, if a senior executive, one that is closely related to the normal operations of the firm.

Guth v. Loft should be one of the most famous corporate law cases, because it involves one of the most iconic companies in the United States, Pepsi-Cola, and the man that built the brand, Charles Guth. 5 A.2d 503 (Del. 1939). Although today Pepsi is a successful public company, during the early years of the twentieth century the company teetered on bankruptcy. The company, then known as the National Pepsi-Cola Company, had failed to establish a national presence, like Coca-Cola, its much larger rival. The Pepsi Company was eventually forced into bankruptcy. Once in bankruptcy, Guth, the defendant, was able to scoop up the assets of Pepsi for a song and reorganized the company. For Pepsi, Guth turned out to be a godsend. He had vast experience in the beverage business and was able to help orchestrate Pepsi's development into a national brand. Guth put together a now famous media (radio) blitz and slashed the price for Pepsi cola to half of the price of a comparable Coca-Cola. Soon, revenues increased precipitously and Guth's interest had grown substantially in value.

The problem, however, was that at all times Guth was the president and director of another company, Loft, a retail soda operation. At this time, "soda" and "cola" were considered vastly different products. Among its beverage products, though, Loft outlets sold a cola drink, which was increasingly emerging as an American mainstay. In 1931, Loft began negotiating with suppliers of cola drinks, principally Coca-Cola and Pepsi. Loft's long-time supplier, Coca-Cola, had refused to negotiate and lower its product price. As the only cola producer with national brand recognition, the Coca-Cola Company had tremendous negotiating leverage. As a consequence, prior to Pepsi's bankruptcy, Loft had been negotiating with Pepsi, a regional cola alternative, to secure cola product. Around this time, Guth also began to play his ownership role in the Pepsi Company. He was, as President of Loft, effectively the buyer of cola from Pepsi and, as owner of the new Pepsi Company, effectively the seller of the same cola.

Although soda shops had their heyday, their popularity was ebbing. Loft, like other soda retailers, would soon face its own insolvency. The company sued Guth for his stake in Pepsi, which was soon worth several million dollars. In their view, Guth's connections with Pepsi were a breach of his duty of loyalty to Loft. Since Pepsi, in which Guth owned a substantial stake, sold cola to Loft, there was a conflict of interest. The more cola Pepsi sold to Loft (at ever higher

margins), the more Guth would benefit. Moreover, it turns out Guth had used
Loft company resources to finance his stake in Pepsi. Guth "borrowed" money
from Loft. Further, he relied heavily on Loft expertise to turn Pepsi around. The
Loft retail network was critical to spreading the Pepsi brand, which was pre-
viously little known. For instance, when Loft switched from Coca-Cola to
Pepsi, it took on great expense advertising the brand.

Guth made three arguments in response. First, Guth argued that the Pepsi
interest was not a corporate opportunity, because he offered it to the board
and the board rejected it. Second, Guth argued that Loft, the retailer, was in
no position to take the Pepsi interest. They were a beverage retailer, not a manufacturer. Third, Guth argued that the Pepsi turnaround was done without
the aid of the Loft. Any Loft funds were merely loans, which he had (mostly)
paid back.

The court rejected all of Guth's arguments. More specifically, the court rejected Guth's claim regarding obtaining the approval of the other directors before proceeding to buy Pepsi. According to the court, the other directors were not
independent decision-makers; they were dominated by Guth. Guth possessed
"some of the qualities of a dictator" and the other directors were "subservient"
to him. The disclosure, in other words, was made to Guth's cronies. Thus, their
approval, if true, would be meaningless. Further, the court found that Guth
would not have been afforded the Pepsi opportunity without his position on the
board of directors. For one thing, consider the timing. Guth was negotiating *on
behalf of Loft* for a better cola deal at the time Pepsi went bankrupt and the opportunity to obtain an interest in the company on the cheap came about. Further, it was Loft's financing, expertise, and retail network that put Pepsi in a
position to market itself nationally. The court reasoned that an insolvent Pepsi
would not have approached Guth if he did not have access to these Loft resources:

> Guth's abstractions of Loft's money and materials are complacently
> referred to as borrowings.... A borrower presumes a lender acting
> freely. Guth took without limit or stint from a helpless corporation,
> in violation of a statute enacted for the protection of corporations
> against such abuses, and without the knowledge or authority of the cor-
> poration's board of directors. Cunning and craft supplanted sincerity.
> Frankness gave way to concealment. He did not offer the Pepsi-Cola
> opportunity to Loft, but captured it for himself. He invested little or
> no money of his own in the venture, but commandeered for his own
> benefit and advantage the money, resources, and facilities of his cor-
> poration and the services of its officials. He thrust upon Loft the haz-
> ard, while he reaped the benefit.

5 A.2d at 515. Finally, the court reasons that the opportunity was in Loft's line of business. Viewed broadly, colas had become a "business necessity" for soda fountains. Additionally, Loft had a unique interest in the Pepsi Company. Recall that since negotiations with Coca-Cola had broken off, it was critical that Loft find a replacement supplier, like Pepsi. In *Guth*, the court laid out in clear terms that the duty that a fiduciary owes to a corporate entity was analogous to a trustee:

> A public policy, existing through the years, and derived from a profound knowledge of human characteristics and motives, has established a rule that demands of a corporate officer or director, peremptorily and inexorably, the most scrupulous observance of his duty, not only affirmatively to protect the interests of the corporation committed to his charge, but also to refrain from doing anything that would work injury to the corporation, or to deprive it of profit or advantage which his skill and ability might properly bring to it, or to enable it to make in the reasonable and lawful exercise of its powers. The rule that requires an undivided and unselfish loyalty to the corporation demands that there shall be conflict between duty and self-interest. The occasions for the determination of honesty, good faith and loyal conduct are many and varied, and no hard and fast rule can be formulated. The standard of loyalty is measured by no fixed scale.

5 A.2d at 510. Further according to the court, any opportunities, which the corporate entity has "reasonable expectancy" interest in belongs to the firm. *See Id.* at 511. Thus, the opportunity was not for Guth to usurp and properly belonged to the corporate entity. The remedy was for Guth to give up his interest in Pepsi, now worth millions, to Loft. Loft was subsequently merged with Pepsi.

The *Guth* opinion is important for several reasons. To begin with, the opinion provides a workable context for what sort of opportunities properly belong to a corporation. As mentioned, a corporate opportunity is usually any opportunity that is reasonably related to an interest of the firm or that the director or officer is privy to, because of her position as a director or officer. However, the court opinion in *Guth* is even more exacting. The court provides a four-part test for corporate opportunities: (1) conflict of interest—whether taking up the corporate opportunity creates a conflict of interest or competition with the firm; (2) financial ability—whether the firm has the financial ability to exploit the opportunity in the first place; (3) reasonable expectancy—whether the firm has a reasonable expectancy in the transaction; and (4) disclosure—whether there has been disclosure to the board.

In *Guth*, the opportunity to acquire a substantial stake in those early years of Pepsi was such an opportunity. First, the Pepsi opportunity was one that created a conflict of interest between Guth and his employer, Loft. Guth would effectively operate as "seller" on behalf of Pepsi trying to exact the highest price and as "buyer" on behalf of Loft trying to get the lowest price for cola. Second, the firm was in a financial position to exploit the opportunity. Indeed, Guth relied on the firm's financial ability to finance the transaction. Third, as the court recounts, the opportunity was in Guth's employer's line of business, since the firm was in dire need of a significant supply of cola product. The court finds that Guth only learns of the opportunity because he was on the board of a well-financed corporation, with the resources and expertise to help turn-around Pepsi. Fourth, Guth's disclosure to the board was inconsequential since the directors were dominated by Guth. That is, the point of the disclosure is to give the firm a chance to make an informed decision about whether the opportunity is a good fit for the organization. If the board of directors is co-opted, such disclosure is meaningless.

In addition, *Guth* is an important decision because it recapitulates the usual remedy in cases of a wrongful seizure of corporate opportunity, which is an extraordinary one. In such cases, the director should give up the opportunity to the corporation. As stated by the *Guth* court, it is as if the director was simply holding the opportunity in trust for the firm. Thus, the director does not get any of the benefit of the opportunity, even if the director's own personal efforts helped develop the opportunity, as Guth's efforts no doubt made Pepsi a viable company. On its face, the rule of disgorgement might seem unfair to individuals who usurp a corporate opportunity. A less draconian and perhaps fairer rule in these cases might be one that called for some split of the benefits of the opportunity. The person who develops the opportunity, albeit wrongfully, might in this view receive some of the benefit of their efforts. However, unlike the rule of disgorgement, a split-benefit rule would do little to deter taking of corporate opportunities and may create incentives for opportunity-taking. That is, those inclined to take a corporate opportunity would have little reason to pass up the opportunity and turn it over to the firm. They would calculate that they are unlikely to get caught and even if caught are will still get some of the gains of exploiting the opportunity, even if sharing is ordered.

However, directors and other insiders do not have a duty to turn over all opportunities to the firm. *Broz v. CIS* is a good example of a case where a director does not have such obligation. 673 A.2d 148 (Del. 1996). In this case, Broz served on the board of directors of cell phone provider, Cellular Information Systems or CIS. He was also the owner of another corporation engaged in a similar line of business, RFB Cellular. When Broz purchased a telephone license for RFB Cellular, some shareholders argued that he had violated his fiduciary duty as a board member to CIS. At the time of the purchase, CIS was not in a position to purchase the cell phone license. However, CIS was being eyed as a takeover target by another corporation, PriCellular. Once PriCellular had taken over CIS, it argued that Broz had breached his duty, since he knew at all times that PriCellular was primed to acquire both CIS and the license in question.

The court held that there was no violation of fiduciary duty, (partly) since Broz owned no such duty to PriCellular prior to its acquisition. Further, the *Guth* factors—expectancy; conflict of interest; ability; and disclosure—were not met. First, Broz was not required, according to the court, to present the opportunity to the board of CIS, since CIS had no expectancy interest in the transaction. CIS had just emerged from bankruptcy reorganization with strict requirements for making new purchases. Further, all the directors of CIS testified that, even if the opportunity were formally presented to the board, they would have rejected it. Second, because of the reorganization in bankruptcy the license was no longer, technically, in CIS' line of business. CIS was in the process of selling off assets, like cell phone licenses, not acquiring new ones. Third, because of the bankruptcy, CIS was not financially able to exploit the opportunity. Fourth, the court found that Broz did not create any new competition for CIS. CIS was fully aware at the time of Broz's appointment of his ownership of a competing company. The fact that Broz bid on the cellular license did not produce any inimical interest that would breach his duty to the CIS.

Importantly also, the court noted that there is no obligation of a director to make a formal presentation to the full board of every opportunity, although the court does continue to endorse formal presentation as a method of creating a *de facto* insulation from liability for breach of duty:

> The teaching of *Guth* and its progeny is that the director or officer must analyze the situation ex ante to determine whether the opportunity is one rightfully belonging to the corporation. If the director or officer believes [based on the *Guth* factors] that the corporation is not entitled to the opportunity, then he may take it for himself. Of course, presenting the opportunity to the board creates a kind of "safe harbor", which removes the specter of a *post hoc* judicial determination that the director or officer has improperly usurped a corporate opportunity.... It is not the law of Delaware that presentation to the board is a necessary prerequisite to a finding that a corporate opportunity has not been usurped.

673 A.2d at 157. *Broz* stands for the importance of turning over opportunities to the board for its consideration. The director-Broz was sure to offer the op-

portunity to CIS, which also created a basis for escaping liability. For instance, under the ALI's *Principles of Corporate Governance* a director (particularly directors also serving as officers) must usually offer corporate opportunities to the firm first. Generally, if the opportunity is properly rejected (or not promptly accepted), the director may take advantage of it. *See* AMER. LAW INST. PRINCIPLES OF CORP. GOVERNANCE § 5.05 (1992) (updated 2008). It appears that Broz attempts to make such an offer, at least informally. In *Broz*, of course, the directors whom were informally presented with the opportunity were cool on the idea. This contrasts with the facts in *Guth*, where the director merely feigns an attempt to offer the opportunity to the board of friendly directors over whom he controlled.

Additionally, *Broz* seems to create a distinction between outsiders who serve as directors and directors who are senior executives. That is, in *Broz* the director is held not to be liable partly because he is an outside director, not an officer in the corporation. This distinction is generally in line with the case law and commentary, which suggest that an outside director's duty of loyalty is more limited than senior executives or other directors who also hold senior executive roles. For instance, compare *Broz* to the holding of director liability in *Guth*, where there arguably was a heightened duty of loyalty because of Guth's dual position as director and president of Loft. Further, the comments to the ALI *Principles of Corporate Governance* provide explicitly that directors who are not senior executives are under no requirement to turn over opportunities that may be in the firm's line of business:

> Because of the importance of encouraging persons who are not employees of the corporation to serve as directors, and the likelihood that many such persons will be engaged in multiple business activities, under § 5.05 directors who are not senior executives have no obligation to offer an opportunity to the corporation simply because the opportunity is closely related to the corporation's business.

AMER. LAW INST. PRINCIPLES OF CORP. GOVERNANCE § 5.05 illus. 1. Thus, inside director's actions regarding corporate opportunities are perhaps analyzed under a tighter level of scrutiny. This makes sense, since inside directors are arguably more likely to come across an opportunity that arises solely because of their connection with the firm. Such opportunities are more distinctively firm property. Consider the beverage opportunity, for instance, presented to Mr. Guth in the last case, which arises because of his role in large soda outfit. However, outside directors are less likely to be liable for usurpation of a firm opportunity, because they likely have multiple posts and arguably, as a consequence, will come across more "opportunities." A highly rigid rule would expose them to perhaps too much liability. Plus, in this case, it would be significantly tougher for judges to distinguish between opportunities that arise out of one directorship over another.

Taken together, *Broz* and *Guth* stand for two important limits on the rule of corporate opportunities. First, directors and others may be protected from liability under the corporate opportunity doctrine by disclosing the opportunity to other members of the board. However, as the language in *Guth* demonstrates, disclosure by itself may not be enough, if the disclosure is not meaningful. Second, the case law suggests that the doctrine of corporate opportunities will be (and should be) applied differently depending on whether the director is an insider. Inside directors, that is, ought to be held to a higher standard of careful conduct with respect to such opportunities.

C. Introduction to Self-Interested Transactions

A second type of violation of the fiduciary duty of loyalty is transactions in which the director transacts business with the firm. A clear example is when the director is simultaneously "buyer" and "seller." If the director has an interest contrary to that of the firm in a particular transaction, the presumption is that the director's judgment might be tainted. Historically, directors were generally prohibited from entering into such transactions, where they were effectively representing the buyer and the seller. However, today, such transactions are generally permitted under state corporate codes, so long as they are approved by a neutral decision-making body.

As a result, today self-interested transactions are much less frequently voided. The law of self-interested transactions, as will be shown, is largely statutory. That is, statutes provide that a self-interested transaction can be approved (or disapproved) by a neutral intermediary, like disinterested, informed members of the board of directors or disinterested, informed shareholders. In cases of approval by a disinterested body, the transaction is not voided. Equally important is that if the proper procedure for ratification is followed, the decision of the board is protected by the business judgment rule, as if no conflict existed in the first place. Thus, if the correct procedure is followed, the board can "reclaim" the protection of the business judgment rule. If the business judgment rule applies, the court does not inquire into the fairness of the transaction. Instead, as always, under the business judgment rule there is a presumption that the director has made a decision in the best interests of the firm.

1. Ratification by Directors

First, the transaction may be ratified by a majority of informed, disinterested directors. If the self-interested transaction is approved by a majority of disinterested directors, the business judgment rule will apply. For instance, the MBCA provides as follows:

> Directors' action respecting a transaction is effective ... if the transaction received the affirmative vote of a majority (but no fewer than two) of those qualified directors on the board of directors or on a duly empowered committee of the board who voted on the transaction....

MODEL BUS. CORP. ACT § 8.62(a). Similarly, the Delaware Code provides as follows:

> No contract or transaction ... shall be void or voidable ... [if the] material facts as to the director's or officer's relationship or interest and as to the contract or transaction are disclosed or are known to the board of directors or the committee, and the board or committee in good faith authorizes the contract or transaction by the affirmative votes of a majority of the disinterested directors....

DEL. CODE ANN. tit. 8, § 144(a)(1). Interestingly, the director with the conflict can participate in the decision-making process. That is, although there are limits on their voting power, the interested director may cajole her colleagues and participate in discussion of the transaction. *See, e.g.,* DEL. CODE ANN. tit. 8, § 144(a).

In the case of such ratification, one of the most important questions is, which directors are in fact independent? Non-interested directors are generally those directors who do not have an interest in the transaction and who cannot be influenced unreasonably by those with an interest. In practice, the cases are somewhat mixed in resolving what that means. The relevant statutes, like the MBCA, provide some guidance:

> A lack of objectivity duty to the director's familial, financial or business relationship with, or lack of independence due to the director's domination or control by, another person having a material interest in the challenged conduct (A) which relationship ... could reasonably be expected to have affected the director's judgment respecting the challenged conduct in a manner adverse to the corporation.

MODEL BUS. CORP. ACT § 8.31(a)(2)(iii). Thus, courts would agree that director independence is undermined if a director has a financial interest in the transaction or is "dominated" by another director with such an interest. For instance, if the firm is contemplating a long-term business relationship with a new company — say, Company X — a director who also happens to be an owner of Company X is not independent. Also, relatively straightforward are cases in which the directors have a close familial relationship with someone with a financial interest in the transaction.

Less clear, however, are cases in which independence in question based on an individual's longtime service on the board, elbow-to-elbow, with a director who may have an financial interest in the transaction. Is director independence undermined by a long-standing board relationship, in other words? Such directors may arguably have an interest in their colleagues' success, which create incentives for biases. Commentators have sometimes referred to such connections as a 'structural bias.' Still, in these cases, courts are unlikely to find a reason to question independence. All told, director independence is usually a determination that centers on analysis of financial incentives and perhaps familial ties.

Recall the *Disney* cases discussed in Chapter 8. *See In Re Walt Disney Company Derivative Litigation*, 731 A.2d 342 (Del. Ch. 1998). Disney agreed to a non-fault termination for its president, Michael Ovitz, which entitled him to a "princely" severance package worth $140 million. Incensed, the shareholders sued for several breaches of fiduciary duty, including a breach of the duty of loyalty. The plaintiffs alleged that Eisner, the CEO and person most responsible for hiring Ovitz, was personally interested in a large compensation package for his underling. They argued that a larger pay package created ample justification for a similar pay package for him. More importantly, they argued that Disney's board was dominated by Eisner and board members were not independent. Thus, they could not approve the rich severance package made available to Ovitz. The court disagreed, holding that a majority of the board was not biased. Thus, the *Disney* opinion is significant, among other reasons, for articulating several factors that courts weigh in considering questions of director independence.

First, directors who are also employees of the firm are arguably less likely to be found to be independent than others. For instance, many interested director transactions involve the CEO of the firm, who also serves on the board of directors. In these cases, other directors who are employees (and subordinates) of the conflicted CEO are hard-pressed to voice dissent, which could create job risks. In *Disney*, for example, the court notes that two directors, who were also employees of Disney, might be unable to reach an unbiased decision. According to the court, as subordinates, they depended on Eisner for their careers and livelihood.

A second point is that wealthier directors are almost always viewed as independent. Courts evaluate independence based on an individual director's reliance on another for their financial well-being. Again, this point is made in the *Disney* cases. Roy Disney, who was an employee of Disney and technically a subordinate to Eisner, was held to be independent, since his family's holdings in Disney stock were worth more than $2 billion. Although technically an employee of Eisner, it was clear according to the court that Mr. Disney did not depend on Eisner to make ends meet. Thus, courts have suggested that wealthy directors are independent, even though they may be subordinates of the alleged interested director.

A third point is that independence is not put in jeopardy by dependence of director fees. That is, although a director may be dependent on his or her director fees, such payments are not thought to undermine independence. Thus, although the wealth of the director is a consideration, the dependence on director fees is not a factor. According to the court in *Disney*, if such payments were to raise the prospect of bias toward approving conflict transactions, then board membership would effectively be limited to those with extraordinary means: "to do so would be to discourage the membership on corporate boards of people of less-than extraordinary means. Such 'regular folks' would face allegations of being dominated by other board members, merely because of the relatively substantial compensation provided by the board membership compared to their outside salaries." 731 A.2d at 360.

2. Ratification by Shareholders

Second, the transaction may be ratified by a majority vote of disinterested and informed shareholders. If such ratification occurs, then the transaction is not voidable. Moreover, the directors are able to reclaim their business judgment rule protection. For example, the MBCA provides as follows:

> Shareholders' action respecting a director's conflicting interest transaction is effective ... if a majority of the votes cast by the holders of all qualified shares are in favor of the transaction after (1) notice to shareholders describing the action to be taken respecting the transaction, (2) provision to the corporation of the information ... and (3) communication to the shareholders entitled to vote on the transaction of the information that is the subject of required disclosures (to the extent the information is not known by them).

MODEL BUS. CORP. ACT § 8.63(a). In significant part, the model code provision tracks the language of Delaware's corporate code with the only noticeable difference being the reference to "good faith" in the Delaware provision:

> No contract or transaction ... shall be void or voidable ... [if the] ma-
> terial facts as to the director's or officers relationship or interest and
> as to the contract or transaction are disclosed or are known to the
> shareholders entitled to vote thereon, and the contract or transaction
> is specifically *approved in good faith* by vote of the shareholders.

DEL. CODE ANN. tit. 8, § 144(a)(2) (emphasis supplied). The shareholders voting to approve the self-interested transaction would have to be both fully informed and disinterested. To begin with, as the above-excerpt shows, shareholder
approval only works to create a safe harbor if the shareholders are fully informed. Similarly, the Delaware code provides that in such instances, voting
shareholders must be informed about "[t]he material facts as to the director's
or officer's relationship or interest ..." DEL. CODE ANN. TIT. 8, §144 (a)(2). Additionally, under statute and cases, the shareholders voting to approve should
likewise be disinterested. Ironically, notice that the statutes do not explicitly
require that the shareholders voting to approve be disinterested. Only Delaware's
provision refers to "good faith," which might be interpreted to require approval
from disinterested shareholders. Regardless of the lack of an explicit, unam-
biguous requirement of shareholder disinterest, courts interpreting the statute
have found that such shareholder approval is only effective if a majority of unbiased shareholders vote to approve.

Fleigler v. Lawrence is a case involving the sale of valuable real property from
the firm's directors to the firm. 361 A.2d 218 (Del. 1976). The board recommended the sale to the firm and the shareholders approved. When the sale was
challenged as a breach of fiduciary duty, the directors raised as a defense the
shareholder approval. The directors were also shareholders who apparently
held significant positions in the company. The shareholder approval, thus, was
unreliable because of their conflict of interest. Yet, since Delaware code technically makes no mention of "disinterested" approval, the defendants made
the argument that shareholder approval (regardless of a potential interest) is
all that is required under the relevant statute. The court rejected this argument
out of hand:

> The purported ratification by the Agau shareholders would not affect
> the burden of proof in this case because the majority of shares voted
> in favor of exercising the option were cast by defendants in their ca-
> pacity as Agau shareholders. Only about one-third of the 'disinter-
> ested' shareholders voted, and we cannot assume that such non-voting
> shareholders either approved or disapproved. Under these circum-
> stances, we cannot say that 'the entire atmosphere has been freshened'
> and that departure from the objective fairness test is permissible.

361 A.2d at 221. The court refused to give business judgment rule protection in the case even though the parties could show that the decision had been approved by a majority of shareholders. As a result, it appears that the board can only reclaim business judgment rule protection, if the conflicting transaction is approved by a majority of *disinterested*, fully informed shareholders.

D. Rule of Entire Fairness

Finally, keep in mind that the statutory ratification procedure that the firm follows might be defective for one reason or another. For instance, approval by disinterested and informed directors may be impossible, because they all may have a serious conflict of interest. Shareholder approval may be impractical because of the cost of making the required notification or because of the time it takes to get such approval. Further, in some cases the conflicting transaction involves a controlling shareholder. In these cases, it is not always enough to get the vote of a majority of disinterested, fully-informed shareholders. Under Delaware case law, the controlling shareholder is thought to have too significant an influence. *See, e.g., In Re Wheelabrator Technologies, Inc. Shareholder Litigation*, 663 A.2d 1194 (Del. Ch. 1995).

However, even in these cases, the self-interested transaction might not create liability for directors under the duty of loyalty. That is, even if a transaction creates a conflict of interest that is potentially a violation of the duty of loyalty, director liability may be limited in cases in which the director can show that the transaction was fair to the corporate entity. This is the rule of entire fairness. The MBCA, for instance, provides as follows:

> A director's conflicting interest transaction may not be enjoined, set aside, or give rise to an award of damages or other sanctions, in a proceeding by a shareholder or by or in the right of the corporation, because the director, or any person with whom or which he has a personal, economic, or other association, has an interest in the transaction, if ... the transaction, judged according to the circumstances at the time of commitment, is established to have been fair to the corporation.

MODEL BUS. CORP. ACT § 8.61(b); *see also* DEL. CODE ANN. tit. 8, § 144(a)(3).

At the end of the day, fairness is determined the courts. For instance, recall the case of *Fleigler*, where members of the board of directors approved a sale of valuable mining property owned by directors in their individual capacity to the firm. Although the court rejected the director-defendant's attempts to ratify the decision based on disinterested shareholder approval, the court ultimately approved the transaction because the transaction turned out to be fair. The court went on an extensive discussion of valuation methods, concluding that the test of entire fairness was met. Thus, unlike in other cases, the courts will undertake a detailed inquiry to ascertain whether the transaction is fair to the firm. This inquiry usually resolves both substantive and procedural aspects of fairness. The substantive element of the requirement entire fairness refers to the sufficiency of the consideration received by the firm. Thus, the firm should not overpay. Additionally, as for procedural elements, the timing of the transaction ought to also be fair.

E. General Limits of the Duty of Loyalty

As mentioned in Chapter 7, the fiduciary duty of care has largely been emaciated by the protections of the business judgment rule and other statutory protections. In contrast, courts and state legislatures have expanded the importance of the duty of loyalty. First, unlike the duty of care, in Delaware (and some other states) the duty of loyalty cannot be contracted around. *See, e.g.,* DEL. CODE ANN. tit. 8, § 102(b)(7)(i). Second, the business judgment rule, the strongest source of insulation for director liability, does not apply in cases of director interest conflicts. Third, controlling shareholders also owe a duty of loyalty to the corporate entity. Fourth, recent cases have suggested that the duty of loyalty also encompasses a broad obligation to make decisions in good faith. *See Stone v. Ritter* No. Civ. A. 1570-N, 2006 WL 302558 (Del. Ch. 2006); *see also* Chapter 8. The duty of loyalty, in this view, might create director liability in cases that would be traditionally thought of as care cases and directors protected under the business judgment rule. Arguably, therefore, the duty of loyalty is a stronger fiduciary duty and more important check against managerial misconduct than even the duty of care. Nevertheless, there are important limits to the reach of the duty of loyalty.

1. Transactions Involving All Shareholders

For instance, the duty of loyalty does not apply in cases in which the shareholders stand to gain equally from the alleged self-interested transaction. If all shareholders stand to gain equally, this establishes that there is good evidence that the transaction is intrinsically fair, as *Sinclair Oil v. Levin* shows. 280 A.2d 717 (Del. 1971). In that case, the giant international oil conglomerated, Sinclair, operated in various countries, like Canada and Paraguay, through various country-specific subsidiaries. The company operated in Venezuela through a Sinclair-affiliated company, the Sinclair Venezuelan Oil Company, known as Sin-Ven. Sinclair later created another wholly-owned subsidiary, Sinclair International, to manage its sprawling foreign operations. It was Sinclair's practice to distribute the earnings of Sin-Ven, and the other subsidiaries, up the chain to Sinclair Corp. However, Sin-Ven was not quite a wholly-owned subsidiary. Instead, Sinclair owned about 97% of Sin-Ven's stock, which gave Sinclair control of Sin-Ven and its board of directors. The other portion appears to have been held by Venezuelan locals.

Sinclair Oil Corp. Organizational Chart

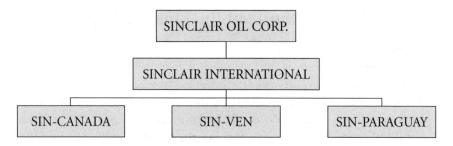

When Sinclair caused Sin-Ven to make a distribution to shareholders of the company, the holders of the minority interest complained. In their view, Sinclair had violated its fiduciary duty of loyalty to the company by forcing the distribution. The call for dividend distributions, they claimed, stunted Sin-Ven's ability to grow. Such complaints may usually be answered by the business judgment rule and the directors and the decision would not be reviewed by the courts. However, in this case, they argued that the duty of loyalty should be involved. As the largest shareholder in Sin-Ven, Sinclair was, after all, a recipient and beneficiary of the decision to call for a distribution. Thus, the plaintiffs posited that this was a self-deal.

The court, however, disagreed. According to the court, the test, in parent-subsidiary cases, is one of intrinsic fairness. The duty of loyalty would only be implicated when the parent made a distribution to itself to the exclusion of other stockholders. In the case of dividend distributions, the court noted that both Sinclair, the majority shareholder, and those holding minority interests in the firm equally benefited. In other words, minority holders also received their *pro rata* share of such distributions and thus the duty of loyalty did not apply. Consequently, one limit of the fiduciary duty of loyalty is the court's definition of self-dealing. Self dealing, as *Sinclair* demonstrates, excludes cases in which all shareholders benefit equally.

2. Trivial Transactions

Additionally, the duty of loyalty does not apply where the director's interest in the transaction is inconsequential. For the duty to apply, the director's self-interest must be significant, not trivial or *de minimus*. In addition to having a significant stake, the director's interest usually has to be a financial one. As mentioned previously, financial interest can be based on an analysis of how the decision implicates the director's wealth or career. Accordingly, the duty of loyalty analysis does not usually apply in cases in which the director has a non-pecuniary interest in the transaction.

Checkpoints

- The duty of loyalty addresses conduct that involves a conflict of interest between a director or senior executive and the firm.

- Two types of conduct could potentially violate the duty of loyalty: seizing a corporate opportunity and self-interested director transactions.

- The duty of loyalty bars directors and officers of the firm from taking advantage of corporate opportunities, if the firm is inclined and able to exploit such opportunities.

- Self-interested director transactions are permissible if approved by a majority of informed, independent directors; or if approved by informed, independent shareholders; or, if approvals are not feasible, if it is shown that the transaction is ultimately fair to the firm.

Chapter 10

Shareholder Rights and Remedies

Roadmap

- Right to Inspect
- Right to Vote
- Right to Sue
- Derivative Actions Versus Direct Actions
- Limitations on the Right to Sue
- Special Litigation Committees
- Recovery of Attorney Fees

Shareholders, discontent with management performance or suspicious of management infidelity, may sell their stock and invest their capital in another company. However, at least conceptually, such shareholders have sold at a loss. That is, consider what the stock would be worth if the oafs were removed from office and replaced by better managers or the wrongful conduct detected and stopped. The value of the shares in the company under proper management would almost certainly rise. Thus, some shareholders may want to avoid selling. Shareholders who cannot or do not want to sell their stakes in the company have additional rights that can be used to affect the direction of the firm and perhaps oust under-performing managers. Of these, three of the most important and basic shareholder rights are the (1) right to inspect the books and records, (2) right to vote, and (3) right to sue. In theory, each of these shareholder rights creates a right to participate in the affairs of the firm. In practice though, each of these shareholder rights have significant disadvantages and may not give shareholders the voice they want to kick out torpid managers.

A. Right to Inspect

To start with, shareholders have a right to inspect the books and records of the company. The right arises under statute and common law principles. *See, e.g.,* MODEL BUS. CORP. ACT § 16.02; DEL. CODE ANN. tit. 8 § 220. This includes a right to inspect public documents, like the firm's articles of incorporation; more private documents, like the list of shareholders and other records; and even in some cases, a right to inspect the books and records of affiliated companies, like wholly-owned subsidiaries. If the firm refuses a proper request to inspect, the shareholder may sue to compel production of the requested documents.

This right to inspect the books and records has at least three good rationales that support the case for shareholder participation in the affairs of the firm. First, this right to inspect the books and records reinforces the shareholders' position as owners or residual claimants of the firm. To be sure, legally the firm is independent of its owners and holds legal title to the books, records, and other firm property. However, as the ultimate owner of the firm or residual claimants, the books and records of the corporation are in a certain sense the shareholders' property. Thus, the right of shareholders to inspect naturally flows from the notion that the shareholders are owners of the firm.

Second, the right to inspect the books creates an avenue for shareholders to monitor the conduct of managers and directors of the firm. That is, this right can have significant consequences for shareholders who want to shine a spotlight on managerial under-performance or misconduct. For instance, shareholders can use the right to inspect the books to help build a case that the managers' performance breaches their obligations and duties to the firm and should therefore be liable. Thus, a request to inspect the books is frequently related to a shareholder lawsuit. Alternatively, shareholders might use the right to inspect the books to mount a takeover of the firm or the ouster of certain directors. Moreover, even if shareholders do not always uncover wrongdoing upon a review of the books and records, the shadow of the right to review still might create a check on potential managerial misconduct. Managers might avoid wrong-doing that could easily be detected by a review of the company's financial statements, for instance. Thus, in all these ways, the right to inspect the books and records serves a shareholder monitoring function.

Related to the right of inspection is the obligation of the firm to maintain books and records. That is, if the firm has no concomitant obligation to maintain books and records, the firm could effectively undermine the right to inspect. Thus, perhaps a third consequence of the right to inspect the books and records is that it creates an obligation on the firm to maintain certain books and records. *See, e.g.,* MODEL BUS. CORP. ACT § 16.01. This requirement to maintain books and records not only facilitates shareholder's property rights in the firm and their ability to detect management misconduct, it also facilitates the ability of public authorities to investigate firm activities. The shareholders' ability to monitor is generally related only to the shareholder's narrow interest in seeing that the firm conducts its business in a way that generates private benefits to the shareholders. The shareholder's interest in private benefit is not always, however, convergent with the interests of non-shareholders, other stakeholders, or the public. The obligation to maintain books and records permits public authorities to more easily ferret out misconduct and prevent the firm from taking acts that violate public law.

1. Limits on Right to Inspect

However, the right to inspect the books is not without hurdles. On the one hand, limits on the right to inspect firm books and records make sense, since otherwise it is conceivable that shareholders would make requests too frequently. The managers at the firm may be unduly distracted by constant requests. Additionally, some books and records should properly stay in the hands of a relative few in order to protect proprietary information or head-off widespread incidence of insider trading. On the other, limits on the right may also have the unfortunate effect of unintentionally weakening the right to inspect. For instance, if discretion for reviewing requests is lodged with the board or senior managers, shareholder requests may too often be refused or delayed out of sheer managerial resistance.

As a procedural matter, shareholders must establish that they are owners of shares in the corporation and identify precisely the documents that they want to view. *See, e.g.,* DEL. CODE ANN. tit. 8 § 220. In some states, another limitation on the right to inspect the books turns on the identity of the shareholder. Smaller shareholders, for instance, who do not own the requisite block of shares, may be precluded from full inspection rights. *See, e.g.,* N.Y. BUS. CORP. L. §624 (2003). Another important limitation on the right to view certain books and records is that the shareholders are often required by state statutes to state a purpose for their request, which is at times the subject of dispute, as in the *Honeywell* case (discussed *infra*). This purpose requirement is one that grows out of both the case law and, to a lesser extent, state statute. Importantly also, even once shareholders have established a proper purpose for the request to inspect, they are limited to inspection rights that will accomplish that purpose. *See, e.g.,* DEL. CODE ANN. tit. 8 § 220(C).

As a general matter, the books and records of the corporation can be divided into two types, *public* books and records and *private* ones. The stringency of the purpose requirement relates to where the requested books and records fall on the public versus private spectrum. Shareholder rights to inspect more public books and records—like the firm's articles of incorporation, by-laws, board resolutions, and annual reports, among others—is generally unfettered. Under some state statutes, in fact, the shareholders need not provide a purpose at all to view the more public books and records of the firm. *See, e.g.* MODEL BUS. CORP. ACT § 16.01-16.02. However, other documents are more private and the shareholders have to demonstrate that they want the documents for a "proper purpose," as the next case shows. More private books and records might include items like the shareholder lists, accounting records, and records of meetings between members of the board of directors or their committees.

Pillsbury v. Honeywell took place during the Vietnam War and, as such, was more about the war than the firm-defendant, Honeywell. 191 N.W.2d 406 (Minn. 1971). Honeywell had significant contracts to supply the U.S. military with munitions. The plaintiff, Charles Pillsbury, bought a few shares of Honeywell stock to create a right of inspection. Pillsbury, the great grandson of the founder of the company bearing the family name, was opposed to the war. He demanded to see the list of Honeywell's shareholders, plus all records dealing with the manufacture of weapons and other munitions. He wanted to use the list to highlight Honeywell's role in the war and contact his fellow shareholders and convince them to vote out Honeywell's directors. Honeywell refused the request. The court agreed with Honeywell that the plaintiff's acknowledged purpose—opposition to the war—was not "germane to his interest as a stockholder." According to the court, the plaintiff, Pillsbury, bought the stock and made the demand request in order to forward a moral cause, which was not in any way tied to his economic interest as a stockholder. Pillsbury, the court surmised, wanted to persuade the firm and its shareholders of the righteousness of his cause, "irrespective of any economic benefit to himself or Honeywell." 191 N.W.2d 412.

Thus, the rule is that a proper purpose includes only things that are of interest to the shareholding community generally. For instance, Delaware's corporate code provides that proper purpose is one that is "related to [one's] interest as a stockholder DEL. CODE ANN. tit. 8 § 220(b). This, the courts have concluded, is a purpose related to a core *economic* interest associated with shareholding. For instance, a proper economic purpose might be valuation of one's residual ownership in the firm; or communication with other stockholders for the purpose of mounting opposition to some value-reducing policy; or to uncover managerial under-performance, since that also reduces value of residual ownership. In addition, a proper purpose is not one that serves an interest primarily geared to harming the firm or a demand that is motivated by bad faith. Thus, a request that is motivated by an interest in competing with the firm would not be allowed under the inspection right. In *Honeywell*, the request might be seen as harming the firm. Recall that the plaintiff wanted to see records related to the manufacture of weapons and munitions. This information likely contains trade secrets, which if divulged, would have the effect of harming the firm's interests.

Interestingly, courts have generally interpreted the shareholder's purpose in light of a subjective standard. Thus, courts tend to look at the shareholder's motivation for the request in the first place. Nevertheless, courts do not necessarily take plaintiff's alleged proper purpose on its face. Courts apply some scrutiny and try to ascertain what the plaintiff's true or actual motivation for the request is. In *Honeywell*, since the plaintiff's motivation appeared to be ending the war and not an interest of the firm, the court denied the request. In *Honeywell*, however, a proper purpose that serves an economic interest might have been if plaintiff could convincingly argue that he wanted the records because he believed that Honeywell's munitions production generated negative publicity for the company, which reduced sales.

Also, as *Honeywell* demonstrates, it is worth mentioning that shareholders still have to overcome managerial reluctance, which is frequently inclined to view such requests as obnoxious meddling. Many times shareholders must file suit to enforce their right. This, of course, can create an enormous upfront cost to shareholders that arguably also eviscerates the right. However, shareholders might be able to recover their attorney fees and other costs, if the denial was wrongful. This depends on whether the denial was made in good faith. *See, e.g.,* Model Bus. Corp. Act § 16.04.

B. Right to Vote

Additionally, shareholders have the right to vote to approve some extraordinary decisions made by management. The shareholder has the right to vote, for instance, on the slate of nominees for the board of directors. Additionally, shareholders may vote on changes in control, like merger or sale of substantially all of the assets of the firm; changes to the articles of incorporation; and eligible shareholder proposals. The shareholder right to vote can usually be exercised at the annual meeting. However, the board of directors or group of the largest shareholders may also call a special meeting at which time shareholders have the right to vote. In order for a proper shareholder vote to be taken, several procedural steps have to be taken, which all arise out of state law. For instance, prior to the vote, the firm must give sufficient notice of the meeting to shareholders. Further, in order to take a proper vote, there must be a quorum present. In the usual case, a quorum will be fifty percent of eligible shares voting. Lastly, and most important, the firm has to make a disclosure to shareholders prior to the vote. This disclosure is frequently extensive and made in the form of a proxy statement, which will be discussed in more detail in Chapter 12.

By all appearances, the right to vote is an important avenue for shareholder democracy. In this rosy view, the right to vote is a way for shareholders to participate in firm decision-making and check management under-performance and intentional misconduct. In theory, for instance, shareholders disgruntled with manager performance may vote to remove such managers or vote for another slate of directors (if there is a competing slate). As a practical matter though, the right to vote is not as important a check on managerial misconduct as one might imagine.

For starters, consider the shareholder meeting, which perhaps in one's imagination is an Athenian-like summit where each attendee gets to offer up her view. The truth of the matter is that shareholder voting usually does not happen at the annual meeting, and few shareholders physically attend the meeting. Instead, these shareholders usually vote or assign their vote prior to the annual meeting. Even shareholders who are disgruntled by management performance and want to wage a campaign to oust the laggards often fail to physically attend the meeting. In most of these cases, shareholders fill out a proxy card, which gives the right to cast their votes to management, the proxy holder. Further, of those shareholders who actually vote, the vast majority of them probably do not actually give substantive review to the materials that the firm is required to disclose. As will be discussed in Chapter 12, the proxy statement is long, tiresome, and complicated. Further, shareholders could receive competing disclosures from parties that oppose management. Instead of reviewing these tedious documents, many of these voting shareholders will simply side with management without much reflection.

Finally, many shareholders do not vote at all. Their vote, after all, can effect very little for the largest public companies with millions of outstanding shares. Thus, the benefit of voting is attenuated, since many shareholders only own a small block of shares. Also, since in the typical case of director elections, shareholders have no alternatives, it makes little difference whether the shareholders vote in favor or vote to withhold support. In many corporations, regardless of the vote, the management-nominees will be elected since there is no alternative slate. Thus, in the normal cases, shareholder voting can probably not be expected to be an extremely important check on managerial under-performance and misconduct. The expected costs of informed voting are high— reading relevant disclosure documents, for instance—while the expected benefit of informed voting is highly uncertain.

1. Voting Methods

If the articles of incorporation do not make a provision regarding how votes are to be allocated among shareholders, the default rule is one vote per share. This matches up well with the other default rules regarding share ownership — e.g., the default rule of equal residual economic rights and the default rule that shares are common shares by default. However, like almost all rules of corporate law, the right to vote is largely a default rule. Under state law, the corporation in its articles of incorporation can arrange any number of voting preferences for any class of shares. *See, e.g.,* Del. Code Ann. tit. 8 § 151(a). Thus, the firm may arrange for a class of shares to have effective voting control and another class to have little or no power to vote at all. Firms routinely do extend certain voting preferences. As mentioned, for instance, the firm can arrange for classes of shares, like preferred shares, that receive different economic preferences and different voting rights.

Still, although firms can tinker with the default rules as they please, most public companies tend to hew closely to the one share-one vote rule. As for director nominations, the one share-one vote rule would mean that each shareholder gets one vote per board position. For instance, assume there are 6 seats up for election to the board and 100 shares of stock. Shareholder A owns 70, while Shareholder B owns only 30. Since there are 6 elections, Shareholder A has 420 votes to case, and Shareholder B has 180 votes to cast. Under straight voting, Shareholder A would cast 70 votes for each of the 6 seats and Shareholder B would cast its 30 votes for each of the seats. Shareholder B would not win any seats, losing every election by 40 votes. Thus, under a straight voting method, Shareholder A would be able to elect all its picks for each of the six seats.

Straight Voting

	Shareholder A	Shareholder B
Seat 1	70	30
Seat 2	70	30
Seat 3	70	30
Seat 4	70	30
Seat 5	70	30
Seat 6	70	30

Perhaps the dominant alternative to straight voting is cumulative voting. Under this method of shareholder voting, shareholders can marshal all their votes for a single candidate or spread their votes across any number of candidates at their choosing. The benefit of cumulative voting is that even minority shareholders may be able to affect the outcome of the election of one or more seats on the board of directors. For instance, assume again there are 6 seats up for election to the board and 100 shares of stock. Shareholder A owns 70, while Shareholder B owns only 30. Under cumulative voting, shareholder A, as before, would have 420 votes. Also, as before, Shareholder B would have 180 votes. However, both shareholders would be able to spend their votes on whichever seat they wished. Assume that Shareholder A spread his votes evenly, *i.e.*, 70 votes per election. Meanwhile, Shareholder B decides to marshal all his votes for one election. In this scenario, Shareholder A would win every election, except for one. Public companies that allow cumulative voting appear to be few and far between.

Cumulative Voting

	Shareholder A	Shareholder B
Seat 1	70	180
Seat 2	70	0
Seat 3	70	0
Seat 4	70	0
Seat 5	70	0
Seat 6	70	0

A third method of director election, a so-called majority vote requirement, has become increasingly important in public companies and is also worth mentioning. Under this voting alternative, directors must receive a majority of the votes cast in order to retain their seat on the board of directors. If a nominee fails to get a majority of shareholder votes, she usually must resign pursuant to company by-laws. Thus, such a rule has important consequences, since many director elections are uncontested, which means shareholders typically have only two options: voting in favor of the nominee or withholding their vote from the nominee. Under the majority voting requirement, if a majority of voting shareholders withhold their support from the nominee, she is effectively removed from office.

2. Interference with Right to Vote

Like the right to vote in political elections, many early courts considered the right to vote in firms to be sacrosanct. Interference with the right was prohibited. The right to vote usually implicates two legal rules important to mention here. First, the board of directors is forbidden under common law from infringing on this right. For instance, as in political elections, the board may not, without compelling justification, create undue procedural hurdles to the right of shareholder voting. Second, vote-buying under early cases was prohibited. Over time, however, the rule against vote-buying has been significantly eroded. Instead, as shall be shown, today many voting arrangements have received the blessing of courts.

First, the board of directors is forbidden from making a decision, even if otherwise lawful, that would frustrate the right of shareholders to exercise the franchise. For example, in the *State of Wisconsin Investment Board v. Peerless*, the defendant firm proposed issuing 1 million new stock options, along with a couple of other routine proposals. No. Civ. A17637, 2000 WL 1805376 (Del. Ch. 2000). SWIB opposed the new issue proposal and mounted a campaign against the plan. SWIB sent a letter to the Peerless shareholders explaining its opposition. The plan was wrongheaded, Peerless argued, because the new issue would dilute the value of the current shares and give the firm too much discretion for deciding how the shares are transferred to managers.

Although the routine proposals were taken to a vote and passed, the contested proposal was not. Instead, the chairman of the board adjourned the meeting prior to completing the vote on the proposal. At the time of the adjournment, the proposal had been rejected by a significant margin. Still, the adjournment appeared lawful, since the company's by-laws provided that the chairman may adjourn such meetings "from time to time." After the meeting was adjourned, the Peerless board continued soliciting votes in favor of the proposal and at the reconvened meeting squeaked out a narrow victory.

The issue in the case is whether the chairman could use his power to adjourn in order to cherry-pick voters in favor of the management-sponsored proposal. The court found that the primary purpose of the adjournment was to frustrate the vote. In such cases, the test is not the business judgment rule, which usually insulates director decisions. Instead, in cases where board action is taken primarily to interfere with the vote, the board's decision is only protected in cases in which the board can demonstrate a compelling justification for the interference.

Second, the courts have outlawed some transactions that contemplate the sale of the right to vote. Importantly, such courts, however, have not condemned all transactions where shareholders assign the right to vote to another. For instance, cases in which the shareholder assigns the right to vote to a trusted confident, advisor, or trustee who is bound to act in the best interests of the shareholders are usually enforceable. State statutes tend to support this rather wide exception to the common law rule against vote-selling. In Delaware, for instance, shareholders may enter into agreements for an indefinite period assigning their right to vote to a "voting trustee." *See, e.g.,* DEL. CODE ANN. tit. 8 § 218. Further, as the next case shows, courts have endorsed voting agreements, as long as the purpose of the agreement was not to defraud other shareholders.

In *Schreiber v. Carney,* the Delaware chancery court considered the plaintiff's claim that a transaction should be voided because the defendant firm, Texas International, had engaged in vote-buying. 447 A.2d 17 (Del. Ch. 1982). In that case, a transaction was hatched to remove Jet International's opposition to a planned merger. Under Texas International's charter, it needed the approval of each class of shares to complete the merger. Jet International owned all of the shares of one of Texas International's classes of shares and had threatened to withhold its support for the merger. Jet International, which at the time held a sizeable number of warrants to purchase shares in the company, complained that the merger would create a taxable event for these warrants. One of the only viable options for Jet International was to exercise its warrants. The problem was Jet International was a holding company with few assets other than its stock and warrants in Texas International. Thus, it would have to borrow the money and incur significant borrowing costs for the small holding firm.

Meanwhile, the other shareholders overwhelmingly approved the merger, since it created the prospect of expanding the business. In order to facilitate Jet International's exercise of the warrants and their support for the merger, Texas loaned the company $3.3 million. The shareholder-plaintiff complained, among other things, that the low-cost loan was a purchase of Jet International's vote for the transaction. According to the court, the purpose of the transaction was hardly to create a fraud on the shareholders. The court held that voting arrangements that do not have such a fraudulent objective are not illegal *per se.* In other words, these transactions, according to the court, are only avoidable if the transaction was somehow unfair to the other shareholders. The other shareholders wanted the merger to go through, as evidenced by their votes in favor after a full and complete disclosure.

C. Right to Sue

Lastly, shareholders have the right to file a lawsuit, another important constraint on management misconduct. The shareholder right to sue has been interpreted relatively broadly to ensure that injured shareholders may have a right to make a claim against the corporation. For instance, consider that the relevant procedural rules — 23 (class actions) and 23.1 (derivative suits) — require that plaintiffs generally be representative of the class of shareholders that the plaintiffs purport to represent. Courts have interpreted these rules to mean merely that plaintiffs cannot have an interest that is "antagonistic" to the interests of other shareholders or the firm. *In re Fuqua Indus.*, 752 A.2d 126 (Del. Ch. 1999). The rationale in broadly interpreting the requirements is perhaps to encourage plaintiffs (or arguably plaintiffs' attorneys) to bring these suits.

1. Derivative versus Direct Actions

In the right case, shareholders can sue derivatively—*i.e.*, on the firm's behalf—or directly—*e.g.*, a class action. To start with, it is important to recognize that distinguishing between whether a suit is a direct or derivative suit is sometimes difficult to do. For instance, consider the American Law Institute treatments of direct versus derivative:

> (a) A derivative action may be brought in the name or right of a corporation by a holder to redress an injury sustained by, or enforce a duty owed to, a corporation. An action in which the holder can prevail only by showing an injury or breach of duty to the corporation should be treated as a derivative action.
>
> (b) A direct action may be brought in the name or right of a holder to redress an injury sustained by, or enforce a duty owed to, the holder. An action in which the holder can prevail without showing an injury or breach of duty to the corporation should be treated as a direct action that may be maintained by the holder in an individual capacity.

AMER. LAW INST. PRINCIPLES OF CORP. GOVERNANCE § 7.01 (1992) (updated 2008). Suffice it to say for now, shareholders may sue directly only if the alleged misconduct has caused a unique injury to the suing shareholders — that is, an injury not shared by the other shareholders.

In *Grimes v. Donald*, the plaintiff-shareholder complained over the lucrative employment agreement that the firm's board had in place with its CEO. 673 A. 2d 1207 (Del. 1996). According to Grimes, the board overstepped the bounds by granting the firm's CEO the ability in the employment contract to be free from "unreasonable interference" from the board. Grimes thought this provision would keep the board from exercising its power as the head of the firm, since the CEO would get a hefty severance package if the board breached the provision. Grimes wrote to the board to complain and ultimately filed suit to have the contract voided as an unlawful delegation or abdication of firm power. Additionally, Grimes claimed that the outsized compensation package to the CEO also constituted a breach of the duty of care. The court held that the latter, breach of duty of care claims, were derivative claims, while the abdication claim was a direct one.

Importantly, according to the court, whether a claim is direct or derivative depends on the nature of the injury and the remedy sought from the courts. On the topic of remedy, the court suggests that when the remedy sought is monetary relief that flows to the corporation, the claim is more likely to be a derivative claim. On the other hand, when the remedy is injunctive, declaratory relief or prospective, the claim is more likely to be construed as a direct claim. Examples of such suits are actions to enforce the right to vote, the right to inspect the books, challenges to an unauthorized act of the board, or actions to force the board to abide by other corporate statutes. Second, courts consider the nature of the injury. If the injury is one that creates an injury to the plaintiff—like, for instance, a contractual breach with the plaintiff—it's a direct claim. Injuries that all shareholders share equally, by contrast, are usually derivative claims.

The legal consequences of whether the plaintiff's complaint is interpreted as a direct suit or derivative are important. For starters, in direct actions, plaintiffs are held to a less stringent pleading standard than in cases of derivative actions. In a direct action, plaintiffs usually only have to give notification of the nature of the claim to the defendant, so-called notification pleadings. By contrast, in a derivative action, plaintiffs are held to the much more exacting standard of pleadings rules, like Delaware's chancery rule 23.1, which requires plaintiffs to plead with "particularity." DEL. CH. CT. RULE 23.1

Another important legal consequence is that in derivative actions, usually only existing shareholders have standing to sue. For instance, the rules of chancery court in Delaware provide that shareholders only have standing to file derivatively if they owned shares at the time of the alleged misconduct and at the time of the suit. Further, Delaware courts have held that if the shareholder-plaintiff sells her shares, then the plaintiff forfeits her standing and the suit should be dismissed. *See, e.g., In Re the Limited, Inc. Shareholders Litigation,* No. CIV. A. 17148-NC, 2002 WL 537692 (Del. Ch. 2002). In other words, courts have interpreted the procedural rules as requiring that plaintiffs continue to hold a stake in the firm of which they complain. However, in direct actions, since the injury is personal to the shareholder, the shareholder will have standing to sue regardless of whether she continues to hold shares in the firm. The one drawback of direct suits is that if the shareholder sues individually, the shareholder has to worry about costs given the usually paltry damages an individual plaintiff might have suffered. That is, direct suits are usually cost-prohibitive, unless the suit is brought as a class action in which case the expected benefit of a successful suit are greatly amplified. Still even in these exceptional cases, like in all class actions, the shareholder would have to show that members of the class share a significant level of commonality in injury.

The right to sue derivatively, meanwhile, is a special situation in corporate law. Usually, the board of directors makes such decisions about whether to sue, when to sue, and whom to sue. Like every other board decision, these decisions to sue or not would be protected under the business judgment rule. However, in cases in which the board of directors cannot be trusted because of a conflict of interest, the shareholder need not leave it to the board to decide whether a suit is prudent. In the right circumstance, the shareholder can bring the case on behalf of the firm. In these cases, if the shareholder is successful, any amounts recovered from the suit would go back to the corporation. However, like the right to vote, the shareholder right to sue in a derivative suit is not a very powerful sword. Specifically, the right to sue derivatively is not an extremely strong shareholder right because of the interaction of three significant procedural rules: (a) the demand requirement; (b) the futility rule; and (c) the advent of special litigation committees.

2. Demand Requirement

To begin with, the first important legal rule to consider in a derivative suit is the demand requirement. As a consequence of the demand requirement, in derivative actions, the plaintiff-shareholder usually must make written demand on the corporation before filing a suit on the corporation's behalf. Although shareholders wanting to pursue derivative litigation must almost always make a pre-suit written demand to the board, the demand requirement does oscillate somewhat from state to state. For instance, in pertinent part, the Delaware demand requirement stems from the pleading rule, which states as follows:

> The complaint shall ... allege with particularity the efforts, if any, made by the plaintiff to obtain the action the plaintiff desires from the directors or comparable authority and the reasons of the plaintiff's failure to obtain the action or for not making the effort.

DEL. CHAN. CT. RULE 23.1. Thus, as seen above, the pleading requirement contemplates in two places — "if any" and "reasons ... for not making the effort" — that no such demand will be made in each and every case. Interestingly though, under the MBCA, there is a universal demand requirement. Under it, shareholders are required to make a pre-suit demand in every case.

See, e.g., MODEL BUS. CORP. ACT § 7.42. The universal demand requirement is also the model recommended by the American Law Institute.

Forcing a complaining shareholder to make a pre-suit demand on the firm reinforces the board of directors as the fount of firm power. For instance, consider a derivative suit that the firm chooses to participate in. The benefit of such suit flows to the firm. Thus, it is logical that the firm should play a leading role in running the suit. Furthermore, this notion has the added benefit of potentially saving judicial resources and encouraging alternative dispute resolution. If complaining shareholders have to first notify the firm of their grievance, for instance, perhaps the firm can address the matter and the dispute can be resolved amicably without a formal lawsuit. A final rationale for requiring pre-suit demand is that it creates an additional obstacle, which might reduce the incidence of frivolous suits and discourage some plaintiff-shareholders from filing in the first place.

Once the firm receives demand, the corporation then has the option of deciding whether it intends to pursue litigation. In theory, if the firm approves of the plaintiff's suit, the plaintiff can pursue the litigation on its behalf. Additionally, if the firm fails to respond to the demand in a timely manner, the plaintiff-shareholder can proceed. A more likely scenario, however, is that the board refuses the demand. The board might refuse to pursue the litigation because the board thinks the claim is weak, or because the board wants to avoid costly litigation, or the board wants to steer clear of negative publicity that arises from a public suit, or the board prefers to resolve the matter through alternative dispute channels, or virtually any other reason. If the corporation refuses the demand and elects not to pursue the litigation, the firm can move to dismiss the shareholder's complaint. The shareholder can only proceed if he can show that the refusal was wrongful, a nearly insurmountable test, since the decision to refuse is protected by the business judgment rule. The case law on showing a wrongful refusal of a demand is scattered and undeveloped. Still, some courts have suggested that a shareholder who suspects a wrongful refusal use the right to inspect the books and records as a start to bolstering such a claim. *See, e.g., Grimes v. Donald,* 673 A.2d 1207.

Further, if the plaintiff fails to make a demand, the corporation can also move to dismiss the complaint for this failure. One author has suggested that corporations move to dismiss in about thirty percent of cases on the grounds that the demand requirement was not met. *See* Randall S. Thomas & Kenneth J. Martin, *Litigating Challenges to Executive Pay: An Exercise in Futility,* 79 WASH. U. L. Q. 569, 579 (2001). As a practical matter, plaintiffs are less likely to file a derivative action because few shareholders will be able to successfully get approval from the corporation after making demand. It is unlikely that the current board would approve a demand for a shareholder derivative suit. The board is likely to see the demand as unwanted meddling in their management of the firm. Further, it is unlikely that the demand would bring to the board's attention any new facts that the board does not already know.

For instance, consider a case a shareholder recently filed against Martha Stewart, the company she is famous for founding, Martha Stewart Omnimedia, and several members of the firm's board of directors. *Beam v. Stewart*, 845 A.2d 1040 (Del. 2004). The plaintiff, Beam, complained that the board had erred in forgoing a possible claim against Stewart for her role in a high profile securities fraud case involving the company. The facts of the cases are well-known and heavily documented by mainstream presses. Stewart received a tip from a friend about pharmaceutical stock that was expected to tank after an announcement that it did not win an important FDA approval. Stewart sold the stock and when investigators questioned her, she obfuscated and lied. Stewart was ultimately sentenced to five months in prison. The shareholder attempted to file suit against Stewart and others for their role in the scandal and media disaster that followed. However, the court dismissed the suit, since the plaintiff had failed to make demand on the firm prior to filing the suit.

3. Futility

Courts have suggested that there is an important exception to the demand requirement. If the shareholder can show that making demand would be futile because the independence of the director/decision-makers is suspect, then demand may be excused. The case may be able to go forward without the shareholder having made demand. This exception for futility makes sense, since in cases of conflict of interest, as previously discussed, directors are not entitled to the presumption of sound judgment under the business judgment rule.

Significantly, this exception appears to be only available in cases in which the plaintiff has *not* previously made demand on the board. That is, if the plaintiff has previously made demand on the board of directors, she has in effect waived her right to argue that making demand would be futile. For instance, exactly this turn of events occurs in *Grimes v. Donald*, the case mentioned above. The plaintiff made demand on the board of directors and, after it was refused, tried to allege demand futility in his subsequent complaint against the firm. The court in *Grimes* held that the plaintiff could not allege demand futility *after* making demand on the firm:

> If a demand is made, the stockholder has spent one—but only one— "arrow" in the "quiver." The spent "arrow" is the right to claim that

> demand is excused. The stockholder does not, by making demand, waive the right to claim that demand has been wrongfully refused.

673 A.2d at 1219. In the end, few shareholders ever make demand, since it is likely that such demand will resolve very little and create unfavorable legal consequences for the demander. As mentioned, making demand creates a waiver of the shareholder's ability to claim futility. Plus, since shareholder-plaintiffs can expect that if they make demand the board will naturally be predisposed to reject the suit and intervene to oppose it, there is little obvious value in doing it.

In order to show demand futility, the plaintiff would generally want to show that more than half of the members of the board are biased or not independent. Put differently, demand would be futile if half of the directors or more cannot be trusted to exercise independent judgment. As a practical matter, the requirement for showing demand futility is a high one.

First, courts have established a common law rule that presumes that directors are independent. The pleading requirements for demand futility are an outgrowth of that presumption. As mentioned, under the usual requirements, the plaintiff must make "particularized" allegations in their complaint sufficient to rebut the presumption. *See, e.g.,* Del. Chan. Ct. Rule 23.1. The standard is higher than the requirement at the pleading/complaint stage of the litigation, where plaintiffs would otherwise, more or less, only have to give notice to the defendant of the plaintiff's claim.

For instance, in *Aronson v. Lewis*, the court claims that the pleadings must be specific. 473 A.2d 805 (Del. 1984). In that case, the plaintiff shareholder complained that the board had violated their fiduciary duties by approving a lucrative employment agreement between one of the directors and the firm. However, according to the court, the allegations would have to raise a "reasonable doubt" that the directors might be independent. The plaintiff's complaint claimed that no demand was made on the firm because it would have been futile for two reasons. First, according to the plaintiff, the defendants were all named in the plaintiff's suit. The court rejects this argument saying that a threat of personal exposure is not enough by itself to create a reasonable doubt of their independence. Second, plaintiff alleged that the defendant-Fink dominated the other members of the board. Fink, according to plaintiff, played a role in selecting the other members of the board, so they would be beholden to him and controlled the board through his substantial ownership stake. The court rejected that Fink's 47% ownership stake would give him control over the board of directors, since it was less than a majority stake. Further, according to the court, without more, even if Fink owned a majority stake in the firm that would not be enough to suggest control and rebut the presumption of sound business judgment. The court also rejected plaintiff's allegation of independence related to the selection of the members of the board. According to the court, "the method of election" to the board does not touch on whether the director is independent. Thus, the court held that none of these allegations would be particular enough to create a reasonable belief that the directors would not be independent. The test for independence, as a general matter, is judged on a case-by-case basis. In fact, from time to time, courts have acknowledged that the test of "reasonable doubt" or reasonable belief is "flexible." *See, e.g., Grimes v. Donald,* 673 A.2d at 1217.

Secondly, courts have increasingly called on plaintiff to offer up firm proof of their allegations of demand futility. In Delaware, for instance, courts increasingly require plaintiff to put forth specific evidence that the board lacked independence such that demand would be futile. Although derivative plaintiffs have no automatic right to discovery to show futility, according to these recent court opinions, shareholders should use the right to inspect the books and records to bring forth specific information that would put in doubt the board's independence. For instance, consider again the *Martha Stewart* case mentioned above. The Delaware Supreme Court is visibly disturbed by the plaintiff's failure to show specific evidence of demand futility:

> Beam's failure to plead sufficient facts to support her claim of demand futility may be due in part to her failure to exhaust all reasonably available means of gathering facts.... Whether or not the result of this exploration might create a reasonable doubt would be sheer speculation at this stage. But the point is that it was within the plaintiff's power to explore these matters and she elected not to make the effort.... Beam's failure to seek a books and records inspection that may have uncovered the facts necessary to support a reasonable doubt of independence has resulted in substantial cost to the parties and the judiciary.

845 A.2d at 1056–57. However, as mentioned previously, the right to inspect the books can be costly if the firm proves stubborn and the plaintiff has to file suit to obtain the documents.

Thirdly, state courts have interpreted independence narrowly and, in effect, limited the class of subjects that might indicate bias and demand futility to the traditional two: personal financial stake in the transaction or domination by someone with a personal stake. Put differently, the factors for considering lack of independence and demand futility are the same as those carved out for establishing a conflict of interest in other areas of corporate law. The plaintiff shows that the board's decision-making ability is compromised because of some personal stake in the outcome of the decision. A good example would be if the plaintiff could show that the board members (or a close family member of the board member) may lose money or her job depending on the outcome of the decision. Alternatively, plaintiff could show that the board members are "dominated" or "controlled" by someone with a personal stake in the outcome of the decision. For instance, consider again the *Martha Stewart* case and the court's rejection of allegations of "affinities" or friendship as a basis for overcoming the presumption of independence:

> Allegations that [the directors] moved in the same social circles, attended the same weddings, developed business relationships before joining the board, and described each other as "friends" ... are insufficient, without more, to rebut the presumption of independence.... Whether they arise before board membership or later as a result of collegial relationships among the board of directors, such affinities — standing alone — will not render presuit demand futile.

845 A.2d at 1051.

In the end, the right to sue has seen significant setbacks from the perspective of shareholders. For one thing, few shareholders will be able to make presuit demand and expect a fair evaluation of their claim. However, those who avoid making demand face a motion to dismiss for their failure to make demand. Although these shareholders can still argue that demand would be futile, the courts are increasingly applying intense scrutiny to those arguments. They will not be able to rely on conclusory allegations without sufficient proof. Today, as a result, fewer and fewer plaintiffs can expect to meet the courts standards for demand futility, at least not without organizing a potentially costly inspection of relevant books and records prior to making a claim of demand futility.

4. Special Litigation Committees

Even if demand is excused because it is futile, the board of directors can still re-claim the protection of the business judgment rule. According to courts, after a lawsuit is filed by a shareholder-plaintiff, the board can refer consideration of whether to intervene in the suit to a committee of directors who are untainted. The committee will investigate the shareholder-plaintiff's allegation and produce a report. The special committee decision is protected by the business judgment rule. If the special committee formed decides that litigation is not in the best interest of the firm, the firm can intervene on the basis of the report and move for dismissal of the plaintiff's suit. If the special committee decides that litigation is appropriate, the firm may still intervene (at the committee's direction) and manage the case, since the recovery is really one for the firm.

Although the committee, in theory, has the ability to decide to pursue the litigation, the committee will probably rarely do this. For instance, even if the committee decides that the firm has a valid cause of action, the special committee is likely to want to avoid pursuing the suit because of, say, the negative publicity such suits create or the costs of legal fees the firm would have to expend for vindication. Thus, the special committee, like the board generally, is predisposed to reject shareholder-inspired suits. However, in order for the SLC's decision to have business judgment rule-type protection, the SLC must be "like Caesar's wife" — "above reproach." As the next case shows, courts only give deference to the decision of the special committee in cases in which the special committee can show an extremely high level of independence.

In *In re Oracle*, the Delaware chancery court lays out an extremely high standard for special committee independence. 824 A.2d 917 (Del. Ch. 2003). In that case, the shareholder had accused certain members of the Oracle board of directors of unlawful conduct and attempted to sue derivatively on the basis of claim futility. That is, the directors could not be expected to fairly evaluate whether the company had a claim in this case, since these very directors were the object of the claim. Thus, the shareholder might be expected to be able to avoid demand and sue derivatively because of the broader board's conflict of interest. However, the Oracle board formed a special litigation committee with members of the board who were not tainted. The members of the Oracle SLC were not accused of wrong-doing and indeed joined the board after the wrong-doing was alleged to occur. The committee, which was composed of two Stanford professors, conducted an exhaustive review of what had transpired at the company. When they concluded, they reported that the company should not sue, a decision which is normally protected by the business judgment rule, unless there is *any* reason to doubt the independence of the special committee members.

In a sweeping and unprecedented opinion, the court suggested that the SLC's independence was in doubt. According to the court, the Stanford professors' independence could be questioned because of the relationships between the Oracle directors and Stanford University and because of the great impact that some of the directors had in the Palo Alto community, where the professors resided and worked. First, the court noted that many of the Oracle directors were significant donors to Stanford University, the school where the members of the special committee worked. Second, according to the court, even in cases in which the directors were not significant donors to Stanford, they were still icons in the Palo Alto area. As such, anyone in the area would be leery of accusing them of wrong-doing, exactly what the special committee was thrust to decide. Thus, in the court's view, proof of financial independence, the usual test for independence was irrelevant and largely beside the point, as this colorful excerpt from the case reveals:

> Delaware law should not be based on a reductionist view of human nature that simplifies human motivations on the lines of the least sophisticated notions of the law and economics movement. Homo sapiens is not merely homo economicus. We may be thankful that an array of other motivations exist that influence human behavior; not all are any better than greed or avarice, think of envy, to name just one. But also think of motives like love, friendship, and collegiality, think of those among us who direct their behavior as best they can on a guiding creed or set of moral values.

Oracle at 824 A.2d 938. Thus, the court refused to give business judgment rule protection to the Oracle SLC. Thus, unlike in almost every other circumstance in corporate law, the SLC enjoys no presumption of independence, good faith, and decision-making protection under the business judgment rule. Instead, the presumption is just the opposite. In order to claim business judgment rule protection, the SLC must establish facts that show that it is comprised of independent decision-makers. Furthermore, as seen in *Oracle*, the facts that the SLC comes up with are particularly scrutinized.

D. Attorneys Fees and the Right to Sue

Lastly, it is worth mentioning one additional rule that has profound implications for the shareholders' right to sue: the right of successful plaintiffs to obtain their attorneys fees. The usual rule, the so-called American rule, is that plaintiffs, even successful ones, do not have a right to the attorneys' fees. The only exception is in cases in which there is a right to attorneys fees provided by statute. However, in shareholder lawsuits, successful plaintiffs normally have the right to obtain their attorneys fees, which grows out of the case law.

1. An Analysis of Attorneys Fees

The right to receive attorneys' fees in successful shareholder suits has been intensely debated. Supporters argue that the right to receive attorneys' fees encourages litigation beneficial to the firm and, by extension, shareholders who would otherwise be apathetic. Opponents argue that shareholders' apathy means that shareholders suits are really the hobby horse of lawyers, without any shareholder interest truly being served.

Accordingly, on the one hand, a benefit of the right of successful plaintiffs to obtain attorneys fees minimizes the natural resistance of shareholders to pursue beneficial suits and creates the prospect of individual firms realizing the benefit of shareholder suits. Such benefits to the firm might include changes to the firm's corporate governance, the ouster of a lackluster board, or return of consideration to the corporate treasury. As mentioned, the shareholders' right to sue is somewhat of a harrowing procedural battle. Equally important to consider is the fact that even a successful shareholder-plaintiff in such suits will realize very little upside. In most direct actions, a shareholder's individual injury is extremely small. In a derivative action, the fruits of the suit do not usually go the shareholder directly at all, but are returned to the firm. Thus, shareholders would normally have no positive incentive to pursue litigation and face significant procedural hurdles. Because the attorneys might be compensated, they have a decent incentive to pursue meritorious claims on behalf of plaintiffs. As a result, these suits are not cost-prohibitive and the firm stands to realize important benefits from these suits. Additionally, the right of successful plaintiffs to obtain attorneys fees ensures that other firms realize benefits from shareholder suits. That is, as long as attorneys are to be compensated for successful shareholders suits, attorneys have an incentive to sniff out corporate wrongdoing. This fact that attorneys are monitoring the conduct of firm managers, no doubt, serves to incentivize these managers careful about their behavior.

On the other hand, the right to receive attorneys' fees may distort the remedy that plaintiff-shareholders ultimately receive. As mentioned, plaintiff-shareholders have little incentive to bring suit, since most shareholders own only small stakes in the firm and there expected benefit from a successful suit is equally small. Similarly, small stakeholders have little economic reason to monitor the activities of their lawyers. Shareholders acting as "lead" need not even have any knowledge of the litigation, other than a basic consent that their lawyer should act on their behalf. Thus, their lawyers, who may be more interested in settlement than pursuing corporate reforms at all costs, may not do what their client-shareholder would want if there was adequate monitoring. However, as one court mentions in a case where the representative plaintiff had no knowledge of the litigation, the interest of private enforcement actions outweighs the potential agency costs:

> [T]he Court of Chancery will not bar a representative plaintiff from the courthouse for lack of proficiency in matters of law and finance and

poor health so long as he or she has competent support from advisors and attorneys and is free from disabling conflicts. This conclusion is both just and sensible.... Our legal system has privatized in part the enforcement mechanism for policing fiduciaries by allowing private attorneys to bring suits on behalf of nominal shareholder-plaintiffs. In so doing, corporations are safeguarded from fiduciary breaches and shareholders thereby benefit. Through the use of cost and fee shifting mechanisms, private attorneys are economically incentivized to perform this service on behalf of shareholders.

In re Fuqua Indus. 752 A.2d at 132. Thus, the rule permitting recovery of attorneys' fees creates the prospect of better corporate governances and increased monitoring of manager conduct by attorneys. However, the rule does not resolve the problem of monitoring with respect to attorneys. In sum, the rule permitting recovery of attorney fees help reduce one agency problem—manager misconduct—but could possibly produce another one—attorney misconduct.

2. Substantial Benefit Test

The common law rule that plaintiffs should get their attorneys' fees in successful shareholder lawsuits grows out of the doctrine of the common law fund. Under this notion, if a party's efforts create a recovery for a class of others, the recovery is analogous to a fund. In these cases, the party responsible for the recovery of the fund should get her costs of attorneys' fees. In shareholder lawsuit cases, the notion of the common fund has been extended to include cases where the shareholder suit generates a monetary recovery or fund *and* cases where the shareholder suit creates positive changes in the firm's corporate governances.

In these cases, it turns out that the most important test, according to courts, is whether the attorney's work created a substantial benefit to the firm. In implementing this test, courts have erred on the side of granting fees. Courts have defined substantial benefit broadly, which fully incentivizes plaintiffs' attorneys to take these cases. To begin with, the substantial benefit test does not require that attorneys obtain some monetary remedy for shareholders. If the attorneys are able to exact other reform—*e.g.*, changes in corporate governance—that create benefit for shareholders, this, too, can be the basis for a benefit to shareholders as a class, such that the firm should pay attorney fees. Additionally, some courts have interpreted benefit to mean even in cases in which the shareholder only hired an attorney who threatened (but never filed) suit against the corporation and was able to extract beneficial changes at the firm. *See, e.g., Blau v. Rayette-Faberge, Inc.,* 389 F.2d 469 (2d Cir. 1968). Lastly, courts can be said to have interpreted "success" broadly, also arguably in an effort to create an incentive for attorneys to take on shareholder suits. In this regards, courts have noted that attorneys are successful, regardless of whether they prosecute a suit to a final judgment; a settlement agreement is usually enough to qualify as a success such that they should be compensated.

Checkpoints

- Shareholders have three basic rights to protect their interest and exert control over the corporation: the right to inspect books and records, the right to vote, and the right to sue.

- The right to inspect books and records allows shareholders to investigate potential mismanagement.

- Shareholders have the right to vote on fundamental corporate matters and may cast those votes at annual or special meetings.

- Shareholders may exercise their right to sue directly (*e.g.,* class action) or by bringing a derivative action asserting a legal right on behalf of the corporation.

- Before bringing a derivative suit, a shareholder must make demand on the corporation, at which point the corporation may either bring the suit itself or refuse, a decision protected by the business judgment rule.

- Special Litigation Committees may be formed by the corporation to consider whether to participate in a shareholder-initiated derivative action and allow the corporation's decision to be protected by the business judgment rule if the corporation can demonstrate the SLC was truly independent.

Chapter 11

Securities Fraud

Roadmap

- Rule 10b-5
- Material Misrepresentation
- Presumptive Versus Actual Reliance
- Causation
- Mental State
- Insider Trading and the "Abstain-or-Disclose" Rule
- Tippee Liability

Section 10(b) of the Securities Exchange Act of 1934 has become a catchall that prohibits any so-called "cunning device" in connection with a securities transaction. More specifically, §10(b) provides that it is "unlawful for any person ... to use or employ, in connection with the purchase or sale of any security ... any manipulative or deceptive device or contrivance" and provides that the SEC should make necessary rules to effectuate the law and protect investors. 15 U.S.C.A. §78j (2008). As a result, SEC Rule 10b-5, perhaps the most famous SEC rule, makes a similar proscription. In pertinent part, Rule 10b-5 provides as follows:

> Employment of Manipulative and Deceptive Devices.
> It shall be unlawful for any person, directly or indirectly, by the use of any means or instrumentality of interstate commerce, or of the mails or of any facility of any national securities exchange,
> (a) To employ any device, scheme, or artifice to defraud,
> (b) To make any untrue statement of a material fact or to omit to state a material fact necessary in order to make the statements made, in the light of the circumstances under which they were made, not misleading, or
> (c) To engage in any act, practice, or course of business which operates or would operate as a fraud or deceit upon any person, in connection with the purchase or sale of any security.

17 C.F.R. §240.10b-5. Under §10(b) and SEC Rule 10b-5, at least two types of securities fraud deserve special attention in this Chapter: (1) private enforcement actions (*e.g.*, class actions) for securities fraud and (2) SEC enforcement actions for insider trading.

A. Securities Fraud

The firm issues a depressing press release that suggests earnings will likely decrease in the next quarter. Some investors might sell the firm's shares in reliance on that press release. If the press release proves false, these traders, no doubt, will be disgruntled. They sold early, too early. In the right case, the duped shareholders might argue that the firm has committed securities fraud. They may band together as a class and sue for the difference between what they sold for and what they would have sold for absent the alleged fraud. Although securities fraud may be a new twist, fraud is a classic tort. In securities fraud, a firm may make a misrepresentation of some sort related to securities transaction that investors would rely on when making trading decisions. Stated more formally, in order to have committed securities fraud there must be: (1) a material misrepresentation; (2) reliance; (3) causation; and (4) scienter, the requisite mental state. The courts have interpreted the rule's rationale as investor protection and, therefore, they have provided an implied private right of action for plaintiffs in cases of basic securities fraud.

1. Material Misrepresentation

The first and perhaps must fundamental point in basic securities fraud cases is that there must be some form of deception or misrepresentation. The plaintiff must ultimately show that the firm has, for instance, issued a false press release, manipulated financial statements, or otherwise gulled shareholders in some way. Without deception, the firm has committed no securities fraud. For instance, *Santa Fe Industries v. Green* involves a tender offer to minority shareholders of Kirby, one of the firm's subsidiaries. 430 U.S. 462 (1977). The buyer provided the minority position-holders with several indications of their shares' value before offering $150 per share. Some of the information provided (particularly information provided by an independent appraisal) arguably suggested that the true value of the shares was much higher than $150. The plaintiffs argued that they should be able to bring a case for securities fraud given the fair market value of the firm's assets, because the plaintiff's tender offer was an unfair lowball. The Court agreed with the defendants that there was no securities fraud because the buyer had not technically deceived any seller. The buyer offered the sellers full information, including copies of the appraisal and analysis about how their tender offer was derived. Without actual deception, there could be no securities fraud.

According to the court, proof of an unfair or unscrupulous action, even if true, would not be enough for securities fraud. Securities fraud, in this view, is not an appropriate remedy for an allegation of an unfair transaction, without more. Plaintiffs, like the ones in *Santa Fe*, may have other causes of action that can handle the unfairness, like state appraisal remedy (discussed in Chapter 12) or breach of fiduciary duty (discussed in Chapter 6). But, in federal actions for securities fraud, the underlying goal is to stamp out deception and promote full and frank disclosures. Another takeaway of the *Santa Fe* decision is that the federal courts are loath to encroach on state jurisdiction by expansively interpreting plaintiff's private right of action under § 10b. For instance, in *Santa Fe*, if the Court had permitted the suit to go forward, the plaintiff would have been in effect able to bring what are normally state law causes of action for unfairness in a federal court. That is, actions for unfairness, the core of the plaintiff's complaint, are usually resolved under appraisal or fiduciary duty breaches in state court.

Additionally, when the firm does misrepresent or deceive, the misrepresentation must go to a material fact. Misrepresentations of trivial facts are not actionable. It is conceivable that without an express materiality requirement, firms might have an incentive to over-supply information, including trivial information, to shareholders in order to avoid liability. This over-supply of information would not serve the general goal of securities law, which is to promote full disclosure. That is, firms over-supplying information may undermine disclosure, as important information might be lost in the weeds of trivial or nonimportant disclosures. Thus, the materiality requirement might keep firms from overwhelming plaintiffs with too much information. In securities fraud litigation, materiality is much like materiality as defined throughout corporate law. That is, a fact is material if a reasonable investor would want to know about it.

Among securities fraud cases, *Basic v. Levinson* is one of the most challenging. 485 U.S. 224 (1988). The basic facts are well-known among legal commentators. Combustion Engineering was a firm with an interest in expanding by acquiring Basic. The two firms began discussions about the possibility of merger, but in several public statements Basic denied rumors that it was in talks. Ultimately, the merger was approved by Basic's board at the relatively rich offer price of $46 per share for the common shares. The plaintiffs filed a class action suit for securities fraud based on Basic's public denials of the merger. Their theory was that members of the class sold their stock prior to the announced merger on the basis of misleading information from Basic.

The more controversial issue in *Basic* is whether the members of the class should be allowed to proceed with the suit, even though many of them had no knowledge—thus, no actual reliance—about the merger denials. (For discussion of this point, see the next section.) Yet, *Basic* is also a good backdrop for a closer inspection of the materiality requirement in securities fraud litigation. For instance, the defendants responded that the alleged fraud did not concern a material fact because the merger talks were just negotiations that could have fallen apart. Because of the uncertainty of the negotiations, they argued, the negotiations would not be significant information to investors. The negotiations, the defendants reasoned, were uncertain and contingent, particularly early on. Furthermore, the defendants pointed out previous decisions by courts that had held that only merger negotiations that reach an "agreement-in-principle" are material for purposes of securities fraud. At trial, the district Court agreed that the negotiations, although on-going at the time of the firm's statements denying a merger in the offing, were too uncertain to be material.

However, the U.S. Supreme Court held that in merger negotiations, as in all other contexts, materiality is based on what a reasonable investor would want to know. The Court endorsed the view of materiality for contingent outcomes taken by prior courts, including the Second Circuit. According to this view, whether information regarding a contingent outcome is material depends on two factors, the likelihood or probability that the contingency will occur and the relative magnitude of the contingency to the firm, the so-called "probability/magnitude approach." In applying its analysis the Court opines as follows:

> Whether merger discussions in any particular case are material therefore depends on the facts. Generally, in order to assess the probability that the event will occur, a factfinder will need to look to indicia of interest in the transaction at the highest corporate levels. Without attempting to catalog all such possible factors, we note by way of example that board resolutions, instructions to investment bankers, and actual negotiations between principles or their intermediaries may serve as indicia of interest. To assess the magnitude of the transaction to the issuer of the securities allegedly manipulated, a factfinder will need to consider such facts as the size of the two corporate entities and of the potential premiums over market value.

485 U.S. at 239. Put simply, for purposes of securities fraud, materiality is defined in the traditional sense as simply whether a reasonable person—here, investor—would want to know. Because a merger is a critical firm event, surely

a reasonable investor would want the truth with respect to almost all potential merger negotiations, even where no agreement had been reached, if an agreement was reasonably likely to occur from them.

2. Reliance

Second, a case for securities fraud must allege that the plaintiffs have relied on the misrepresentation. That is, the misrepresentation must have led the complaining party to have changed their position in some way. Taken literally, the requirement of reliance can be the death knell to many potential plaintiffs, as many potential plaintiffs will have no direct notice of the misrepresentation. Shareholders are typically passive investors, not busy, professional traders. As a result, most shareholders might not, for example, have actually been in the audience when the press conference was held and may have never reviewed the firm's fraudulent financial statements. If these shareholders rely on a misrepresentation at all, their reliance is indirect and remote.

Recall again, for instance, the *Basic* case. 485 U.S. 224 (1988). The plaintiffs appear to have no direct knowledge of the misrepresentations because they were not actually aware of the merger denials. Yet, the plaintiff class argued that class members relied on the misstatements and sold their shares at artificially low prices because of Basic's denials about the impending merger. The defendants argued against class status on the grounds that the class members were not similar and should be required to each individually show reliance on the misstatements. As the Court observed, if the plaintiffs were required to individually demonstrate direct allegations of reliance, then it "would have prevented respondents from proceeding with a class action, since individual issues then would have overwhelmed the common ones ..." 485 U.S. at 242.

More fascinating, the Court argued that a cramped notion of reliance should be rejected because of a theory of efficient capital markets. According to the court, in such cases, the plaintiffs need not show actual reliance. Reliance could be presumed. Specifically, the U.S. Supreme Court in *Basic* agreed with prior lower courts that the allegations of misrepresentation essentially amounted to a fraud-on-the-market. That is, the market for securities in public companies like Basic involves many anonymous buyers and sellers. Each of these buyers indirectly trades on the basis of presumed market efficiency; that is, the belief market price incorporates all relevant publicly-available information. When, as alleged, Basic made misleading statements, it fraudulently depressed the shares of the firm in the market. Thus, even if the purchasers had not directly relied on the misstatements (and may not have known about them), they did indirectly rely on such statements when they made purchases on an efficient capital market. Put another way, the purchasers relied directly on the market to incorporate in price all relevant public information, which, in turn, included the misstatements. Although the underlying theory here leaves much left to question, the Court is firm in a rule of presumptive reliance in public markets:

> Indeed, nearly every court that has considered the proposition has concluded that where materially misleading statements have been disseminated into an impersonal, well-developed market for securities, the reliance of individual plaintiffs on the integrity of the market price may be presumed. Commentators generally have applauded the adoption of one variation or another of the fraud-on-the market theory. An investor who buys or sells stock at the price set by the market does so in reliance on the integrity of that price. Because most publicly available information is reflected in market price, an investor's reliance on any public material misrepresentations, therefore, may be presumed for purposes of a Rule 10b-5 action.

485 U.S. 247. Thus, the Court held that the class could continue, on the basis of "presumptive reliance." Thus, in order to receive the benefit of the presumptive reliance, the plaintiff need only show that (1) public misstatements were made and (2) that they traded in (and relied on) an efficient market, regardless of whether the traders had actually learned of the misstatements themselves.

Importantly, though, the presumption of reliance is rebuttable. At least in theory, the defendant might offer evidence that the plaintiffs are not entitled to the presumption by offering up direct evidence either that the market price was not affected by the misleading disclosure or that the plaintiffs were not fooled by the deception. To begin with, the rule of presumptive reliance might be rebutted by showing that the plaintiffs had better information than other market participants or otherwise did not rely on the misleading statements. For instance, perhaps the plaintiffs sold the stock for reasons unrelated to the misstatements or perhaps the plaintiffs have credible counter-intel that the misstatements were actually false. In either of these cases, plaintiffs would not be entitled to the presumption. Alternatively, the defendants could rebut presumptive reliance by establishing that that the misstatements did not artificially swing trading prices, because the market did not move on the basis of the public statements. One example of this would be if market participants had reason to ignore the misstatements. Perhaps major market players had been privy to more credible information regarding the on-going merger talks, or perhaps news of merger talks had otherwise seeped into the market.

The rule of presumptive reliance is in many ways a rule of convenience because it would be too difficult for plaintiffs to show direct reliance in these cases. Placing the burden on plaintiffs to come up with proof of reliance in these circumstances would set the bar too high and miss too many plaintiffs who also suffered harm as a result of misleading statements. That is, many plaintiffs who suffered harm by buying at artificially set prices will be unable to show direct reliance because they may never personally have heard the false statements. At the same time, presumptive reliance makes it possible for individual plaintiffs to band together in a class action suit. Recall that the main rationale behind securities fraud prohibitions is the protection of investors. Without the class action, investors would have to individually pursue litigation, which would likely only be cost effective for the largest defrauded stakeholders. That is, on an individualized basis, plaintiffs are not likely to be able to bring suit and get legal redress, given the high cost of litigation and the low levels of damages for typical plaintiffs on an individualized basis.

It is worth nothing that *Basic* has been the subject of a substantial amount of academic commentary, much of it contrarian. Perhaps the most obvious critique is that the court's notion of efficient capital markets (and, thus, presumptive reliance) is not found in the text of §10(b). Thus, the Court's analysis essentially expands on a literal reading of the section. The holding provides, in effect, that plaintiffs have an implied right of action even in cases where there is no reliance. The *Basic* holding shifts the burden of proof as to reliance to the defendant—in other words, after *Basic* it is the defendant who must show that the plaintiffs did not rely.

Moreover, and somewhat related to this last point, other commentators have suggested that the opinion is not consistent with other recent court opinions that put fiduciary duty at the center of fraud cases. In these earlier cases, which are examined closely in this Chapter as well, the Supreme Court emphasized breaches of fiduciary duty as the way to resolve what type of conduct creates securities fraud. For instance, misleading omissions are only actionable when the failure to speak represents a breach of a fiduciary duty. Commentators, like Jonathan Macey and Geoffrey Miller, would argue that *Basic* undermines the focus on breaches of fiduciary duty. In their view, it is not clear that the directors in *Basic* have breached their duty to Basic shareholders when they made the alleged misstatements. In fact, they would argue that the misstatements may actually benefit shareholders, being that such misstatements are more likely to keep merger negotiations in tact. *See generally* Jonathan Macey & Geoffrey Miller, *Good Finance, Bad Economics: An Analysis of the Fraud-on-the-Market Theory*, 42 Stan. L. Rev. 1059 (1990). However, on the other hand, the rule makes sense, because the firm in *Basic* could have remained silent about the negotiations. That is, they could have kept the negotiations in tact by not talking at all. There was no need to mislead. At bottom, this argument is simply that the Court articulates a rule that sweeps too broadly or that is over-inclusive.

Last, critics have suggested that the presumptive reliance rule, which depends on efficient capital markets, is impractical. The Court does not give lower courts any reliable way to judge whether markets are efficient. Instead, the Court seems to presume that this finding will be easy to make for courts. However, the notion of efficient capitals markets is not a notion that is so easily defined or applied. Indeed, even in academic circles, which markets are efficient is debatable. This failure of the Court to provide additional guidance as to how to identify efficient markets is likely too problematic for judges who are not also economists.

3. Causation

Third, the misrepresentation must be the proximate cause of loss. The nature of loss was clarified in *Dura Pharmaceuticals v. Broudo*. 544 U.S. 336 (2005). In that case, the Court says that actual loss, not potential loss, was the requirement. In *Dura Pharmaceuticals*, the shareholders claimed that the firm's misstatements led them to purchase shares at artificially inflated prices. Interestingly, the plaintiffs in *Dura* claimed that the right to bring a securities fraud action is instantaneous, from the moment the shares were purchased at prices manipulated by misinformation. The contrary view was that the right to redress became available only after the "revelation" or truth become public and the shares tumbled as a consequence. In the case, Dura had made public statements that suggested a new asthmatic spray device would soon receive FDA approval and that drug sales would pick up as a consequence. This announcement of positive news resulted in active trading in Dura's shares. When Dura made subsequent announcements that the device was not approved by the FDA and that sales were flagging, the stock price halved.

The Court, however, argued that the misstatements had resulted in no actual loss for the plaintiffs, at least not while they continued to hold the shares of the firm. According to the Court, even if the plaintiffs had bought at artificially high prices, there is no way to determine their losses until such time as the truth is reveled and after measuring the effect of the revelation on the shares' trading price. The point is that the plaintiffs, who allegedly bought at (artificially) high prices, might also be able to ultimately sell at (artificially) high prices. Alternatively, assuming the plaintiff did ultimately sell at a large loss, the loss on the transaction might be explained by other factors not related to the misstatements—like "economic circumstances, changed investor expectations, new industry-specific or firm-specific facts, conditions, or other events." 544 U.S. at 343. Thus, the opinion in *Dura* suggests that plaintiffs have to wait until they have suffered actual economic loss as a consequence of a revelation, before they might seek redress for securities fraud.

The Court's analysis is open to criticism on a couple of fronts. First, the Court's analysis seems to create incentives for firms to continue to hide information after an initial misrepresentation. Recall that under the *Dura* court's analysis, the longer the time period between purchase and revelation of the information, the less likely the misrepresentation could be described as a cause of economic loss. Thus, prevaricating firms have an incentive after a misleading disclosure to conceal the truth for as long as possible, or at least until such time as other factors will interpose to arguably affect trading prices. Concealment is bad for the markets because it prevents market participants from accurately pricing shares in the firm. Related to this last point, the Court's opinion seems to confound basic notions of equity. That is, the longer the firm can conceal the misstatements the less likely the fundamental goal of investor protection is served and more likely that those committing fraud go unpunished, since other intervening events might make disclosure less relevant.

4. Scienter

Finally, plaintiffs must allege the requisite state of mind or scienter for there to be securities fraud. According to courts, defendants must have intentionally or, in some cases, recklessly undertaken the acts that form the basis for securities fraud. Misconduct that is merely negligent would not be enough to constitute fraud. For instance, the U.S. Supreme Court in *Ernst & Ernst v. Hochfelder* faced the mental state requirement head-on. 425 U.S. 185 (1976). In *Ernst*, the predecessor firm to Ernst & Young, one of the Big Four auditing firms, was accused of securities fraud for merely negligent acts. According to the plaintiffs, the auditors, then operating under the trade name Ernst & Ernst, had failed to act with ordinary prudence in the conduct of their audit, which would have revealed their client's fraud. Apparently, the President of one of Ernst's clients was secreting client money that was supposedly destined for "high-yield" investments. In failing to discover the fraud by giving a reasonably thorough audit, the plaintiffs claimed that Ernst & Ernst had aided and abetted in securities fraud. Plaintiffs made no allegation that the auditor's misconduct was intentional or reckless.

The Court rejected the plaintiffs' allegations as insufficient, given the Court's interpretation of the language and history §10(b) and SEC Rule 10b-5. In the Court's view, the use of words like "deceptive," "manipulative," "device" and "contrivance" all "strongly suggest that §10(b) was intended to proscribe know-ing or intentional misconduct." 425 U.S. at 197. Also, if the plain language of the statute was not enough, the Court turned to the legislative history. The Court examined some of the language of legislators, like Congressman Thomas Corcoran, at the drafting of the statute. The Court concluded that the legisla-tors intended for the statute to be a "catch-all" for new acts of cunning, not a device to stop those who are simply negligent. *Id.* at 202. Thus, according to the opinion, only intentional misconduct and perhaps reckless conduct can create the basis for securities fraud. *Ernst* is a unique case, as in most cases of securities fraud the mental state requirement requires only a cursory analysis. That is, the mental state requirement is a small hurdle for perhaps most plain-tiffs in securities fraud litigation. In most securities fraud cases, showing that the acts were intentional or reckless are not usually difficult because firms usu-ally intend the acts that create the basis for the fraud in the first place. The firm, for instance, surely intends to issue a press release and it would be an odd defense to argue that the firm had not.

5. Standing

Lastly, the courts have clarified some standing issues with respect to a basic right to sue in securities fraud litigation. According to the text of SEC Rule 10b-5, one only has standing to sue "in connection with the purchase or sale of a security." Thus, plaintiffs cannot bring a securities fraud case based on an expectation that they would have traded in the securities of the firm, if not for the fraud. This requirement makes sense, even though surely there are some potential plaintiffs out there who would have traded 'but-for' the misleading statement. The rule makes sense as a matter of practicality because it would be too difficult for the courts to figure out what plaintiffs would have done but-for the misleading statement.

B. Insider Trading

Insider trading is a species of securities fraud and occurs when an insider trades on the basis of material non-public information. Insider trading viola-tions are different from general securities fraud cases in several important ways. Significantly, for instance, in insider trading cases it is generally the SEC that brings the enforcement action. Private parties may also bring an action, but usu-ally the damages at issue are too paltry to make it worth the cost of litigation. The SEC can bring an action and ask for penalties ranging from disgorgement, punitive damages, or even jail time. Not all insider trading is prohibited. For instance, insiders are not barred from trading on the basis of their own independently developed expertise or educated guesses about the firm's outlook. However, in other circumstances insider trading is sharply curtailed by legal regulation, if not flatly prohibited. The statute that arguably bars insider trading is SEC Rule 10b-5, which of course is a catchall that very generally bars fraudulent practices in connection with a securities transaction. Courts have provided most of the nuance for what specific type of conduct constitutes a violation of insider trading rules. Some of these court opinions are easy to apply; others are more difficult.

1. Theory of Insider Trading

The theory behind prohibition of insider trading, although still hotly contested by several commentators, is at least three-fold. First, insider trading represents a fiduciary breach to the shareholders of the firm. The shareholder has a reason to trust insiders and that trust is broken by the insider trades. The insider who trades with this information takes advantage of his trading counterpart. In theory, secondly, insider trading may affect securities prices in unusual ways. That is, if insider trading is allowed, those with inside information may have an incentive to hoard the information crucial to accurate pricing, lest they lose a profitable tactical advantage. As a result, insiders will have incentives to avoid or delay disclosure of information that they think they could use to generate profit. Third, insider trading may do damage to the integrity of capital markets. If investors believe that insiders have a decisive trading advantage and are allowed to profit unfairly, they may be more hesitant to invest in capital markets. This may create a liquidity problem — that is, fewer buyers and sellers of security interests.

On the other hand, some thoughtful commentators, including the redoubtable Henry Manne, think insider trading regulation is misguided. *See generally* HENRY MANNE, INSIDER TRADING AND THE STOCK MARKET (1966). In Manne's view, insider trading should be permitted because it serves a useful purpose in that it is an efficient, low-cost way to compensate insiders for their innovation and entrepreneurial efforts. In addition to compensation for corporation managers, Manne argues that insider trading actually helps promote better pricing because insider trading is a form of disclosure. That is, market participants may get a fuller sense of a firm's earnings prospects by carefully monitoring insider traders. As a result of this monitoring, they will make trades that indirectly incorporate the inside information and this results in more accurate pricing of a firm's securities.

2. Introduction to "Abstain-or-Disclose" Rule

The general rule in insider trading is "abstain-or-disclose." As to the "abstain" principle, insider trading rules are a flat prohibition of trading for insiders on the bases of material non-public information. Such trades may be unlawful because the insider owes a fiduciary duty to the firm and, by extension, shareholders of the firm. If the insider was permitted to trade in the firm's shares, this would be a breach of that duty. As for "disclose," an insider may trade if the insider discloses the information to the trading partner. The disclose part of the "abstain-or-disclose" rule is somewhat of a straw target because other principles will likely prevent the insider from making such a disclosure. Specifically, an insider may not have discretion to simply disclose and trade because other legal rules might constrain an insider's ability to disclose, including SEC regulations, listing requirements, and common law principles. For instance, the SEC has a full disclosure rule. Thus, if the insider were to make a disclosure to his trading counterpart, the insider would have to disclose publicly, which in some cases might jeopardize the firm's interest. Additionally, they could not disclose because of the agency principle that agents have to keep confidential information. *See* RESTATEMENT (THIRD) OF AGENCY § 8.05(2). Thus, when the firm, as a matter of policy, has a rule that firm strategy should not be disclosed, the only viable option for insiders is to avoid trading.

SEC v. TGS is one of the classic insider trading cases because the cases contains all the stereotypical elements: positive news about the firm's prospects, greedy insiders who trade on the basis of that news, and, to boot, a potential cover-up to keep the gravy train going. 401 F.2d 833 (2d Cir. 1968). In the case, TGS finds a potentially large mineral deposit in eastern Canada. Many of the rocks are sent out for test results, but even the initial eyeball inspection showed that the find would be a great one. Over several months, the firm devises a strategy to buy up all the promising land, while executing a strategy to keep the find a secret, lest the firm be forced to pay exorbitant prices for the surrounding lands. In the meantime, TGS employees, directors, and corporate managers bought an unprecedented level of securities in the firm. Rumors of a find and insider trading picked up quickly. Along the way, the firm issued a press release that tried to beat back the rumors of a find. The court held that the insiders had violated insider trading prohibitions because they had traded on nonpublic material inside information.

TGS helps clarify the rule regarding non-public information and disclosure. On its face, the rule is that an insider may trade on the basis of information, but only if the information is first disclosed. However, *TGS* demonstrates that in most cases of insider access to valuable information the disclosure part of the rule is, as mentioned, a dead letter. That is, the insiders in *TGS* could not disclose the discovery without violating the firm's strategy of keeping this important find a secret. *See* 401 F.2d at 844. A premature disclosure would have foiled the firm's plans to continue buying up all the available land. Thus, if the insiders had prematurely disclosed in order to avoid violating insider trading laws, the disclosure would have concurrently exposed them to liability to the firm for their disobedience.

Moreover, even when the firm does not have a strategy of secrecy, *TGS* demonstrates that simple disclosure may not be enough to avoid violation of the insider trading prohibition. Recall one rationale of the insider trading prohibition is that the insider should not have an unfair advantage over other market participants to whom a duty is owed. Under these lights, simple disclosure to the markets is not enough because in the immediate moments after a disclosure a nimble insider could still have an advantage over most market participants. According to the *TGS* court, the insider must give the market a reasonable period of time to react. The court points out that several trades, even though they occurred *after* the press release announcing the discovery, could still be unlawful insider trades, because an insider must wait a reasonable amount of time for the market to digest the news. Although the courts gives no firm guidance as to how long insiders have to wait after disclosure of the news the court does suggest that Coates, one of the TGS directors, "should have waited until the news could *reasonably* have been expected to appear over the media of widest circulation, the Dow Jones broad tap, rather than hastening to insure an advantage to himself and his broker son-in-law." 401 F.2d at 854 (emphasis supplied).

3. Insider Breaches of Fiduciary Duty

The classic rationale of insider trading rules, as seen in *TGS*, is that liability flows from the insider's violation of a trust relationship. That is, the insider is privy to information that he uses to trade with the shareholders in the very corporation for whom the insider has a fiduciary obligation. In this circumstance, the classic rule is clear. The insider has a duty to make a disclosure to these ignorant shareholders or simply abstain from trading with them at all. Strictly construed, this classic rule of insider trading leaves much conduct out of the ambit of insider trading regulation. For instance, the classic rule does not, perhaps intentionally, abjure trading on the basis of insider information that is casually overheard (say, in an elevator) because the eavesdropper likely has no relationship of trust with shareholders.

Consider, for instance, *U.S. v. Chiarella*, a case where a print shop employee learns about impending takeover bids by deciphering certain closing documents that were delivered to the print shop prior to the actual closings. 445 U.S. 222 (1980). The printer used this information to trade in the stock of the target companies, amassing about $30,000 in just over a year. The Court held that the defendant was not guilty of insider trading and the abstain-or-disclose rule did not apply. Because the print shop was retained by the buying firm (as opposed to the target firm), the employee had received no information from the target firm, did not work for the target firm, and was not a fiduciary of the target firm:

> No duty could arise from petitioner's relationship with the sellers of the target company's securities, for petitioner had no prior dealings with them. He was not their agent, he was not a fiduciary, he was not a person in whom the sellers had placed their trust and confidence. He was, in fact, a complete stranger who dealt with the sellers only through impersonal market transactions.

445 U.S. at 233–34. As a result, the individual who trades on the basis of inside information without disclosing such to the counterpart, according to the Court, may be guilty of fostering unfairness. But, because he owed no duty to the target firm or, more to the point, the shareholders of the target firm, he was not guilty of insider trading.

Chiarella is important because the Court rejects the competing rationale that the insider trading prohibition is about parity of information. Chiarella clearly had an information advantage over his trading counterpart. But, the question is not simply whether he was in possession of nonpublic information. The more important point is whether that information was ill-gotten. Individuals may have information if, say, the information is gained by their own independent, lawful research regarding the firm's prospects or if the insider overhears the information or learns of the information without breaching a fiduciary duty. In *Chiarella*, the Court suggested that he had not breached a duty to the target firm's shareholders in acquiring the information. Thus, at least on that theory, Chiarella's information advantage was not wrongfully obtained.

4. Derivative Insider Breaches of Fiduciary Duty

Additionally in subsequent cases, the courts have expanded on the classic rule, such that the insider trading prohibition seems to sweep more broadly. For instance, the prohibition on insider trading applies not just to insiders, but to those who receive tips from insiders. In these cases, the tippees might still be liable as if they were actually insiders themselves. Liability in these cases turns on whether the insider who passes along the information does so in violation of her position of trust with the firm. However, insider trading liability has important limitations. For instance, someone who overhears a conversation discussing an impending merger and trades on the basis of that information has done nothing unlawful and perhaps not even untoward. Assuming the person was a stranger, the tippee likely had no reason to know that the information was public or non-public or whether the disclosure was authorized or unauthorized. Thus, the tippee in this case may trade safe from the prospect of an SEC enforcement action (though perhaps not safe from the risk that tip might have been false or other normal market risks). The classic case discussing the tippee's immunity from liability is *SEC v. Dirks*.

In *Dirks*, a senior analyst learns that a fraud is on-going at one of the companies he covers. 463 U.S. 646 (1983). Dirks conducts an investigation of the alleged fraud and, what's more, passes the information along to several parties, including many of his clients who trade on the basis of that information and the *Wall Street Journal*. Some of the clients liquidated their positions on the basis of the information and ultimately the firm was delisted from the NYSE as word of the fraud spread. If Dirks had learned of the information as part of a *quid pro quo*, then he would be liable as if the insider himself had traded on the information. However, Dirks learns of the fraud from an employee who is trying to blow the whistle and bring the firm to justice. Thus, the original disclosure to Dirks was not improper. Just as one who overhears a conversation has little reason to believe the inadvertent disclosure is wrongful, so, too, did Dirks have no reason to suspect that this disclosure was improper.

Importantly, the Court analyzes what would be an improper disclosure. According to the Court, an improper disclosure would be one whereby the tipster makes the disclosure for personal gain, broadly defined:

> It is clear that neither Secrist nor the other Equity Funding employees violated their *Cady, Roberts* duty to the corporation's shareholders by providing information to Dirks. The tippers received no monetary or personal benefit for revealing Equity Funding's secrets, nor was their purpose to make a gift of valuable information to Dirks. As the facts of this case clearly indicate, the tippers were motivated by a desire to expose the fraud. In the absence of a breach of duty to shareholders by the insiders, there was no derivative breach by Dirks. Dirks therefore could not have been "a participant after the fact in [an] insider's breach of a fiduciary duty."

463 U.S. at 666 (citations omitted). Thus, it appears that disclosures not motivated by *quid pro quo*, such as inadvertent disclosures, do not create tippee liability. In these cases, the tippee has no reason to know that the disclosure was improper.

Also, whether a disclosure is proper or not, appears to be a function of property interests. Confidential and proprietary information, after all, is a form of intellectual property. However, in *Dirks*, arguably the Court should not countenance the firm having a property-type interest in the fraudulent information. If the firm has no property interest in the information (at least no interest that should be recognized by courts), then those who learn of the information are free to share it. On the other hand, if the tippee has reason to know that the disclosure is an improper one—similar to wrongful conversion of any type of property—the tippee is the equivalent of an insider owing (derivative) fiduciary duties. Upon improper disclosure, the tippee must abide by the abstain-or-disclose rule as if she were an insider owing a fiduciary obligation to the firm and its shareholders.

Additionally, the Court adds further clarification to the understanding of the fairness rationale for proscribing insider trading. In *Dirks*, the Court, again, reasons that fairness does not mean that all traders have equal information or parity-of-information. A parity-of-information rule would be untenable in the Court's view, because it would undermine the work of market analysts, who are paid to ferret out information and get an information advantage for the clients they serve. Incentives to get information should be maintained because traders with superior information affect market pricing in positive ways. Thus, the ability to gain an information advantage is not enough to create liability. Rather, the Court suggests that there must be both an information advantage and a breach of duty to the source of the information.

5. Misappropriation

A second basis, according to courts, for prohibiting insider trades is based on a theory of misappropriation. In the view of these courts, the information belongs to the firm and one who takes and uses that information for her own benefit has in effect misappropriated the property of another. Before *U.S. v. O'Hagan*, the U.S. Supreme Court had declined to opine on the matter, even though it had its chances to do so. Recall, the *Chiarella* case, for instance. Although the Court found that Mr. Chiarella could not be liable for an insider trading violation under the classic theory because he owed no duty to the target companies, the Court punted as to whether Mr. Chiarella's acts violated his duty of trust to his employer, the print shop and the acquiring firm.

In *O'Hagan*, a prominent Midwest law firm was working on a tender offer that one of the firm's clients, Grand Met, was in the process of making to takeover Pillsbury, a Minneapolis manufacturer of a famous line of foodstuffs and marketing icons, like the Pillsbury Doughboy and the Jolly Green Giant. 521 U.S. 642 (1997). One of the partners at the firm, O'Hagan, was not working on the merger transaction, but learned of the impending tender offer. He began purchasing securities, call options and common stock. When the tender offer was announced, the price of Pillsbury stock rose from the high $30s to around $60 per share and Mr. O'Hagan netted more than $4.3 million in profits. The classical theory of insider trading, based on breach of fiduciary duty, would fail in this case. O'Hagan had no relationship with the shareholders of Pillsbury. Nevertheless, the Court held that O'Hagan had committed securities fraud. He had traded in securities on the basis of information procured deceptively. He had violated the trust relationship he had with several others, like the partners at his firm and the firm's client, Grand Met. O'Hagan could only avoid exposure, like any violator, by abstaining from trading or disclosing. Interestingly though, the Court in *O'Hagan* describes the disclosure option differently than in the classic case fiduciary breach case. In *O'Hagan*, and presumably in other misappropriation cases, the Court suggests that the disclosure is owed to the source of the information, not necessarily to the trading partner. 521 U.S. at 652. Thus, in this view, O'Hagan would not have been guilty of securities fraud if he had gotten permission to use the information from the firm and the firm's client. However, because he was not technically an insider of Pillsbury, he need not make a disclosure to those shareholders.

Checkpoints

- In order to have committed securities fraud there must be: (1) a material misrepresentation; (2) reliance; (3) causation; and (4) the requisite mental state. The courts have interpreted the rule's rationale as investor protection and, therefore, they have provided an implied private right of action for plaintiffs in cases of basic securities fraud.

- A standing rule requires a potential plaintiff to have actually purchased or sold the security in question. Those who may have bought but-for the alleged misstatement do not have standing.

- Rule 10b-5 also prohibits trading by insiders with knowledge of non-public information, so-called "insider trading."

- The general rule in insider trading cases is 'abstain-or-disclose.'

- As to the 'abstain' principle, insider trading rules are a flat prohibition of trading for insiders on the bases of material non-public information. As for the 'disclose' principle, an insider may trade if the insider discloses the information prior to trading to their counterpart.

- An outsider who trades on an inside tip must abide by the same abstain-or-disclose rules when they are aware (or should have been aware) that the disclosure was improper.

Chapter 12

Proxy System

Roadmap

- Proxy Contests
- Independent Proxy Solicitations
- Proxy 'Solicitations'
- Proxy Statement Expenses
- Proxy Statement Fraud
- Shareholder Proposals

A. Introduction

Firms are able to make some of the most important business decisions and communicate to shareholders largely by way of the proxy system. For instance, consider the annual shareholder meeting. State corporate codes require the firm to have the yearly meeting, which the board uses to secure shareholder approval of various corporation actions, including (among others) changes in the corporate charter, authority for a new issue of securities, approval of an independent auditor, ratification of a transaction between the firm and the directors, approval of a plan of merger and, importantly, election of directors to the board. DEL. CODE ANN. tit. 8, § 211(b) (1999); MODEL BUS. CORP. ACT § 7.01 (2005). Ahead of the meeting, the firm sends out various disclosures regarding the upcoming meeting, like the annual report and the expected agenda, the so-called proxy statement. In addition to sending out the proxy statement, the board will also send out a proxy card, which permits shareholders to vote by mail (or over the Internet) without actually showing up at the meeting. *See, e.g.,* MODEL BUS. CORP. ACT § 7.22(b) (2005); DEL. CODE ANN. tit. 8, § 212(c) (1999); Rule 14a-16, 17 C.F.R. § 240.14a-16(a)(1) (2007).

As a consequence, the proxy system creates several advantages of convenience for the firm and its owners, the shareholders. For instance, shareholders need not waste resources to show up at the shareholder meeting. The cost of traveling to the annual meeting, frequently at the company's headquarters, would be an extravagant expenditure for most shareholders with only small holdings. Instead, many shareholders may vote their interests by proxy based on the proxy statement and the recommendation of the board. Thus, shareholders are permitted a low-cost way to participate in firm governance.

Equally important, the firm's ability to secure votes by proxy is critical for the firm to be able to establish a quorum and conduct business. State laws frequently require that at least half of eligible shareholder interests be represented before certain business, like the shareholder meeting, can be conducted. *See* DEL. CODE ANN. tit. 8, § 216 (1999); MODEL BUS. CORP. ACT § 7.25(a) (2005). Finally, the proxy system also creates a mechanism for interested shareholders to gain extensive information regarding upcoming matters of importance to the firm, regardless of whether they actually intend to vote or attend the meeting. Although few shareholders likely review in detail the exhaustive proxy statements, this sort of routine communication establishes an important mechanism for interested shareholders to become informed, without having to independently gather information about the firm, the value of their shares, and the performance of managers.

The proxy system has great potential for fostering shareholder democracy by giving shareholders a practical way to effect beneficial changes at the firm. For instance, shareholders can mount an independent proxy solicitation and attempt to seat a competing slate of directors. The goal here would be to convince their co-shareholders to vote for the challenger slate and against the incumbent board. Also, shareholders may use the proxy system to make proposals about how the firm is operated. This strategy creates the prospect of a challenge on other firm operational points, not exclusively director elections. For instance, shareholders might make a recommendation that a firm abandon a strategy, change the by-laws, or simply hold the annual meeting in a different locale.

As mentioned, both of these actions—independent proxy solicitations relating to particular director elections and proposals relating to non-election issues—could potentially give shareholders a voice in the firm's trajectory. However, the proxy system rules largely leave these actions without much real power for shareholders, as shall be seen in this Chapter. The expense and exposure of a proxy challenge makes this option less of the sharp sword that shareholders interested in the economic condition of the firm would be apt to turn to. As for shareholder proposals not related to a particular election, shareholders must still rely on the approval and grace of the incumbent board before any such proposal sees the light of day.

B. Independent Proxy Solicitations or Proxy Challenges

Any person or entity that plans to "solicit" shareholder votes must also follow the rules of the proxy system. This includes, most interestingly, challengers pushing reform by mounting a challenge to the incumbent board. They must issue their own proxy statement and collect as many proxy votes preceding a shareholder meeting as possible. Thus, shareholders who want to oppose the board-recommended slate can do so when the board nominees are up for election at the annual meeting. If the board is not staggered, all of the board members will come up for election annually and a shareholder may counter-propose her own slate. However, these contests for elections, like any controversial business to be taken up at the annual meeting, are done by proxy. Thus, shareholders who want to nominate a competing slate cannot wait until the annual meeting to do so. They must send out their own proxy statement preceding the meeting and try to collect as many proxy votes for their own slate as possible. By initiating an independent proxy solicitation, a challenger-shareholder might be able seat their own slate of directors and oust under-performing or corrupt managers.

However, the general legal rules regarding proxy solicitations create huge, although not insurmountable, obstacles for challengers, while virtually ensuring the board nominees will be seated. *See generally* Rules 14a-4, 14a-5, 14a-6, 17 C.F.R. §§ 240.14a-4, 240.14a-5, 240.14a-6 (2007). For instance, the rules provide that shareholder-challengers may have to foot their own bill for a proxy challenge. Moreover, shareholders who want to engage the proxy system to mount a challenge to the board also expose themselves to liability by private actions under rather expansive theories of proxy fraud. Last, shareholders have to be aware that almost any conduct can constitute a solicitation.

Additionally, challenges to the incumbent board by way of an independent proxy solicitation are also problematic from an economic perspective. That is, the gains of a proxy challenge, as opposed to some other methods of pushing a change in control, are shared by the shareholder community generally. If, say, the successful challengers are about to replace the incumbent board of directors with a new slate of individuals who are able to increase firm value and the price of the company's shares, the gains to the challengers will continue to be a function of her shareholder stake. The successful challenger will, in other words, have to share the gains from challenge with other shareholders. Thus, compared to other methods of reform, a successful challenger will have less incentive to mount a proxy campaign, when she cannot capture all of the value that accrues from winning the challenge, and from the beneficial changes at the company that follow.

As a consequence perhaps, one would expect that very few independent proxy solicitations occur from shareholders seeking to change the management of the company. The truth of the matter is not far from that expectation. In fact, one of the most prolific corporate law commentators, Lucian Bebchuk, has found that very few shareholders mount a proxy challenge from year to year. According to his research, in the last decade, 1996–2005, shareholders made a true challenge to the incumbent managers by way of a proxy challenge in only about a dozen instances each year. Lucian A. Bebchuk, *The Myth of the Shareholder Franchise*, 93 VA. L. REV. 675, 685–86 (2007). For large companies—*i.e.*, those with a market capitalization of over $200 million— Bebchuk finds that there were fewer than 3 such challenges per year. *Id.* at 686–87. Furthermore, according to Bebchuk's statistics, less than 40 percent of all contested proxy solicitations focused on installing an alternate management team for the governing company. *See id.*

1. "Solicitations"

To start with, consider the current rules regarding solicitations. Generally, any person or entity who intends to "solicit" the authorization of another to vote their shares must issue a proxy statement to those solicited. Solicitations are broadly defined to include any conduct "reasonably calculated" to influence shareholder votes. Rule 14a-1, 17 C.F.R. § 240.14a-1 (2007). This means that, in order to avoid legal liability, shareholders have to follow relatively exacting and costly disclosure requirements in many circumstances. Because "solicitations" are relatively broadly defined, a challenger who, say, merely contacts a couple dozen other shareholders about an upcoming election to the board of director might have unwittingly mounted a proxy campaign with the accompanying regulatory requirements. This means that the average shareholder, who likely only holds a small stake in the firm, will likely avoid conduct that could possibly be construed as a solicitation, because this is safest way to also avoid accompanying disclosure obligations. Thus, the cost of communicating with other shareholders about even possibly beneficial changes at the firm may be cost-prohibitive for the vast majority of shareholders. In many cases, challenger communications, even non-traditional ones, might create an obligation for challengers to issue a costly proxy statement.

Long Island Lighting v. Barbash is somewhat representative of the regulatory consequences of conduct that could conceivably fit the code's definition of a solicitation. 779 F. 2d 793 (2d Cir. 1985). In that case, a political candidate made a campaign issue out of the management of the utility company and its plan to construct a nuclear power facility. He, along with other citizen groups, took out newspaper advertisements opposing the utility's plan and ran radio spots against the proposed plan. The utility's board of directors brought suit to enjoin the activity on the grounds that the plaintiff's communications were in fact "solicitations" to other shareholders and not permissible without issuing a proxy statement with the relevant disclosures. The group defended that the advertisements were protected under the First Amendment because the issue was of public concern. The Second Circuit remanded the case. The important takeaway from cases like *Long Island Lighting* is that shareholders need to be wary. Even newspaper ads, if they were designed to influence the vote, could create the prospect of a challenge as a solicitation within contemplation of the rules.

To be sure, not all acts are solicitations. *See* Rule 14a-1, 17 C.F.R. § 240.14a-1 (2007). For instance, a challenger does not "solicit" for purposes of the statute when she makes a public speech or otherwise publicly indicates how she intends to vote. Thus, large shareholders may inform the media of their intention to, say, oppose management. Even though such an interview will likely generate press and steer some other shareholders to consider following their lead against the management slate, such conduct is excluded from the "solicitation" sphere. Nor does a challenger need to worry about issuing a proxy statement if she only intends to communicate with a small number of shareholders—*i.e.*, solicitations directed at ten or fewer persons. Rule 14a-2(2), 17 C.F.R. § 240.14a-2(2) (2007).

2. Proxy Statement Expenses

Additionally, consider the rules regarding recovery of expenses in a proxy contest. The incumbent board members can rely on the firm for these expenses, if reasonable. Meanwhile the challenger normally has to pay for their own proxy expenses. Challengers may only cover their expenses *ex post*—that is, after a challenge—if they succeed in their challenge, which is broadly defined. Further, their recovery will also depend on shareholder approval. *See, e.g., Rosenfeld v. Fairchild*, 128 N.E.2d 291, 293 (N.Y. 1955).

To be sure, the rules regarding expenses in a proxy contest create a significant advantage for incumbent directors who are able to charge their expenses for a proxy contest to the firm. However, the rules seem to have several sensible rationales. For instance, the rule that forces challengers to cover their own expenses initially makes some sense insofar as it prevents frivolous challenges. The cost of the disclosure by way of proxy statement along with other expenses probably dissuades the vast majority of challengers. A challenger would only bare the expense of a proxy challenge if the expected benefit of success outweighed the costs of the fight in the first place. Considering that many shareholders have relatively small stakes, only outsized gains would merit mounting a contest.

At the same time, a more balanced approach—for instance, an approach that permitted both challengers and incumbents to recover their expenses— would create an incentive for too many challengers. If challengers could always rely on the firm to fund their challenges, they would have little compunction about waging challenges. These challenges may undercut firm interests, force the incumbent board to spend precious resources in defense, and unnecessarily distract the manager and directors from their work. Additionally, the rules regarding proxy expense that permits the incumbent board to use firm resources makes sense because it reinforces other rules. For instance, it reaffirms the notion of the incumbent board as being the nucleus of the firm's operations, and as being the body with the power to shape the firm's interest, including what is in the firm's best interest during a proxy contest. If the board of directors was seriously limited from making expenditures in defense, the board would become a feckless body at the mercy of well-financed challengers. Board members willing to serve on the boards would be hard to find under such circumstances.

In a contest for control by proxy, the expenses are not trivial. The challenger faces several expenses in a proxy contest, including the expense of printing the proxy statement for hundreds of thousands (or perhaps millions) of shareholders, postage to transmit the proxy statement to shareholders, and the legal fees paid for drafting the proxy statement in compliance with state and federal disclosure rules. One source has suggested that the cost of a proxy solicitation can range from several hundred thousand dollars to several million dollars. *See* Bebchuk, *supra* at 689–91. The federal disclosure rules are extensive, including information regarding the date and time of the meeting, the identity of the solicitor, a description of the methods of solicitation, and the source of the solicitor's funding. *See, e.g.,* Schedule 14A, 17 C.F.R. §240.14a-101 (2007).

From afar, the general rules for recovery of expenses in a proxy challenge are simple: The incumbent board may pass along their expenses to shareholders, while the challenger can only recoup their expenses from the firm if they win the proxy challenge. However, on closer inspection, the recovery of proxy expenses is more nuanced. For instance, according to the case law, although the incumbent board may pass along their proxy expenses to the firm, there are at least some nominal parameters. The incumbent board, that is, may not pass along expenses that were not reasonable in scope and that served no clear firm interest. As a practical matter, however, an incumbent board can easily meet both of these standards.

Rosenfeld vs. Fairchild, for instance, involved a successful challenge to the incumbent board. 128 N.E.2d 291 (N.Y. 1955). The challengers passed a resolution (approved by shareholders) to reimburse them for their costs of the campaign and to recompense the incumbents for some outstanding costs of the incumbent's campaign. The majority opinion approved the expenditures. Both of the aforementioned thresholds—reasonable expenses and firm interest—were easily met. First, courts traditionally have given incumbent boards wide latitude when it comes to determining the level of expenditure that is reasonable. In fact, it appears that the only type of expenditure that might be considered unreasonable would be expenditures that are wasteful, an impossibly high standard. The parties in *Rosenfeld* both agreed that several expenditures were reasonable, including expenditures to hire proxy solicitation firms, a public relations firm, expenses for entertainment, and chartered travel. *See Id.* at 295–96 (J. Van Voorhis, dissenting).

Second, the board is technically limited to making expenditures that are related to a firm interest. The upshot of this limitation is only that the board may not recommend expenses solely to maintain their office. However, few, if any, firm decisions are naked power plays by the board; most proxy battles have some elements of both personal and firm interest. No doubt, the incumbent board is likely motivated by a personal desire to stay in office, but also a genuine belief that the challengers have misguided plans for the firm. For instance, in *Rosenfeld* the challengers claimed to wage their proxy contest to cut off a long-term pension contract for a former director of the board. The incumbent board probably had a personal stake in seeing the former director prosper in his retirement, given that his successful retirement is related to their own prospects after leaving the board. However, a firm interest can also be easily offered up in such a circumstance, because lavish pension benefits are a way for the firm to recruit good talent. In the end, since the incumbent board is almost always able to come up with a firm-related justification for their waging a proxy battle, this criterion is not limiting at all.

As for the challengers, they may only recover if they succeed in their proxy challenge, though as a practical matter "success" is in the eye of the beholder. In the traditional view, the challenger may recover if they win control of the board of directors, at which time the new board will simply resolve to reimburse the challenger for its reasonable expenses. Because this type of resolution creates the prospect of a conflict of interest—*i.e.*, the challenger dominates the board—it is customary that the resolution regarding reimbursement be approved by a majority of shareholders as well. However, this is not the only way a challenger can get reimbursed for their expenses. A challenger, one would expect, might also get their expenses for preparing to mount a proxy contest as part of a settlement with the board. For instance, an activist investor may threaten an independent proxy solicitation unless certain changes are made at the firm. Such investor may back down if the firm agrees to such changes and sweetens the pot by also promising to pay the challenger's heretofore incurred expenses. A third way a challenger may be able to get their expenses is by winning *some* seats on the board, although she may not win control. In this circumstance, it is also possible that the new board members may be able to negotiate with the current board for reimbursement.

At the same time, it is worth mentioning that in some cases a nominally successful challenger, in theory, may not be reimbursed for their expenses. For instance, some proxy challenges involve other matters not involving a shareholder-nominated slate to the board. For instance, a proxy challenge might emerge over a shareholder proposal to change some aspect of the firm's operation, like proposals to amend the firm's bylaws or charter, particularly in cases involving the redemption of a poison pill. The number of proxy contests about issues not involving the election of directors, according to Bebchuk, was relatively numerous, representing about one-quarter of all proxy contests in the last decade. *See* Bebchuk, *supra,* at 686. In these cases, even a successful challenger may not necessarily have a right to a reimbursement of their expenses. In this case, the successful challenger has no control of the board and it is still the board which would decide whether to pass a reimbursement resolution.

3. Proxy Statement Fraud

Finally, when an entity communicates by proxy, another significant consideration is the potential exposure to liability if the proxy statement fails in some regard. The rules regarding proxy statement fraud also seem to create a relatively high hurdle for plaintiffs interested in communicating with other shareholders by use of the proxy system. As mentioned, the proxy statement is heavily regulated from the form of the proxy statement to the procedure for filing a preliminary statement with the SEC. *See generally* Rule 14a-1 et seq., 17 C.F.R. § 240.14a-1 et seq. (2007). The party seeking proxies can be liable for issuing a proxy statement that is misleading as to a material fact or fails to include a material fact. *See* Rule 14a-9, 17 C.F.R. § 240.14a-9 (2007). The incumbent board of directors, in fact, might mount a suit funded by the corporate treasury alleging proxy fraud on the part of their pesky challengers. Meanwhile, in contrast to the incumbent board, the challengers have to bear their own costs of making a complete and frank disclosure and the legal fees of defending a challenge over their disclosure. In both cases, liability depends on the whether the fact was material—that is, a fact which a reasonable investor would want to know.

Consider *Case v. Borak*, a case where the U.S. Supreme Court first suggested that plaintiffs have an implied cause of action when the firm issues a false or misleading proxy statement. 377 U.S. 426 (1964). In that case, the plaintiff sought to enjoin the merger between Case and the American Tractor company on the grounds that the Case had issued a misleading proxy statement, among other issues. According to the plaintiffs, because of the misleading proxy statement, which failed to alert shareholders to stock market manipulation, shareholders were gulled into voting to approve the merger.

The court finds that shareholders have an implied private right of action, which serves as a backstop to the SEC policing power. That is, although the SEC reviews proxy statements, it, according to the court, has few resources to detect proxy statement fraud among the thousands of statements it receives annually. Thus, the private right of action serves a private policing mechanism to detect failure to conform to the proxy disclosure rules.

Importantly also, the court notes that the right to bring an action for proxy statement fraud can be brought as either a direct or derivative suit:

> The injury which a stockholder suffers from corporate action pursuant to a deceptive proxy solicitation ordinarily flows from the damage done the corporation, rather than from the damage inflicted directly upon the stockholder. The damage suffered results not from the deceit practiced on him alone but rather from the deceit practiced on the stockholders as a group. To hold that derivative actions are not within the sweep of the section would therefore be tantamount to a denial of private relief.

377 U.S. at 432. The right of a plaintiff to bring a case as a derivative suit is significant, as it greatly expands the case for awarding attorneys' fees. That is, in derivative litigation, successful plaintiffs are usually able to recover their attorney's fees from the corporation if they create a substantial benefit to a class of investors. *See Ramey v. Cincinnati Enquirer, Inc.*, 508 F.2d 1188, 1199 (6th Cir. 1974). In a later case, in fact, the U.S. Supreme Court confirms that because of the substantial benefit to shareholders, plaintiffs should be able to recover their attorneys' fees if they succeed in establishing a cause of action for proxy fraud. *See, Mills v. Electric Auto-Lite Co.*, 396 U.S. 375 (1970). As a consequence, both the rights described in *Borak*—the private right of action and the right to bring a private action as derivative suit—creates significant incentives for the private parties to police the content of proxy statements, their conformance with the proxy rules, or, as the Supreme Court later puts it, vindicate statutory policy. *Id.* at 627.

For three reasons the chances for liability for proxy statement fraud are significant for both challengers and the incumbents. First, the proxy rules, as mentioned, require extensive disclosure. Due to the wide-ranging disclosure requirements, the chances of making an inadvertent, but still misleading, statement are amplified. In fact, it appears that even a merely negligent misrepresentation may be the basis for proxy fraud. Second, liability turns principally on whether the statement in question is "material," which, in these cases, has been expansively defined. As mentioned, materiality turns on the reasonable investor standard, rather than on whether the misstatement actually caused any change in conduct on the part of shareholders. *See, e.g., Mills* at 384. Third, liability for misleading proxy statement is relatively severe because the courts have read into federal proxy regulations an implied right of plaintiffs to bring an action. Because of the operation of other rules, this means that plaintiff's lawyers have a significant incentive to uncover evidence of proxy fraud.

In the end, shareholders who want to challenge managers through an independent proxy solicitation face an uphill battle because of the intersection of at least three important rules: the requirement to make disclosures for solicitations; the rules regarding proxy expenses; and the real prospect of liability for proxy statement fraud. Partly as a consequence, challengers make few proxy challenges against the incumbent managers, as the Bebchuk research shows. More disheartening still for proponents of shareholder democracy are the statistics regarding the likelihood of success when challengers do make a challenge. Again, measured by success rates, it appears that proxy contests are heavily tilted toward the incumbent board. In fact, Bebchuk finds that in the last decade approximately 62% of challengers lost proxy contests. *See* Bebchuk, *supra* at 687.

C. Shareholder Proposals

Shareholders, in the right circumstance, may piggyback off the firm's proxy statement. In this way, they might be able to avoid issuing their own proxy statement (and the accompanying expense, not to mention some exposure to liability). In these cases, a shareholder might make an application for their proposal to be included in the firm's statement to shareholders. Thus, another way shareholders might communicate with their co-investor colleagues is by submitting a shareholder proposal via the firm's proxy statement. *See generally* Rules 14a-7, 14-a8, 17 C.F.R. §§ 240.14a-7, 240.14a-8 (2007). For instance, the shareholder might make a proposal that concerns executive compensation, or financial reporting, among other business issues. The shareholder proposal right has also been used by shareholders to garner media attention for the issue *de jure*. Thus, a notable number of shareholder proposals concern social and political issues, like divesting from apartheid South Africa, affirmative action, opposition to the Vietnam war, animal rights, or worker rights in China.

However, like the rules regarding recovery of expenses, the rules on shareholder proposals also seem to create a high hurdle for shareholders interested in using the proxy machinery to communicate with other shareholders. On the face of it, with a proper shareholder proposal, a shareholder gets an opportunity, at low-cost, to make a short pitch to shareholders through the firm's proxy statement. The shareholder's proposal, along with a short supporting statement, is sent with the firm's proxy statement. Thus, the shareholder need not bear the expensive of printing and posting. Because the proxy statement is only required in connection with a solicitation of votes, shareholders who do nothing more than send out a proposal, are not usually thought to have solicited votes and, thus, they are not required to send out a statement. *See generally* Rule 14a-8, 17 C.F.R. § 240.14a-8 (2007). Further, many of the procedural barriers to entry are relatively minimal. For instance, a shareholder must usually hold only a modest number of shares for at least one year, keep the proposals and any supporting statement short (*e.g.*, limited to 500 words), and transmit the proposals a reasonable time in advance to the board, among others. *See generally* Rule 14a-8, 17 C.F.R. § 240.14a-8 (2007).

On the other hand, in only a very limited set of circumstances must the firm include the shareholder proposal as part of its proxy statement. Other rules regarding shareholder proposals, if taken at face value, effectively shut out many of the most important shareholder proposals. The rules exclude thirteen types of proposals, including proposals that relates to an election; proposals that contemplate unlawful activity; violate proxy rules; usurp the powers of the board under state law; proposals concerning insignificant items; proposals that the board has no power to effectuate; and proposals related to dividends, among others. *See, e.g.*, Rule 14a-8, 17 C.F.R. § 240.14a-8.

Luckily for shareholders, courts have interpreted these exclusion rules as narrowly as possible. For instance, in a recent case, *AFSCME v. AIG*, the second circuit court of appeals held that the exclusion for proposals relating to an election did not apply to proposals concerning election procedures generally. 462 F.3d 121 (2d Cir. 2006). In that case, AFSCME, a union, brought an action to compel AIG, a corporation, to include the union's proposal that AIG's bylaws be amended to permit shareholder nominees to be included in the proxy statement for certain shareholders. AIG objected to the proposals on the grounds that it related to an election and the SEC issued a no-action letter, which gave AIG the go-ahead to initially exclude. The Second Circuit, however, disagreed.

Even though the proposal, on its face, related to election, the court held that the language was ambiguous:

> The relevant language here — "relates to an election" — is not particularly helpful. AFSCME reads the exclusion as creating an obvious distinction between proposals addressing a particular seat in a particular election (which AFSCME concedes are excludable) and those, like AFSCME's proposal, that simply set the background rules governing elections generally (which AFSCME claims are not excludable). AFSCME's distinction rests on Rule 14a-8(i)(8)'s use of the article "an," which AFSCME claims "necessarily implies that the phrase 're-lates to an election' is intended to relate to proposals that address *particular elections*, instead of simply 'elections' generally." It is at least plausible that the words "an election" were intended to narrow the scope of the election exclusion, confining its application to proposals relating to "a particular election *and not* elections generally." It is, however, also plausible that the phrase was intended to create a comparatively broader exclusion, one covering "a particular election or elections generally" since any proposal that relates to elections in general will necessarily related to an election in particular. The language of Rule 14a-8(i)(8) provides no reason to adopt one interpretation over the other.

462 F.3d at 126–25. Because the language was susceptible to multiple reasonable interpretations, the court noted that other interpretive tools must be resorted to, like previous interpretations of the SEC. After an exhaustive review of historical interpretations by the SEC, the court decided the exclusion should be viewed narrowly as limiting the board's discretion to exclude proposals that deal with a particular election, not elections more generally.

Similarly, in another case, *New York City Employees' Retirement System v. Dole*, shareholders were the New York City Employees' Retirement System, a public pension fund. NYCES proposed that Dole study the possibility of universal healthcare. 795 F.Supp. 95 (S.D.N.Y. 1992). Specifically, the proposal directed the board to establish a committee to study the three predominate models for moving toward national healthcare: a single payor system, limited payor system, and a system of employer mandates. Dole objected on three grounds, arguing that the proposal concerned "ordinary business operation;" insignificant matter; and insofar as it concerned universal healthcare, the proposal centered on a topic that the firm could not effectuate. 795 F.Supp. at 99.

The district court held that Dole had not met its burden of showing that one of the statutory exclusions applied to the proposal for national healthcare. To be sure, usually setting the terms of employee relationships, wages, and benefits are quintessentially "ordinary" operational tasks. However, the court found that the proposal was extraordinary, considering that it "may affect the entire scope of Dole's employee health insurance policy." The court also found that that the proposal concerned a significant part of Dole's expenditures, likely far greater than the 5% threshold. Finally, the court suggested that Dole had the power to take up the proposal, if it was to pass, because it only called for Dole to issue a report on the three national healthcare proposals.

Thus, *Dole* reinforces shareholder democracy insofar it stands for the notion that courts may be generally predisposed to interpret the exclusion rules narrowly. In this way, well-advised shareholders have a decent chance of having their proposals issued along with the firm's proxy statement and can communicate with other shareholders. Additionally, the case represents good guidance to shareholders keen on avoiding exclusion of their proposals. For instance, the court speaks favorably of the language the pension fund uses, how the proposals in Dole were "couched." Shareholders would be well-advised to structure the language of their proposals accordingly. In many instances, well-advised shareholders would make their proposals precatory or non-binding in order to make sure that the proposal does not unnecessarily usurp board power and give the board a reason to exclude. Further, shareholders intent on making a proposal that centers on an important social or political issue, like healthcare in *Dole*, need to also be able to connect their proposal and supporting statement to some interest of the firm. For the most hot-button of political issues this is somewhat easy to do with many larger corporations that have operations that touch many different areas. Otherwise the proposal might be excluded as irrelevant to the firm's interests.

Checkpoints

- A shareholder can influence the corporation by mounting an independent proxy solicitation (or proxy challenge).
- A challenger's individual gain will be a function of the size of his stake in the company because any gains realized from a successful proxy challenge are shared by all shareholders.
- Solicitations are broadly defined as any conduct that is reasonably calculated to influence shareholder votes. Solicitations require the issuance of a proxy statement to those solicited.

Checkpoints *continued*

- Proxy challenges can be both costly and risky for a shareholder because she must finance the costs associated with issuing a proxy statement in compliance with the law and is exposed to potential private legal action under expansive theories of proxy fraud.

- Shareholder proposals are an alternative to full-fledged proxy challenges. Shareholder proposals allow a shareholder to communicate with other shareholders by attaching the proposal to the firm's proxy statement and avoiding the costs associated with an independent solicitation.

- Rules governing shareholder proposals impose multiple limitations. Importantly, for instance, thirteen types of proposals can be excluded by the board, including proposals related to director elections.

Chapter 13

Takeovers

Roadmap
- Dissenter Rights: Notice, Vote, and Appraisal
- Statutory Mergers
- Sale of Assets
- Triangular Mergers
- Short-Form Mergers
- De Facto Mergers
- Hostile Takeovers
- Defensive Measures

A. Introduction to Takeovers

As mentioned in the last chapter, the proxy contest is one way of gaining control of the firm and ousting under-performing corporate managers. The second, perhaps more frequently used and higher profile action for control of the firm, is the takeover. In a takeover, one firm (the acquirer) buys up the assets and franchise of another firm (the target). The goal is, of course, to realize significant value or synergies (like cost-savings) from the combination. Takeovers frequently occur when a firm is performing poorly in the marketplace, creating a plum opportunity for a takeover artist. An acquirer might buy the target company at the beat-down price, sack the current managers, sell off assets, and take other action to improve company value.

Takeovers, as opposed to proxy contests, allow the shareholders to appropriate significantly more of the intrinsic value of the firm itself than in a proxy contest. Recall that in a proxy contest, the challenger faces huge upfront cost to wage a proxy battle, although the result is far from certain. Additionally, recall that in successful proxy contests, the successful challenger's potential profits are a function of the size of their shareholding. If the proxy contest is successful and the new leaders are able to improve company value, those gains will be shared *pro rata* among the shareholders. However, in a successful takeover, the buyer will realize significantly more value from their attempt to improve company value. In a takeover, the acquirer buys up all (or a controlling majority) of the depressed stock. Other shareholders are bought out. If the acquirer is able to turn the company around, the gains from the turnaround rebound mainly to the acquirer's benefit.

Takeovers can occur under very different scenarios in terms of funding, deal structure, and management approval. The substance of the transaction though is largely the same: The productive assets of the target company are merged with those of the acquirer. To begin with, in terms of funding, an acquiring firm could mount a takeover by offering to the target cash consideration, assets, or securities in the acquiring firm. Thus, the prospect of a takeover increases as companies find themselves awash in cash, which would otherwise be used to make a dividend to shareholders or expand current operations. Frequently, however, the acquiring company spends relatively little of their free cash flow to make a takeover. Instead, these acquirers finance a portion of the takeover consideration using the target firm's assets as collateral. These are called leveraged buyouts or management buyouts if the target firm's managers participate.

Additionally, the takeover could be legally structured as a statutory merger, a purchase of the target firm's assets, or a tender offer directly to the target firm's shareholders. The combined firms might consolidate into a new firm, the bigger firm, or the firm with the better franchise. Finally, a takeover could be friendly, meaning the board approves of the takeover approach. Management, in many cases, may effectively put the target firm up for sale and subsequently play a substantial role in selecting the buyer. In these friendly approaches, managers are conflicted. Corporate managers will negotiate the terms of the takeover on behalf of the shareholders, in addition to perhaps quietly negotiating a severance package or future position for themselves. Alternatively, takeovers can be hostile, a situation where the board of the firm that has been targeted for acquisition disapproves. The board, as shall be explained in more detail, may find the terms of the takeover inadequate and decide, as a consequence, that the takeover should be resisted.

B. Dissenter Rights

Many takeovers raise the prospect that some shareholders might be treated unfairly. For instance, some takeover offers include shares in the acquirer firm in exchange. In the event of such an acquisition, some shareholders could find themselves holding stock in a firm they are unfamiliar with, managed by strangers, with markedly different assets. Furthermore, in many cases, takeovers can be approved by a simple majority of shareholders or even a single controlling shareholder. Thus, in these cases minority shareholders might find themselves bound to merge under terms that they find unfavorable or even derisory. Nevertheless, shareholders have a few rights in statutory mergers (and, in some states, assets sales), which on their face appear to provide shareholders with protection.

1. Right to Notification

First, shareholders have the right to be notified of an impending merger. The notice is a particularized requirement to ensure that shareholders know when the shareholder meeting is taking place, plan of merger, possibility of appraisal rights, and the purpose of the meeting, along with some information about the acquiring firm. *See, e.g.*, MODEL BUS. CORP. ACT §§ 11.04(d), 13.20 (2006).

2. Right to Vote

Second, in many statutory combinations, dissenting shareholders have a right to voice their approval or dissent from the transaction by shareholder vote. The breadth of the shareholder's right to vote frequently depends on whether the corporate combination is organized as a sale of assets, statutory merger, or tender offer. For instance, in a statutory merger, shareholders of both firms (the acquirer and the target) usually have a right to vote on the transaction.

However, it is important to note that shareholder voting power is counterbalanced by the operation of other rules. For example, combinations under other corporate code provisions, depending on the state, might not provide for a shareholder vote for both firms. In Delaware, shareholders do not have the right to vote upon the sale of firm assets, even though substantively this transaction might be comparable to a statutory merger. DEL. CODE ANN. tit. 8, § 271 (2008). Also, in most cases, a simple majority in favor of the takeover will suffice. Thus, many of the firm's largest shareholders effectively determine the firm's fate, leaving minority holders with little real voting power. Additionally, the right to vote can be substantially diluted on the eve of the corporate combination. That is, many firms have authorized but unissued stock, which they may issue to buyers in order to ensure that the acquirer wins control.

3. Right to Appraisal

Third, and most important, under most state corporate codes shareholders in a target firm have the right to statutory appraisal. When this right is applicable, shareholders cannot be forced to participate in a merger transaction and must be cashed out at fair value *prior* to the merger. (The "prior" is intended to signal that shareholders are not normally allowed to gain the value from the merger, the merger premium. *See, e.g.,* DEL. CODE ANN. tit. 8, § 262 (2008); b*ut see Weinberger v. UOP*, 457 A.2d 701, 713 (Del. 1983)). If dissenting shareholders follow the right procedure, they can be cashed out for the fair value of their stake in the firm. As with the right to vote to approve the transaction, the right to statutory appraisal, while creating a sufficient protection for dissenting shareholders, is far from perfect.

For one, shareholders must strictly follow requirements for dissent, like making separate and timely written demand for payment from the firm prior to the vote for merger, and often state corporate codes provide that shareholders interested in appraisal remedy dissent or vote to abstain from the merger. *See* MODEL BUS. CORP. ACT § 13.26 (2006); DEL. CODE ANN. tit. 8, § 262 (2008). The procedural requirements to perfect the appraisal right can be particularly devastating to shareholders. For instance, shareholders routinely fail to vote in opposition to the proposed merger or vote at all and may fail to send demand for appraisal in the time permitted under the statutes. Second, dissenting shareholders, in order to get the benefit of their appraisal right, might have to bring a court action at their own cost. Many courts find that appraisal actions cannot be brought as a class action and even more courts hold that the appraisal remedy is not proper as a derivative action. Thus, it is difficult for appraisal plaintiffs to find a lawyer to take an appraisal action on contingency. Because most shareholders only hold a small position in the firm, this may make statutory appraisal too costly to pursue. Third, in half of the states (including Delaware), the right to shareholder appraisal is generally not available in cases of publicly-traded companies or companies with widely-dispersed ownership. The thought behind this market exception is that there is no need for court intervention to value the shares since the marketplace already has done it. In this view, dissenting shareholders who find the offer to be inadequate have an easy alternative: They can sell their shares in the marketplace.

C. Statutory Takeovers

The relevant state corporate codes and cases provide a window into the various mechanisms for effectuating a takeover of a firm, including basic statutory mergers, sale of assets, triangular mergers, freezeout mergers, and short-form mergers between parent firms and their subsidiaries.

1. Statutory Merger

First, in a basic statutory merger, the board of directors and the shareholders of both the acquirer and the target have to approve the transaction. *See, e.g.*, MODEL BUS. CORP. ACT § 11 (2006); DEL. CODE ANN. tit. 8, § 251 (2008). Generally in statutory mergers, the board of directors approves the terms of the merger agreement, and then puts that agreement to a vote by the sharehold-ers. Assuming both the board and a majority of shareholders approve the merger, the merged entity is born under the terms of the agreement and the constituent firms are no longer. The merger agreement might provide that the new entity will operate under the acquiring company's trade name or the trade name of the target company. Either way, the merged entity will take on all the assets, debts and liability of its constituent firms, while the constituent firms no longer have a legal existence.

Because the merged entity by operation of law succeeds to all the liabilities and assets of the formerly separate firms, the merger likely saves on transac-tion costs. That is, the merged entity need not make countless filings in the states where the constituent firms once operated in order to have legal rights over assets. The disadvantage of the statutory merger is that the shareholders of both the target and the acquiring firm have voting and appraisal rights. The voting rights raise the prospect that the combination might not be completed because shareholders may reject the deal even if it is one for fair value and has the board's approval. Further, the appraisal right makes statutory merger un-appealing because the combined firm might have to spend down precious cash resources to appease dissenting shareholders.

2. Substantial Sale of Assets

A second type of combination set out in state corporate codes is the sale of substantially all of the target firm's assets. One unique advantage of asset sales is the limited nature of shareholders' right to vote and appraisal. Both the board and the shareholders of the target firm would usually have to approve the transaction. MODEL BUS. CORP. ACT § 12.02 (2006); DEL. CODE ANN. tit. 8, § 271 (2008). Worth mentioning, however, is that shareholders of the sell-ing firm may not have approval rights when the sale is less then "substantial." Generally, substantial sells are those that are outside of the ordinary course of business. *See* MODEL BUS. CORP. ACT § 12.01 (2006). At the same time, the shareholders of the buying firm do not necessarily have to approve of an asset purchase. This can be a significant advantage for the buying firm because they do not have to waste resources to gain their own shareholders' approval.

Additionally, at the end of a typical asset sale, the target company still exists. This is significant because the target firm may have latent liabilities. In an asset sale, such liability would not flow to the acquiring firm. Thus, another big advantage of sale of assets is that the acquirer is able to limit its exposure to those liabilities agreed to in the asset purchase agreement. Related to this last point, another advantage of asset sales is that the target firm continues, which keeps the target's relationships with other parties in tact and unaffected by the combination. In some cases, the target has built up a significant brand presence or franchise that is worth keeping around. Further, the target's relationships with others contracting parties, like creditors, may depend on the continued legal operation of the target. The counterpoint is that, unlike statutory mergers, sale of assets are high on transactions costs. Each asset sale must be documented and appropriately filed with the relevant state or regulatory agency.

3. Triangular Merger

The triangular merger is a third type of merger, which combines some of the advantages and disadvantages of the other two types. In the triangular merger, the acquiring firm sets up a subsidiary with no real operational responsibility (a so-called "shell"). The acquiring firm then capitalizes the shell subsidiary and merges it with the target. The shell firm has no shareholders except for the parent corporation, which means that the parent board's makes all decisions for the shell. The advantage of the triangular merger is that the acquiring firm is able to reduce its exposure to liability and the scope of dissenter rights (like in a sale of assets) and is able to benefit from the relatively low transaction costs (like in a statutory merger).

First, consider dissenter rights in the type of merger transaction just described. To be sure, the shareholders of the target entity would still have a right to vote down the transaction. However, because the acquiring firm's subsidiary rather than the acquiring firm itself is entering the merger, the voting rights of the acquiring firm would be cut off. Only the acquiring firm's subsidiary shareholders would be entitled to vote. However, remember there aren't any such shareholders. Essentially, the board of directors of the parent would decide. Second, in a triangular merger, the acquiring firm still receives the benefit of a relatively low-doc transaction, as in a straight two-party statutory merger. That is, the target and the acquirer are merged, which effects a legal consolidation of ownership in the formerly separate firms' assets and liabilities. Thus, since the target is to be merged with a subsidiary of the acquirer, there is no pressing need for multiple, voluminous state-specific filings. Third, even though the acquiring firm has combined with the target, the triangular merger cuts off liability. This is because there is a layer of insulation from liability between the parent and its' subsidiary, the entity created to consummate the transaction with the target. The parent is the sole owner of the subsidiary, but liability is limited as it would be for any shareholder in a corporate entity.

4. Freezeout Merger

Because the controlling shareholder dominates the board of directors, the controlling shareholder can easily push through board approval as required in the statutory merger. Equally, the controlling shareholder is also in a position to vote its stake in favor of the merger, even in cases in which there is a strongly coordinated minority dissent. Thus, a statutory merger orchestrated by a controlling shareholder is variously referred to as a "freezeout" or "squeeze out" to take into account the relatively weak role minority interests might play. Still, in the case of controlling shareholder mergers, the controlling shareholder still has to live up to the fiduciary duty of entire fairness to other shareholders (a la *Sinclair v. Levien*) and dissenting shareholders who perfect still may have the right to have their shares appraised. All told, therefore, the non-controlling shareholders will have to either tender their shares under the terms of the merger agreement, seek appraisal of their shares, or attempt an action for breach of fiduciary duty and entire fairness.

In *Weinberger v. UOP*, the Signal Corporation, a large, publicly-traded conglomerate, devised a strategy to acquire one hundred percent control of UOP, a publicly-traded petro-chemical services company. 457 A.2d 701 (Del. 1983). At the time of the plan, Signal already owned a majority interest in UOP, which it had previously acquired in a friendly transaction with the board of directors and UOP shareholders. Signal, as a result, also controlled 7 out of the 13 director positions on UOP's board. Thus, through these directors and other executives who had long-standing relationship with Signal, the company had access to significant proprietary information about UOP's prospects.

Notably, for instance, several senior executives at Signal, who were also on the board of UOP, prepared an internal report based on UOP proprietary information that suggested that UOP could be purchased "at any price up to $24 each." *Id.* at 705. Signal, however, never shared the internal report with other members of the UOP board or with UOP shareholders. Instead, based on the report and flush with cash, Signal decided to make an offer of $20 to $21 for the remaining stake it did not already owned. Signal approached UOP's president and CEO with the proposed offered, which represented approximately 50% over the trading price of the stock. The UOP chief thought $21 would be a fair offer and presented it to the non-Signal members of his board of directors. He also directed Lehman Brothers to turn around in fairly short-order a fairness opinion, which the investment bank delivered a few days later suggesting that the $21 per share offer was fair. Signal's board and the board of UOP, which was dominated by Signal insiders and former insiders, approved the terms of the cash merger at $21 per share. One of the minority shareholders who would have been cashed out at $21 sued.

The *Weinberger* court establishes that the controlling shareholder must also live up to their fiduciary duty to the minority shareholders. Thus, the appraisal remedy is not the only remedy for dissent shareholders in a freezeout merger. Dissenting shareholders may also have a claim for breach of fiduciary duty, which in controlling shareholders transactions like these are analyzed under the entire fairness standard, which is a more exacting level of scrutiny. Recall from above that the appraisal remedy has significant limitations, including the requirement that the shareholder perfects his right and the market exception. Thus, the ability to bring a case for entire fairness has significant benefit to a non-controlling shareholder who believes the consideration was inadequate, but would otherwise be limited in an appraisal proceeding.

The controlling shareholders, as a consequence, most show fairness, both substantive (fair price) and procedural fairness (fair dealing). In terms of procedural fairness, the controlling shareholder/purchaser must show that the transaction makes sense for the company in terms of timing, structure and overall process of negotiation. 457 A. 2d at 711. The court in *Weinberger* found that the process of the transaction lacked many of key elements of fairness, which would arise out of arms length negotiation. The whole transaction, according to the court, felt rushed. The Lehman Brothers fairness opinion was drafted in a hurry. Signal was able to secure the UOP board's approval in four days. 457 A.2d at 711. No negotiation team set out to get the best value for UOP shareholders. The UOP chief merely acceded to the offer terms as presented, without nary of a complaint or attempt at raising the bid.

In terms of substantive fairness, the court suggested that the firm may meet its initial burden if the freezeout transaction was approved by a majority of the non-controlling shareholders. However, the *Weinberger* court finds that Signal was not entitled to this burden-shifting benefit because the minority holders were not fully informed at the time of their approval. At the time of the vote to approve, the non-controlling shareholders were not told of Signal's internal report that showed that a high range of $24 for the shares of UOP, which meant approximately $17 million of additional value for shareholders. *Id.* at 712. Thus, their uninformed approval was "meaningless." *Id.*

Finally, the appointment of an independent negotiating committee is good evidence of substantive fairness. Specifically, the *Weinberger* court, in a footnote, suggests that one way of establishing fairness in a freezeout is by establishing an independent negotiating committee:

> [T]he result here could have been entirely different if UOP had appointed an independent negotiating committee of its outside directors to deal with Signal at arm's length. Since fairness in this context can be equated to conduct by a theoretical, wholly independent, board of directors acting upon the matter before them, it is unfortunate that this course apparently was neither considered nor pursued. Particularly in a parent-subsidiary context, a showing that the action taken was as though each of the contending parties had in fact exerted its bargaining power against the other at arm's length is strong evidence that the transaction meets the test of fairness.

457 A.2d at 709. The thought here is that if the controlling shareholder established such a committee, then the transaction might be protected under the business judgment rule. It turns out, however, according to later Delaware courts, even if a decision is approved by an independent committee it is still subject to meaningful judicial review. *See Kahn v. Lynch*, 638 A.2d 1110 (Del. 1994). The only difference is that if there is approval by such a committee, the burden of showing a failure of fairness shifts to the plaintiff.

In sum, what cases like *Weinberger* and its progeny seem to establish is that firms should adopt a variety of mechanisms in order to demonstrate that non-controlling shareholders have been treated fairly, including the following: (1) approval from a majority of the non-controlling shareholders; (2) obtain a timely fairness opinion; and (3) appoint an independent negotiating committee.

5. Short-Form Merger

A final type of takeover worth noting here is also orchestrated by a controlling shareholder. Corporate codes typically include a specific method for some controlling shareholders to execute a merger that wipes out the minority interest. The controlling shareholder may take advantage of these statutes, which make mergers easier for parents and their subsidiaries. This is a statutory merger between a subsidiary and a parent corporation, which owns 90% or more of the outstanding shares of a subsidiary. In these cases, the parent firm may merge with its subsidiary in short-order, with nothing more than the approval of parent firm's board. Because of the ease of executing this type of combination, it is frequently referred to as a short-form merger. The unique advantage of the short-form merger is that the parent firm need not obtain the approval of the subsidiary's shareholders. *See, e.g.*, MODEL BUS. CORP. ACT § 11.05 (2006); DEL. CODE ANN. tit. 8, § 253 (2008). Additionally, unless the parent corporation will cease to exist, the short-form merger does not trigger any dissenter rights for the parent firm's shareholders. However, the parent firm still must give at least one important dissenter right, the right to appraisal, to minority holders.

6. *De Facto* Mergers

Because statutory mergers permit shareholders to vote on the transaction and a statutory appraisal remedy, many firms will want to avoid a straight statutory merger. Put another way, creative transactional lawyers may recommend different methods of corporate combination of company assets, without effectuating a statutory merger and the accompanying appraisal and voting powers. In most states, the rule of statutory construction holds that each corporate statute has an independent significance, or "equal dignity," which protects a firm's choice of combination method. *Hariton v. Arco Elec.*, 188 A.2d 123, 125 (Del. 1963). The upshot of the rule is that parties may elect to use whatever statute they desire without fear of courts re-characterizing the transaction. Despite this rule of interpretation adopted by most courts, a minority of courts look to the substance of the transaction (not just technical compliance with the statute) to decide whether a statutory merger has occurred.

Farris v. Glen Alden involved two unmatched firms. 143 A.2d 25 (Pa. 1958). List was a firm with diversified holdings in real estate, oil and gas, textile, and the movie industries. Glen Alden was a relative small scale operator of a Pennsylvania mining concern. List had acquired a substantial stake in Glen Alden and had concluded that acquiring the rest of the company would produce positive synergies. Perhaps counterintuitive, however, the deal was structured such that Glen Alden, a relatively tiny firm, would buyout List, the much larger company. Under the deal's terms, Glen Alden would "buy" all of the assets of List and List would be dissolved. In exchange List shareholders would get newly-issued shares in the new combined firm, which would be known as the List Alden Corporation. The hope of the parties was that by structuring the deal as a sale of assets, as opposed to a statutory merger, the combined entity could avoid the appraisal remedy and, thus, preserve its cash. The plaintiff complained that the so-called purchase of assets was actually in substance a merger of the two firms. As such, plaintiff argued that shareholders deserved rights, like fair notice and right to appraisal. The court agreed. Thus, although the deal was structured as a sale of assets, according to the court the practical effect was no different than a statutory merger. After the transaction, the court found that the plaintiff would effectively hold shares in a different company against his will, if the court allowed the firms to avoid the protection afforded in the merger statute. According to the court, thus, the transaction was a *de facto* merger.

The case is important for a variety of reasons. To begin with, the case is important from a transactional perspective. The case illustrates how the substance of the same transaction can be accomplished by resort to various code provisions. The same transaction can take the form of a "sale," "merger," or "consolidation" without a real substantive difference for the owners. Yet, the characterization of the transaction as a sale of assets or merger has significant legal effects. If the acquiring firm is able to avoid appraisal rights, they are able to preserve cash. Furthermore, although substantively identical, structuring the transaction as a sale also means that the purchaser has limited liability. In a statutory merger, of course, the merged entity has continuing exposure to the liabilities of the component entities. Notwithstanding *Farris*, many state courts would hold that a deal structured as a sale, even though substantively the same avoids appraisal rights, based on the doctrine of independent statutory significance. Even in Pennsylvania, where *Farris* was decided, the state legislature, soon after the case was decided, passed a statute that purported to abolish the *de facto* merger doctrine.

Additionally, the case is important because it creates decent guidance as to what type of conduct might create the basis for a court re-characterizing an asset sale as a statutory merger. One fact in particular stands out. As in *Farris*, a court is more likely to deploy the *de facto* merger doctrine when the firm selling all the assets promises to dissolve after the sale as part of the agreement. This agreement-to-dissolve makes the substance of the transaction distinguishable from a true asset sale, where the company can be expected to continue in business, even if at a reduced capacity or in a different line.

D. Hostile Takeovers

Some merger proposals are not greeted with approval from the board of directors, but, instead, are met with hand-wringing. In these circumstances, the takeover artist can avoid the board of directors and take her case directly to shareholders in the form of a tender offer to shareholders or a proxy contest (previously discussed in Chapter 12). In a tender offer, the acquirer deals directly with shareholders. She makes an offer of cash, assets, securities or other consideration in exchange for the shareholders' holdings. The hope is that the acquirer will be able to gain control by convincing a majority of the shareholders to tender or turnover their shares. If the acquirer can get a controlling stake, the acquirer may then attempt a freezeout of the minority holders. For instance, if the acquirer can reach 90% ownership, the acquirer can then execute the short-form merger.

In one sense, using "hostile" to describe the acquirer tactics that bypass board approval and deal directly with shareholders is perhaps an inappropriate and overbroad use of the word. For starters, the term suggests that the buyer is somehow hostile, uncivil, or impolite. This can be far from the truth. After all, even in these so-called unfriendly approaches, shareholders are frequently paid a premium above the current trading price of their shares. Further, shareholders who decide whether to tender still have a say in whether the transaction is completed. Although coordination problems are rife, the shareholders can elect not to accept the hostile acquirer's offer. Finally, hostile bids likely effects management conduct in positive ways. That is, without sufficient monitoring, corporate managers may have incentives to shirk responsibility or convert corporate assets to personal uses. Hostile bids (or even the threat of hostile bids) create a check on such misconduct; that is, when manager performance dips, the attractiveness of the company as a takeover target increases. The appeal of increased value from sacking the wayward managers becomes clearer.

Yet, in another sense, bypassing the board's approval does create certain coercive or hostile effects and amplifies shareholders' vast coordination problems. That is, in a tender offer, an acquirer may be able to low-ball shareholders by setting a short deadline or making an offer to earlier tendering shareholders that is more appealing (e.g., cash) than the offer to later shareholders (e.g., securities). Further, in contrast to statutory takeovers, tender offers and proxy contests are generally regulated by federal law, as opposed to state corporate codes. Even though hostile approaches have advantages for acquirers, there are some disadvantages. In particular, in the case of hostile takeovers, the acquirer will still have to overcome the holdouts. That is, in any tender offer, it is virtually certain that some shareholders will not tender. Thus, in order to "buy" these shareholders, the acquiring will still have to rely on a statutory merger, albeit a lot quicker if the acquiring controls 90% of shares.

If there is a hostile party in these transactions, then it is almost certainly the target's board of directors. That is, the buyer has bypassed the target board because he is certain that the board of directors will resist the offer. Perhaps, for instance, the target board believes the prices is inadequate; or because the target board believes that they might be sacked if a takeover occurs; or because the target board believes the eve of a takeover is a golden time to secure financial advantage in terms of rich severance package or increased equity stake in the firm. Either way, the target board has resisted the takeover approach and perhaps even pursued defensive measures.

E. Defensive Measures

In many cases, the board of directors may initiate or rely on defensive measures to stop a takeover attempt. First, the incumbent board may be able to hold off an undesirable takeover attempt by changing the terms of the shareholders' relationship with the firm. For instance, the incumbent board may introduce changes to the charter of the organization that attempt to make it impossible to effect a quick takeover without dealing with the incumbent board of directors. A simple, but effective, delaying tactic might be for the board to recommend changes to the terms of election to the board of directors so that only a third of directors come up for a vote in one year. The takeover artist, even one able to acquire a majority stake in the firm, will not be able to effectuate a quick takeover by replacing members of the board of directors at a single meeting. In the interim, would-be buyers might lose their financing or move on to other pursuits.

Alternatively, the board may recommend changes that make it substantially more expensive to effectuate a takeover of the firm. For instance, the firm may devise a "rights plan" that gives shareholders the right to buy shares in the company (or acquirer) at fire-sale prices in the event of a takeover. Or, the incumbent board may attempt to undermine a takeover attempt by entering into transaction with a more appealing buyer. The incumbent board usually promises to give these so-called white knights lavish deal terms with exotic names, like "no-shops," "lock-ups," and "cancellation fees." A final type of defensive measure involves the firm's search for an appealing seller. In these instances, the incumbent board might recommend that the firm acquire another entity to create complexity and regulatory havoc for the hostile bidder. For instance, an incumbent board in the newspaper industry might recommend the firm make a defensive acquisition of a local radio station or other newspapers to raise potential antitrust concerns that frustrate a hostile bidder.

The law of takeover defenses does not fit neatly with traditional paradigms. On the one hand, a board's defensive crouch may be justified and motivated by an interest in seeing shareholders receive adequate value for their stakes. If this were the case, the board's conduct should be reviewed under the highly deferential business judgment standard. On the other, the danger is that because the livelihood of the incumbent board members may be on the line, these sorts of defensive tactics may be also motivated by their selfish interests in resisting a takeover rather than by an interest to serve the firm and its shareholders.

Thus, the problem is that in takeovers, the board of directors has a real conflict of interest. It expects that the takeover would not result in a nominal change in control, but a substantive one: new corporate managers and new members of the board. Thus, board members possibly have a unique incentive to avoid takeovers and the presumption of the business judgment rule seems inappropriate. Thus, with the increased risk of bad behavior, it makes sense that courts should scrutinize this type of conduct more closely. In fact, defensive measures are not judged by the business judgment rule. Instead, they are judged by an "enhanced" level of judicial scrutiny. This "enhanced" or "proportionate" or "intermediate" level of scrutiny is perhaps most famously presented in *Unocal v. Mesa Petroleum*, the next case.

In *Unocal*, the board of directors attempted to stave off a takeover approach from Mesa, a company with a history of corporate raiding. 493 A.2d 946 (Del. 1985). Mesa, a Texas company, made a two-tiered tender offer to shareholders. In the first part, shareholders who tendered early would be received $54 cash in exchange for their shares. Mesa's offer of cash was available for the shareholders until Mesa owed just over half of Unocal. In the second part of their offer, Mesa would offer the remaining shareholder securities that it claimed were also worth $54 a share.

The board of directors met to consider the offer, but considered it grossly inadequate in light of the firm's liquidation value of more than $60 a share. Further, the board was particularly incensed that shareholders on the back-end, in the second step of the transaction, would be compensated with junk bonds, securities whose value is often speculative and carry a high risk of default. Such two-tiered offers are frequently thought to be coercive because shareholders may be duped to tender their shares in order to avoid the perceived worst outcome in the second step. Recall that the first part of the offer involved a cash exchange, while shareholders tendering on the back-end were only promised junk bonds. Thus, the structure of Mesa's offer gave risk-adverse shareholders an incentive to tender their shares quickly, so as not to be left with an arguably weaker offer of risky securities.

The board resolved to attempt to block the transaction by making an alternative offer to shareholders. The offer provided that Unocal would buyout millions of tendering shareholders for $72 in securities. Interestingly, the terms of the self-tender provided that the offer was exclusive and not available to Mesa. The effect of Unocal's selective exchange offer or selective self-tender was that it would undercut any incentive effects from Mesa's two-step proposal in at least a couple of ways. First, the self-tender would be extremely costly. The board would have to spend down their firm's capital or borrow in order to buyback shares from tendering holders. As a result, the company, either laden with additional debt or a depleted treasury, would be less attractive as a takeover target. It would be more difficult for Mesa to finance their acquisition based on the highly leveraged assets of Unocal. Further, if Mesa were to acquire the company, much of the value would have been dissipated to shareholders (other than Mesa). Second, and perhaps more important, the self-tender creates an incentive for shareholders to refuse Mesa's first-step cash offer. That is, shareholders would have little incentive to be a part of the initial step because they could rely on the self-tender even if Mesa was successful. That is, many shareholders would have an opportunity to tender their shares for the much higher consideration promised under the terms of Unocal's self-tender.

Mesa argued that the discriminatory self-tender was a violation of fiduciary duty. The Delaware court endorsed the board's action to take defensive measures and articulated a relatively low-hurdle for evaluating defensive measures: reasonableness. The reasonableness-based test that the court crafts in *Unocal* breaks out into two components, both of which are relatively easy to satisfy.

First, in order for defensive tactics to pass muster, the target board has to be able to demonstrate that there is a good faith belief that there is a threat from a bidder. The *Unocal* court suggests that the judgment of outside directors that an offer was inadequate is good evidence that the takeover represents a threat. *Id.* at 955. Problem is, outside directors are in many ways as conflicted about the takeover as inside directors. Outside directors also have a personal interest in avoiding the takeover and keeping their directorship. *Unocal* also suggests that the board show some reasonable investigation of whether the proposal was a threat to the firm. *Id.* Delaware courts have suggested a fairness opinion commissioned by the board of directors might also establish whether the takeover offer represents a threat. *See Cheff v. Mathes*, 199 A.2d 548, 556 (Del. 1964). Again, however, the opinions come from investment banks, which may have a long-standing relationship with the target firm, might also have conflicts of interest that might create incentives for them to issue an opinion that backs up the target board.

Second, the board must be able to show that its response to the threat was reasonable; that is, proportional to threat posed. In particular, the court held that the board could adopt defensive measures so long as they were reasonably calibrated to thwart the threat posed and the director's conduct served a firm interest. The court noted several factors to consider whether the measure was reasonably calibrated given the threat:

This entails an analysis by the directors of the nature of the takeover bid and its effect on the corporate enterprise. Examples of such concerns may include: inadequacy of the price offered, nature and timing of the offer, questions of illegality, the impact on "constituencies" other than shareholders (*i.e.*, creditors, customers, employees, and perhaps even the community generally), the risk of nonconsummation, and the quality of securities being offered in the exchange.... While not a controlling factor, it also seems to us that a board may reasonably consider the basic stockholder interests at stake, including those of short term speculators, whose actions may have fueled the coercive aspect of the offer at the expense of the longer term investor.

493 A.2d at 955–56 (citations omitted). Thus, the court suggests that the firm need not just consider shareholder interest, but interests of the firm more generally. Because the list of considerations is extremely broad, it is likely that under *Unocal* the target's board of directors will almost always be able to come up with a firm-related reason for its defensive measure. For instance, in the case, the court approves of the selective exchange offer as a reasonable response to the Mesa two-tier tender offer. In the end, under *Unocal*, the target board can erect defensives to a takeover and expect little judicial interference. To be sure, in *Unocal*, the court acknowledged that defensive measures are not to be judged by the business judgment rule, which would effectively permit virtually every action by the board without much inspection. Yet, as discussed, *Unocal* established review of defensive measures in reality gives a target board wide latitude to pursue defensive measures.

Also, in *Unocal*, the court says that the board is not a "passive instrumentality." 493 A.2d at 954. Thus, the *Unocal* opinion tends to undercut at least one major strand of legal theory regarding board behavior in change of control transactions. That is, one theory best articulated by Dan Fischel and Frank Easterbrook, is that the board of directors should be passive in cases of self-tender. In their view, board passivity encourages takeover attempts and takeover attempts in turn encourage corporate managers to perform well. Put another way, actual takeovers (and the threat of takeovers) creates incentives for managers to perform well, lest they want the company taken over by some buyer who intends to squeeze value by sacking the incompetent managers. Thus, they argue that board passivity serves the interests of shareholders best because the threat of a takeover (whether or not one occurs) incentivizes good manager performance and minimizes agency costs.

Revlon v. MacAndrews was a roll call for some of the biggest names in takeover history: Lazard Freres was advisor to the target firm; Martin Lipton, inventor of the "poison pill" and founder of Wachtel, Lipton, the most famous mergers and acquisitions law firm, was the lead lawyer; Ron Perelman, once the richest person in the country and perhaps the most famous takeover artist, was the broker behind the hostile bid; Michael Milliken, the so-called inventor of junk bond financing, provided the financing; and Revlon, a dynamic beauty products conglomerate. 506 A.2d 173 (Del. 1986).

Ronald Perelman was an experienced takeover artist and set his sights on the Revlon Corporation, his biggest potential acquisition to date at that point. He first tried to negotiate on friendly terms with chief of Revlon only to be rebuffed. Revlon's chief thought his offer range, $40–50 per share, was inadequate. Lazard Freres pitched in with an opinion that suggested that the firm was worth at least $50 as a going concern and worth $60–$70 if the some of the company assets were sold. Perelman persisted and threatened to make a tender offer directly to shareholders for $45 per share, if the board did not negotiate.

On the advice of Martin Lipton, the firm instigated three defensive measures. First, the firm would repurchase about one-sixth of the outstanding shares. Frequently the thought behind this maneuver was that the repurchase of shares would spend down some of the corporate free cash flow, which might make the target less appealing to an acquirer who anticipates having access to a target flush with cash. At the same time, the repurchase would also increase the relative market value of the shares. That is, with fewer shares on the market, the relative value of the remaining shares usually increases. As the market value of the target goes up, so, too, does the price tag to purchase enough shares to gain control for an acquirer.

Second, the firm backed a "rights" plan, which since *Weinberger* has become a common defensive tactic. The rights plan gave very lucrative rights to shareholders in the event that an acquirer gained control of 20% of Revlon's shares. They would be able to exchange their shares for a $65 note payable at 12% interest.

Under a third scheme, the board would make a selective offer to 10 million shareholders in exchange of their shares for a note with even richer terms. Importantly, the notes contained restrictive covenants, which would have made it difficult for Perelman to takeover the company. For instance, the notes prohibited the firm from incurring new debt obligations or selling of assets without board approval, the principal financing mechanisms for Perelman. The notes also prevented the firm from paying a dividend without board approval, also something Perelman might have relied on in order to make the acquisition.

Meanwhile, Perelman made his first tender offer to shareholders at $47.50, which the incumbent members of the board advised shareholders to reject. As the war between the incumbent board and Perelman escalated, Perelman continued to raise his bid. Less than two months after his initial bid, Perelman had offered a little over $57 to tendering shareholders.

Revlon tried yet another defensive tactic: identifying a white knight or outside friendly acquirer. Revlon found one in Forstmann, a small buyout shop. Forstmann would offer $56 cash per share in a board recommended acquisition, while the board would redeem the defensive measures, including the rights plan and covenants. Furthermore, because the board preferred Forstmann, the incumbents offered several enticing deal provisions exclusively to Forstmann. For starters, the board offered Forstmann confidential financial information, which was not made available to Perelman's group. Additionally, the Forstmann group also asked for and received a lock-up provision, a no-shop provision, and a termination fee. Each of these devices would protect Forstmann in the event that a deal was not closed because another buyer offered more to shareholders. Under the lock-up provision, the incumbents entered into agreement whereby they promised to sell at least one of the Revlon units to Forstmann regardless of whether a deal with Forstmann was consummated. Under the no-shop provision, the incumbent board of directors was barred from negotiating with other potential acquirers. Lastly, under the termination fee, Forstmann would receive $25 million as a fee if for some reason the deal broke apart. Perelman sued to enjoin Revlon's friendly hook-up with Forstmann and to redeem the defensive measures.

The court held that many of the incumbents' strategies were unenforceable. Thus, the case represents a relative bookend to the *Unocal* case, which effectively suggested that directors could create defensive measures with little fear of court oversight. In direct contrast to *Unocal,* the *Revlon* court held that once a board of directors has decided to put the firm up for sale, it has to try to get the maximum value for its shareholders:

> [W]hen Pantry Pride increased its offer to $50 per share, and then to $53 it became apparent to all that the break-up of the company was inevitable. The Revlon board's authorization permitting management to negotiate a merger or buyout with a third party was a recognition that the company was for sale. The duty of the board has thus changed from the preservation of Revlon as a corporate entity to the maximization f the company's value at a sale for the stockholders' benefit. This significantly altered the board's responsibilities under the Unocal standards. It no longer faced threats to corporate policy and effectiveness, or to the stockholders' interest, from a grossly inadequate bid. The whole question of defensive measures became moot. The di-

rectors' role changed from defenders of the corporate bastion to auc-
tioneers charged with getting the best price for the stockholders at a
sale of the company.

506 A.2d at 182. Thus, once a firm is up for sale, the directors should no longer
consider the firm interest generally, as under the very broad *Unocal* standard. Rather, directors who want to fulfill their fiduciary obligation have a
very narrow objective: to get the most value for the company's shareholders. These have been variously described as the *Revlon* duties. In *Revlon*,
once the incumbent board sought out and received a competing bid from
Forstmann, the directors had effectively decided to put the firm up for sale.
Once that happens, the protections of *Unocal* to mount defensive measures
evaporate. At that point, the directors could not use their powers to erect
obstacles for bidders, even hostile bidders, like Pantry Pride. Thus, the defensive measures that tended to give Forstmann an edge, including the lock-
up, no-shop, and termination fee, were not enforceable according to the
court.

However, *Revlon* did provide an opening for future dealmakers to continue
to insist on defensive measures. For instance, the *Revlon* court suggested that
these provisions were not illegal *per se*, but were inappropriate if they undermine market forces and the board's ability to get the highest value for shareholders. Future dealmakers would try to retain many of these same provisions
by including new language, like "fiduciary out" provisions that permit the
board to consider other competing bids under the right circumstances. In addition, the *Revlon* courts' mandate that the directors should facilitate an active bidding war only applies in cases in which there is a change in control.
Future parties would be able to argue that the transaction did not represent a
change in control and, thus, *Revlon* should not apply. They would argue that
the much lighter standard of review of defensive measures, the *Unocal* standard,
should apply in these cases.

In the next case, *Paramount Communications v. QVC Network*, the Delaware
Supreme Court begins to clarify (though not completely) some of the factors that courts would consider to ascertain whether a change in control
had occurred. 637 A.2d 34 (Del. 1993). At the time of the case, Paramount
had previously tried without success to combine with Time. Their approach
was famously rebuffed by Time's board and Paramount renewed its search
for a new partner to merge. *See Paramount v. Time*, 571 A. 2d 1140 (Del. 1980).
Paramount's latest overtures piqued the interest of two powerhouse media
companies, Viacom and QVC. Viacom's bid was favored by the Paramount
board. As a condition of Viacom's offer, Paramount agreed to include sev-

eral deal protection devices in the merger agreement to deter a competing bidder. Among the most important, the Paramount board agreed to a no-shop provision, a termination fee, and a (stock) lock-up. QVC responded to the impending Viacom-Paramount hookup by offering Paramount a deal worth substantially more. This encouraged more bidding from Viacom, which ultimately bid $85 per share, and still another bid from QVC, which ultimately bid $90 per share. QVC brought a claim to stop the merger between Viacom and claimed that the various provisions, or poison pills, were not enforceable as they would frustrate the ability of the board to consider all comers.

According to the court, the transaction was a change in control, which kicks in *Revlon* duties. The most important factor according to the court is that Viacom-Paramount transactions contemplated Paramount being under the control of a single person:

> In the case before us, the public stockholders (in the aggregate) currently own a majority of Paramount's voting stock. Control of the corporation is not vest in a single person, entity, or group, but vested in the fluid aggregation of unaffiliated stockholders. In the event the Paramount-Viacom transaction is consummated, the public stockholders will receive cash and a minority equity voting position in the surviving corporation. Following such consummation, there will be a controlling stockholder who will have the voting power to: (a) elect directors; (b) cause a break-up of the corporation; (c) merger it with another company; (d) cash-out the public stockholders; (e) amend the certificate of incorporation; (f) sell all or substantially all of the corporate assets; or (g) otherwise alter materially the nature of the corporation and the public stockholders' interests ...

637 A.2d at 43. Thus, if the transaction simply called for a combination with no single controlling person or entity, no change of control would be effectuated for *Revlon* purposes. Thus, the court reasons this is a classic shift in ownership that requires the board to actively seek out the best possible price by "conducting an auction" or "canvassing the market" or other methods to secure the highest value for shareholders.

Checkpoints

- Shareholders generally have three rights that afford them a measure of protection against a potential takeover: the right to notification, the right to vote, and the right to appraisal.

- Statutory mergers generally save on transaction costs, while having the downside of requiring approval from the shareholders of both firms.

- Asset sales are advantageous because they create only limited shareholder rights and cut off liability for the acquiring firm, among other benefits. However, asset sales have the disadvantage of generally creating higher transaction costs than statutory mergers.

- Other alternatives include triangular mergers, where the acquiring firm merges the target firm into a subsidiary firm, sidestepping the need for shareholder approval from the acquiring firm while simultaneously limiting liability; and freeze-out mergers, where a controlling shareholder ultimately buys out minority holders.

- The minority rule of *de facto* mergers expands the rights of dissenting shareholders in some combinations, regardless of whether such combinations are technically statutory mergers.

- In a hostile takeover, the acquirer avoids the board of directors and takes her case directly to shareholders in the form of a tender offer to shareholders. In response, the incumbent board will often erect an array of defenses to prevent the takeover.

Mastering Corporations and Other Business Entities Checklist

Chapter 1 · Agency Law
- ❏ An agency relationship is formed when two parties agree that one party (the agent) will act on the other party's (the principal) behalf, and the principal provides general control over the agent's actions.
- ❏ An agent's authority to bind the principal in contract may be created by an express statement of the principal (express authority), the circumstances or the principal's conduct (implied authority), a "holding out" by the principal that suggests authority (apparent authority), or from the customary powers of an agent's position (inherent authority).
- ❏ A principal may face vicarious liability when her agents act within the scope of their employment. Acts outside the scope of an agent's authority are not normally attributable to the principal.

Chapter 2 · General Partnerships
- ❏ The general partnership is the default organizational form. Thus, the parties need not make a formal filing to form a general partnership.
- ❏ Unless otherwise agreed, partners in a general partnership have an equal right to ordinary operational management of the partnership. Similarly, partners in a general partnership have an equal right to share in profits (or losses) of the partnership.

Chapter 3 · Introduction to Limited Liability Entities
- ❏ In limited liability entities, investors generally do not bear the risk of inappropriate conduct by firm managers beyond their investment.
- ❏ The rule of limited liability creates several advantages. The rule encourages investment, reduces the need for monitoring, matches up well with notions of fairness, and creates the opportunity for uniform valuation.

Chapter 4 · Limited Partnerships

❏ The general partner in a limited partnership controls operations of the limited partnership, while the limited partners are usually passive investors.

❏ The general partner is liable for the unsatisfied obligations of the limited partnership.

❏ The limited partner is generally shielded from liability, except for the limited partner's contribution to capital of the partnership.

Chapter 5 · Limited Liability Companies

❏ The operating agreement governs internal relations in an LLC.

❏ The default rule is that an LLC is member-managed and each member has an equal right in decision-making. An LLC may also be manager-managed in which case professional managers execute policy on behalf of the LLC.

Chapter 6 · Corporate Formation

❏ To form a corporate entity, one need only file articles of incorporation, also variously known as a charter with the appropriate state body, usually the Secretary of State.

❏ A promoter's liability on pre-incorporation contracts depends on three factors: the intent of parties at time of transaction, whether the corporation was ultimately formed, and whether the corporation, once formed, "accepted" the contract.

Chapter 7 · Corporate Characteristics, Capital Structure, and Management

❏ While shareholders are not liable for the misdeeds and misrepresentations of the corporation, they may be personally liable for their own acts or misconduct and in rare cases of veil-piercing.

❏ While the courts differ in their views of veil-piercing, factors that may be considered are commingling of personal and corporate funds, underfunding the entity, plundering of assets by investors, and using funds of one corporation to pay obligations of another.

Chapter 8 · Fiduciary Duty of Care

❏ The standard of review of director decision-making is normally referred to as the business judgment rule, the notion that courts should not second-guess director decisions, absent exceptional circumstances.

❏ While courts defer to the decisions of the board under the business judgment rule, there are exceptions to the rule for directors who fail to provide some oversight to prevent misconduct, who fail to reasonably inform themselves before making decisions, and who make irrational or unlawful decisions.

Chapter 9 · Fiduciary Duty of Loyalty
❏ Two types of conduct could potentially violate the duty of loyalty: seizing a corporate opportunity and self-interested director transactions.
❏ The duty of loyalty bars directors and officers of the firm from taking advantage of corporate opportunities, if the firm is inclined and able to exploit such opportunities.
❏ Self-interested director transactions are permissible if approved by a majority of informed, independent directors; or if approved by informed, independent shareholders; or, if approvals are not feasible, if it is shown that the transaction is ultimately fair to the firm.

Chapter 10 · Shareholder Rights and Remedies
❏ The right to inspect books and records allows shareholders to investigate potential mismanagement. The right is limited to specific document requests and those documents for which the shareholder states a proper purpose.
❏ Shareholders have the right to vote on fundamental corporate matters and may cast those votes at annual or special meetings.
❏ Shareholders may exercise their right to sue directly (*e.g.*, class action) or by bringing a derivative action asserting a legal right on behalf of the corporation.

Chapter 11 · Securities Fraud
❏ In order to have committed securities fraud there must be: (1) a material misrepresentation; (2) reliance; (3) causation; and (4) the requisite mental state.
❏ A standing rule requires a potential plaintiff to have actually purchased or sold the security in question. Those who may have bought but-for the alleged fraud do not have standing.
❏ The general rule in insider trading cases is 'abstain-or-disclose.'
❏ As to the "abstain" principle, insider trading rules are a flat prohibition of trading for insiders on the basis of material non-public information. As for the "disclose" principle, an insider may trade if the insider discloses the information prior to trading to their counterpart.

Chapter 12 · Proxy System
❏ A shareholder can influence the corporation by mounting an independent proxy solicitation (or proxy challenge).
❏ Shareholder proposals are an alternative to full-fledged proxy challenge. Shareholder proposals allow a shareholder to communicate with other

shareholders by attaching the proposal to the firm's proxy statement and avoiding the costs associated with an independent solicitation.

Chapter 13 · Takeovers

❑ Shareholders generally have three rights that afford them a measure of protection against a potential takeover: the right to notification, the right to vote, and the right to appraisal.

❑ Statutory mergers generally save on transaction costs, while having the downside of requiring approval from the shareholders of both firms.

❑ Asset sales are advantageous because they create only limited shareholder rights and cut off liability for the acquiring firm, among other benefits. However, asset sales have the disadvantage of generally creating higher transaction costs than statutory mergers.

❑ In a hostile takeover, the acquirer avoids the board of directors and takes her case directly to shareholders in the form of a tender offer to shareholders. In response, the incumbent board will often erect an array of defenses to prevent the takeover.

About the Author

The author is a law professor at the University of Memphis Cecil C. Humphreys School of Law, where he teaches Corporations, Mergers & Acquisitions, and Contracts. He has also held previous appointments at the George Washington School of Law in Washington DC and the Grenoble Ecole de Management in France. Professor Harris has published over a dozen articles in prominent legal journals. Prior to entering academia, Professor Harris practiced law at a large corporate law firm. He graduated from Yale Law School, where he was both a Coker Fellow in Contracts and Economics Teaching Fellow. He graduated from Morehouse College in Atlanta, GA and has also been a visiting student at the London School of Economics.

Index